Political Philosophy

by suggestions for further reading, including sources of the more important positions discussed.

★

My greatest debt is to those political philosophers whose original thoughts are presented here in simplified form. I hope they forgive the simplification. Much of my understanding of their ideas comes from arguing about them with my students – listening to essays, trying to work out what they are saying, and challenging it. (Yes, I get paid for this.) I'm grateful to all of you and well aware of how lucky I am.

Martin O'Neill first suggested that my lectures might make a book. Angie Johnson turned tape into text, Clare Chambers helped with research assistance and indexing, and Lin Sorrell provided secretarial support. Sophie Ahmad's wise editorial advice and Janet Moth's expert copy-editing decisively improved the book in its final stages. Many friends, colleagues and current students read a draft and offered helpful suggestions. Thanks to Bill Booth, Selina Chen, Shameel Danish, Natalie Gold, Sudhir Hazareesingh, Margaret Holroyd, Sunil Krishnan, Kirsty McNeill, David Miller, Naina Patel, Mark Philp, and Micah Schwartzman. I'm grateful also to a number of anonymous referees, but especially to two non-anonymous ones – Harry Brighouse and Matt Matravers – whose efforts far exceeded the call of duty. Where it's still wrong, the fault is mine.

The book was finished while enjoying the luxury of a British Academy Research Readership. Since I was given that award to work on something else, I'm not sure whether the Fellows of the Academy will appreciate my gratitude, but they have it anyway. Nuffield College very generously offered me a Research Fellowship for the period of my leave. Thanks to it for taking me in and to Balliol for letting me go.

My father's inability to make any sense of one of my journal articles stiffened my resolve to write something even he might understand. I dedicate the book to him, with much love and fingers crossed. Danny and Lillie are already argumentative enough. I'm glad it'll be a few years before they're ready to read it.

Preface to Third Edition

As well as bringing the suggestions for further reading up to date, and tidying up a few points of detail, I've taken the opportunity to add discussions of global justice and gender equality, and to say a bit more about how political philosophy can be applied to the real world. Some of the examples and allusions have been brought up to date: Tiger Woods has become Usain Bolt; the 'Big Society' has come onto the scene; Seamus Heaney has turned into Doris Lessing; death dates have been added, alas, for Ronald Dworkin and my dear friend Jerry Cohen. I'm grateful to Dan Butt and Zofia Stemplowska for advice on the new bits and two anonymous referees for their suggestions. For Polity, Emma Hutchinson and Sarah Lambert have been patient and supportive editors, Sarah Dancy the perfect copy-editor. To my surprise and delight, a dramatization of some of the discussion of Berlin on liberty has made it to YouTube, thanks to Liam Shipton who was using the book at school. Those who can cope with Sir Isaiah as a young black woman in a miniskirt and extremely strong language can find it at http://www.youtube.com/watch?v=K2qvoESODOk. Those interested in the ethics of the comedy of gendered abuse may enjoy the discussion at http://crookedtimber.org/2010/11/07/swift-versus-berlin-on-positive-liberty/.

Introduction

Politics is a confusing business. It's hard to tell who believes in what. Sometimes it's hard to tell whether anybody believes in anything. Politicians converge on the middle ground, worrying about focus groups, scared to say things that might be spun into ammunition by their opponents. There is some serious debate about policies, but little about the values that underlie them. When it comes to principles, we have to make do with rhetoric, the fuzzy invocation of feel-good concepts. Who is against community, democracy, justice, or liberty? This makes it look as if values are uncontroversial. Politics comes to seem a merely technical matter: politicians disagree about how best to achieve agreed goals and voters try to decide which of them has got it right.

The reality is different. Beneath the surface, concealed by the vagueness of these grand ideals, lurk crucial disagreements. Politicians who share the view that liberty matters, or that community is important, may have very different ideas about what they involve. Even where they agree about what values mean, they may weight them differently. These disagreements feed through into policy. What we ought to do about tax rates, welfare, education, abortion, pornography, drugs and everything else depends, in part, on how and what we think about values. Some politicians may be clear about which interpretations of which ideals guide their policy preferences, and how important each is compared to the others. Many are not. And even where they are, that doesn't necessarily help those of us whose job it is to choose between them. To do that we need to be clear about our own principles. We need to be aware of the different interpretations of these ideals. We need to see where claims presented in their terms conflict and, when they do conflict, we need to decide which is right. We need political philosophy.

Clarity is more important than ever before. Of course, it has always been better to work out exactly what you think than to rest content with vague generality. But vague generalities are less of a guide than they used to be. To simplify extravagantly, political views used to come in blocks, pre-packaged. If you were on the left, right, or somewhere in the middle, you knew what you thought about a wide range of issues, and you knew what your opponents thought too. This made life much easier. It was easier for politicians because they didn't have to grope around trying to work out their precise position on difficult questions − the kind where competing considerations pulled in different directions. They just referred to their block of views, which usually supplied an answer. It was easier for voters because we knew which block politicians subscribed to and could judge them by seeing what we thought about that, without getting involved in the messy details. (What we thought about it often depended on our identification with a particular party − usually the one we had inherited from our parents − so there wasn't all that much thinking going on in any case.)

Today we are suspicious of these pre-packaged blocks. Politicians are keen to leave behind the old dogmas and orthodoxies, to move beyond left and right, to adopt a mix-and-match approach. They have to make it up as they go along. They are willing to look at what works, to borrow good ideas from the other side. In the UK, one can now be a 'Red Tory' or endorse 'Blue Labour'. This brings the charge of opportunism, of lacking any clear guiding principles. Politicians reply that they are not selling out; rather, they are adapting the traditional values of their party to a new context, which may include an electorate less sympathetic to those values than it used to be. Political philosophy provides the tools that politicians, and the rest of us, require to work out what they – and we – really think about the values and principles that can guide us through these complexities.

★

This book does not tell the reader what to think. Its aim is clarificatory and expository, not argumentative. It tries to present some of the more important arguments developed by political philosophers in a way that will help the reader to understand the issues at stake and to decide for herself what she thinks about them. True, getting a clearer sense of what a particular position involves may make that position less attractive or plausible than it seemed when things were less clear. True, I am critical of the way in which some arguments are formulated, mainly when they obscure what is really at stake. (Part 4 gives some appeals to 'community' a rough ride.) But I'm not trying to persuade the reader of any particular political views. When abstract topics like social justice, liberty, equality or community come up in political debate, or in my students' essays, my usual reaction is not 'I disagree with this person. Can I persuade her to change her mind?' It is more: 'This person is confused. Can I help her see some distinctions that would help her understand what she really thinks and why?' I don't pretend that my own views are irrelevant, or inscrutable to the careful reader. Making a distinction, or clarifying the precise meaning of a claim, is often the first step towards exposing the kind of simplification or ambiguity that leads people to get things wrong. ('Now that you've seen what you're actually saying, you can't go on believing it, surely?!') But it really wouldn't bother me if, having read this book, somebody continued to hold all the political views that she did before she started, however mistaken. What matters is that she should understand better why she holds them, and have considered the reasons others might have to reject them.

Some of the book is 'conceptual analysis'. Don't worry. This is just a fancy name for the obviously important job of working out what people mean when they say things. (Asked at a New York cocktail party what philosophers actually do, one replied: 'You clarify a few concepts. You make a few distinctions. It's a living.')

But this is just a first step. Philosophers – at least my kind of philosopher – want to know what statements mean in order to decide whether they are true. We decide that mainly by thinking hard about all the reasons there might be to think them true (including whether they follow logically from other propositions there are reasons to believe are true) and all the reasons there might be to think that they are not true. We make arguments in support of particular conclusions, trying to explain where those who disagree with us have gone wrong. So although this book doesn't argue that one view is right and others mistaken, that's only because this is a beginners' guide. I do care about truth and trust that readers will make their own judgements about which of the various arguments gets closest to it.

This distinguishes me from a different kind of philosopher, the postmodern kind who regards my interest in truth and reason as terribly old-fashioned. Postmodernism comes in a variety of (dis) guises, but, applied to politics, it tends to involve scepticism about the idea that there is such a thing as 'truth' and a mistrust of 'reason' as itself 'socially constructed' rather than a genuinely independent or objective basis for assessing and criticizing society. Since some postmodernists are doubtful about the idea of truth in sciences such as physics and biology, it's hardly surprising that they should be wary of the suggestion that one can apply that category to claims of the kind made in politics. I don't know a better defence of my approach than the rest of the book, so I will leave it to the reader to judge whether the kind of thing we 'analytical' philosophers do is indeed worth doing.

This is not a guide to the history of political philosophy. That history is fascinating and important but it's not – for me – what matters. I know something about Plato, Aristotle, Hobbes, Locke, Rousseau, Kant, Tocqueville, Mill, Marx and the rest of the gang. Occasionally they'll get a mention (with dates). But, when I read or teach the writings of these great thinkers, what grabs me is not the historical context in which they were written, or how what they thought developed over their lifetime, or anything 'historical'. I want to know what they believed, how their arguments went, and whether what they believed is true, their arguments valid. Of course, working out what they believed – exactly what they meant when they wrote something – may well require detailed knowledge of the intellectual and other contexts in which they were writing. Of course, tracing and explaining changes in their ideas, or apparent inconsistencies between their various writings, can help us render their views more precise. I greatly respect those historians of political thought whose careful scholarship and interpretative sensitivity has brought us a clearer understanding of what these great thinkers believed. But, for me, this is all preparatory to the task of analysis and assessment, of deciding whether they were right. I certainly don't think that the pantheon of all-time greats holds a monopoly on wisdom. Just as scientists working today hold many more true beliefs about the world, and more precise ones too, than the greatest, most brilliant, scientists of the past – Galileo, Newton, Darwin – so even ordinary political philosophers can have profited from the genius of a Hobbes or a Rousseau without needing to spend their lives in historical scholarship, and without knowing all that much about what those extraordinary thinkers had to say.

Political philosophy is philosophy about a particular subject – politics. Any definition of 'the political' is controversial. If the personal is political, as the feminist slogan has it, then institutions like the family, and other personal relationships, have a political dimension. Perhaps politics happens wherever there is power. There is a lot to be said for such a view. Nonetheless, for the purposes of this beginners' guide I'm going to stick to the narrower perspective that sees 'the political' as concerned specifically with the state. Political philosophy asks how the state should act, what moral principles should govern the way it treats its citizens and what kind of social order it should seek to create. This isn't as narrow as it looks actually, since it includes the question of what we should do, as individuals, when the state isn't doing what it should be doing. It also includes the crucial question of what should and should not be subject to political control – what is and is not the proper business of the state. (Recent enthusiasts for the 'Big Society' in the UK think that the state has taken on too much, getting into areas that should be left to private or voluntary associations.) So even on my narrow view, political philosophers have plenty to think about.

As those 'shoulds' suggest, it is a branch of moral philosophy, interested in justification, in what the state ought (and ought not) to do. The state, as political philosophers think about it, isn't – or shouldn't be – something separate from and in charge of those who are subject to its laws. Rather, it is the collective agent of the citizens, who decide what its laws are. So the question of how the state should treat its citizens is that of how we, as citizens, should treat one another. The state is a coercive instrument. It has various means – police, courts, prisons – of getting people to do what it says, whether they like it or not, whether they approve or disapprove of its decisions. Political philosophy, then, is a very specific subset of moral philosophy, and one where the stakes are particularly high. It's not just about what people ought to do, it's about what people are morally permitted, and sometimes morally required, to make each other do.

From the range of concepts addressed by political philosophy, this book looks at five: social justice, liberty, equality, community and democracy. I've limited myself to five to keep the book manageable. I've chosen these five partly because they form a reasonably coherent group and partly because they are the ones that come up most frequently in actual political debate. This means they are the most relevant to those seeking guidance through the confusions of contemporary politics and increases my chances of presenting philosophical arguments in an accessible way. The cost is that some very important concepts are left out. Two are the closely interrelated issues of authority and obligation. What, if anything, gives the state the authority to make people do what it says? Under what conditions, if any, do citizens have an obligation to do what it says? These are touched on, in passing, in the discussion of democracy, but are not the focus there and receive nothing like the thorough treatment they get in other introductions to the subject.

One last warning. The fact that the book is written for politicians as well as students does not mean that it is practical or policy-oriented. This will frustrate some, perhaps confirming the suspicion that philosophy – even political philosophy – is so much hot air or self-indulgence. (The 'intellectual masturbation' take on my chosen career.) On the few occasions when I have been at think-tank seminars bringing together political philosophers and politicians, that sense of frustration has been all too evident. For many politicians, a seminar (and presumably a book) is useful only if it yields a policy, or at least a slogan, ideally one that will go down well with focus groups and electorates. This is a problem, sometimes two. In the first place, philosophers do not take kindly to the suggestion that they should tailor their conclusions to what other people happen to be willing to vote for. So even where sound principled arguments yield clear implications for policy, the policy that's implied might well be an electoral disaster and hence of little use to politicians. But there can be a second, deeper, problem. It can be genuinely unclear what policies are implied even by clear principles. Conclusions about what we should do, in a particular context, can depend on a whole range of facts about the world that philosophers may know little or nothing about. It's social scientists – economists, sociologists, psychologists, political scientists – who are (supposed to be) the experts when it comes to questions about how the world works. Take a simple example from Part 1. Suppose one agrees with the most influential political philosopher of our time, the American John Rawls, that inequalities in the distribution of income and wealth are justified only if those inequalities help, over time, to maximize the income and wealth enjoyed by the worst-off members of society. It is still a very good question, as Rawls himself acknowledges, what kinds and extents of inequality are indeed justified by that principle, what tax rates, what kind of welfare state it implies, and so on. Rawls even accepts that the principles he comes up with are indeterminate between capitalist and socialist ways of organizing the economy.

It's not only politicians who get frustrated, and the problem isn't only that we need social science as well as philosophy to tell us what to do. Over the past decade or so, the kind of political philosophy that Rawls goes in for has come under attack from other philosophers (and anti-philosophers) for being utopian and irrelevant. (Greek *topos* = place, *ou* = 'not', so 'utopia' = 'not a place'.) These critics object to 'ideal theory' – theory which tells us what the ideal society would be like – though it's worth noticing that there are two versions of the critique. Some focus on the utopianism. The charge here is roughly that philosophers who come up with 'ideal theory' are naive about human beings, overestimating their capacity for altruism and putting too much faith in rational moral principles. According to these 'realist' critics, the results are implausibly ambitious visions of an ideally just or good society – visions that can never be realized and that it might even be dangerous to aim for. Some claim that these philosophers misunderstand the nature of the political, neglecting the irrational, the emotional and sometimes the downright nasty that are inevitable parts of the struggle for power. From this perspective, philosophers who work on ideal theory are too idealistic.

Others worry more about the irrelevance. Even where philosophers' visions are realistic and desirable as long-term goals, they aren't that helpful when it comes to the here and now. There is a gap between the principles that would be followed in the ideal society and those that apply in the, alas far from ideal, real world. Suppose you believe that, in a just society, rich parents would not be allowed to buy their children a better education than is available to poor children. The principle at stake here is some version of equality of opportunity (see Part 3) and it tells you that elite private schools should not exist. Does it follow that it would be wrong for you to send your own child to such a school if you had the money? The law allows it and other people are doing it; perhaps your local state schools are really poor. (Perhaps they're poor partly because the law allows it and other people are doing it.) Does it follow even that you should vote to abolish elite private schools if you were given the option? Other countries permit them. Maybe we need to allow rich parents the option or they will simply send their children abroad, or move abroad themselves. It's not obviously wrong to send your child to, or vote to allow, the kind of school that would have no place in an ideally just society. The issues are complex. But ideal theory doesn't help us. What's needed, according to this second criticism, is more non-ideal theory. Theory that helps us think not about the perfect society but about what to do in our actual circumstances. From this perspective, philosophers who work on ideal theory are answering the wrong question.

I'm sympathetic to some of this. Political philosophers could helpfully devote more attention to the practical questions that confront us. They could do more to help us as citizens, when we come together to make, or at least to decide who is going to make, policy. And they could do more to help us as individuals, in our daily lives, as we make choices about how to act within the existing policy framework. (In another book I had a go at the issue of school choice.) But it's not either/or. Philosophers who work on ideal theory don't only tell us what the ideal society would look like, they also explain why that kind of society would be ideal. They explore and articulate the values that are needed for us to judge whether one policy, or personal decision, is better than another. Even if some of their overall visions are indeed utopian, we need careful thinking about ideals – such as social justice, liberty, equality, community and democracy – simply to understand the issues at stake in the choices that we make, implicitly or explicitly, here and now.

Nonetheless, those hoping for guidance on policy – like those wanting to be told what to think, those interested in the history of political thought, and deconstructors of truth and reason – will be disappointed and might do best to stop here. This book is for those who want to think for themselves about the moral ideas that structure political argument. The concepts to be discussed form the backdrop in front of which everyday political debate is played out. Consciously or otherwise, and with less or more clarity and control, politicians conceive and couch their positions – including their positions on specific policies – in terms that invoke particular interpretations of those concepts. This book aims to help those politicians, and those of us judging between them, to become more conscious of these background ideas, and better able to assess the interpretations and arguments framed in their terms.

Further reading

Four introductions to political philosophy stand out from the crowd. One is Jonathan Wolff's *An Introduction to Political Philosophy* (2nd edn, Oxford University Press 2006), which manages at once to cover all the big areas in political philosophy (including democracy and authority) and to give readers a glimpse of the big names in the history of political thought (Aristotle, Plato, Hobbes, Locke, Rousseau, Mill, Marx). And all this in a genuinely introductory and accessible way. Another is Will Kymlicka's *Contemporary Political Philosophy: An Introduction* (2nd edn, Oxford University

Press 2002). This is not really the introduction it says it is, but it is an extremely helpful guide to contemporary debates, and should be useful both for advanced undergraduates and for the more determined lay reader. Catriona McKinnon's *Issues in Political Theory* (2nd edn, Oxford University Press 2012) assembles an authoritative collection of survey articles and is linked to an Online Resource Centre. David Miller's *Political Philosophy: A Very Short Introduction* (Oxford University Press 2003) is very short and very good.

The brief remarks about the nature of politics are filled out in my 'Political Philosophy and Politics', in Adrian Leftwich (ed.), *What is Politics?* (Polity 2004). The book about school choice is *How Not To Be A Hypocrite: School Choice for the Morally Perplexed Parent* (Routledge 2003). For ways into the debate about 'ideal theory' and the practical relevance of political philosophy, I'd suggest Raymond Geuss's polemical *Philosophy and Real Politics* (Princeton University Press 2008), Amartya Sen's *The Idea of Justice* (Allen Lane 2009), and Adam Swift and Stuart White's 'Political Theory, Social Science and Real Politics', in David Leopold and Marc Stears (eds.), *Political Theory: Methods and Approaches* (Oxford University Press 2008).

Part 1

Social Justice

The idea of distributive justice has been around for a very long time – the Greek philosopher Aristotle (384–322 BC) wrote about it. Social justice is different. That idea is relatively recent, creeping into use from about 1850 on, and not everybody likes it. It developed only as philosophers came to see society's key social and economic institutions, which crucially determine the distribution of benefits and burdens, as a proper object for moral and political investigation. Some philosophers aren't happy with it. People can act justly or unjustly, but what does it mean to say that society is just or unjust? Some politicians aren't crazy about it either. For them, those who talk about social justice tend to hold the mistaken belief that it is the state's job to bring about certain distributive outcomes, which means interfering with individual freedom and the efficient working of a market economy. (To get a common confusion out of the way, let's be clear from the start that social and distributive justice are usually regarded as different from retributive justice. That is concerned with the justification of punishment, with making the punishment fit the crime. So we're not going to be dealing with the kind of justice administered by the criminal justice system, the kind where we would talk about 'miscarriages of justice'.)

Given that it is controversial, and relatively new, wouldn't it make more sense to begin with liberty, or community – ancient ideas that everybody values? I start with social justice for two reasons.

First, and most important, most political philosophers would say that it was the publication of a book on social justice – *A Theory of Justice* (1971) by the American philosopher John Rawls (1921–2002) – that transformed and revived their discipline. I would agree with them. For many years before Rawls, academic political philosophy was either the history of political thought or quasi-technical linguistic analysis of the meaning of political concepts. Since Rawls, there has been systematic and substantive argument about what the societies we live in should actually be like. ('Substantive' means 'to do with substance or content, not just form'.) Much of what has been written since then can helpfully be understood as engaging with Rawls's theory – like it or not, those writing in his wake have to think about how their arguments relate to his – so it makes sense to lay out the basics of his position right at the beginning. His theory invokes and incorporates ideas of liberty, equality and community. These concepts are all closely interrelated, and thinking about his approach to justice provides the most convenient way in.

Second, one of Rawls's most famous claims is that 'justice is the first virtue of social institutions'. That is debatable, as we shall see: one might judge that other goals, goals that conflict with justice, are more important. But it is at least quite common for people to believe that other goals can only be pursued to the extent that that pursuit is compatible with the claims of justice. Think about the situation where one can make a lot of people very happy by killing an innocent man. (Suppose they mistakenly think he is guilty and that's why they would be happy.) Most people feel that to do that would be wrong, because the most important thing is not to treat people unjustly. Something similar underlies the thought that it is better to let the guilty go free than unjustly punish the innocent. On this kind of view, justice is a constraint on what we can do. It doesn't tell us everything – remember we are talking about the virtues of social institutions, not the virtues we might exemplify in our individual lives. But it does tell us what must be our top priority when it comes to deciding the rules we are going to live under.

Concept v. conceptions: the case of justice

Let's begin with an elementary but very useful analytical tool: the distinction between a concept and the various conceptions of that concept. Much confusion can be avoided by holding on to this distinction, which applies to many political concepts, not just those discussed in this book. With this clearly in mind, it gets a lot easier to see what is going on in political debates where, typically, those on different sides use the same word to mean things that, when probed, turn out to be rather different. Understanding how they differ, and what underlies the disagreements, is the first step towards deciding which side is right.

The 'concept' is the general structure, or perhaps the grammar, of a term like justice, or liberty, or equality. A 'conception' is the particular specification of that 'concept', obtained by filling out some of the detail. What typically happens, in political argument, is that people agree on the general structure of the concept – the grammar, the way to use it – while having different conceptions of how that concept should be fleshed out. Take the case of justice. The basic concept of justice is that it is about giving people what is due to them, and not giving them what is not due to them. (This, at least, is how a lot of people think about it, though it is true that there might be disagreement even about this. I don't want to get on to that, more properly philosophical, terrain.) What is due to them. Not what it would be nice for them to have. Not what it would be polite to give them. Not even what it would be morally good to give them. (I'll explain this one in a minute.) What they have as their due.

This analysis, then, ties justice to duty – to what it is morally required that we, perhaps collectively through our political and social institutions, do to and for one another. Not just to what it would be morally good to do, but what we have a duty to do, what morality compels us to do. And, of course, there are many different

conceptions of this concept, because people who agree that this is
what 'justice' means, as a concept, can still endorse different conceptions of justice, can (and do) disagree about what justice 'means'
in terms of the content fleshing out the grammar of that term. This
part of the book will say a bit more about the overarching concept
of justice, and then lay out three influential conceptions – Rawls's
justice as fairness, Robert Nozick's justice as entitlement, and the
conception of justice as desert. Most people endorse bits of all
three. Sometimes this is done in an informed self-reflective way
that has worried about whether the overall package of beliefs about
justice is consistent (for there are ways of combining elements of
these – and other – conceptions into a coherent whole). More
often, however, it happens unthinkingly, in a way that turns out,
on inspection, to contain a deal of confusion.

Back to the concept of justice. There might be things it would
be morally good to do that aren't requirements of justice. Think of
justice as a specific subset of morality. If Rawls is right that justice
is the first virtue of social institutions, then that means that the
most important set of moral considerations relevant to politics and
the organization of society is that which concerns giving people
their due. And what is due to people has a good deal, though
not everything, to do with what they have a right to. That's why
justice and rights are so closely connected. Consider the contrast
between justice and charity. One might think it was morally good
to give charitably to those in distress without thinking that it was a
requirement of justice. Indeed, if one thought of oneself as giving
charitably, then one would precisely not be thinking of one's act
as a requirement of justice. (Of course you might give to particular
needy individuals or organizations calling themselves 'charities'
because you felt that their claims on you were indeed claims of
justice, but then you would not be giving charitably.) It is quite
common, I think, for people to regard their reasons for helping
those who are starving in far-off countries as reasons of charity,
or as deriving from a principle of humanity (say, a concern and
respect for fellow human beings), but not as reasons of justice. We
ought to help them in times of need, it is morally praiseworthy to
do so, and the reasons to do so are moral ones, but there is no duty
to do so, for their claims on us are claims of common humanity,

not claims of justice. The same kind of thinking is applied by some – such as the libertarian Nozick, whose views we'll examine shortly – to our obligations to help needy members of our own society. It's a morally good thing to do, but justice is about protecting legitimate property rights and it should be up to the individual to decide whether to help or not.

This brings us to the big reason why the distinction between justice and other kinds of moral claim is typically seen as so important. The state is justified in making sure that people carry out their duties to one another. It is justified in using its coercive power to force people to do what they might not do voluntarily. This is a big deal. As I said in the introduction, the state, as political philosophers think about it, is not something separate from and in charge of those who are subject to its laws. It is – or should be – the collective agent of the citizens, who decide what its laws should be. So to say that the state is justified in forcing people to comply with their duties is to say that citizens are justified in using the coercive apparatus of the state (laws, police, courts, prisons) to force one another to act in certain ways – including ways that some citizens might believe to be wrong. This, of course, raises big and difficult issues to do with the justification of state authority and whether, or in what circumstances, individuals are obliged to obey (and perhaps sometimes to disobey) laws they disagree with. Fortunately, this book is not about those big and difficult issues. What matters here is the significance of justice, given a common and plausible view of what the state can and cannot make people do. If you think that the state can justifiably force people to be charitable to one another, you are guilty of conceptual confusion. But thinking that the state can justifiably force people to carry out their duties to one another is, for many, part of the point or significance of the concept of duty. So justice is central to political morality, because of the widely held claim that once we know what our duties are to one another then we also know when we can justify using the machinery of the state to get people to do things they might not otherwise do, and might even regard as wrong.

Clearly, if justice is about identifying the scope and content of coercively enforceable duties, or if we think that by definition the duties that arise are coercively enforceable, then it becomes particularly important correctly to identify the scope and limits of justice. And it's not surprising that there are big disagreements about that scope and those limits. Everybody will agree that it is legitimate for the state to (try to) enforce the law against murder. We all have a duty not to murder one another, and a duty to do what we can to prevent people performing the unjust act of murdering others. That some people might want to murder others, or might disagree that they have a duty not to, is neither here nor there. But claims about social or distributive justice go way beyond this kind of claim, in terms of the extent of the duties they imply. Do talented, productive people have a duty to forgo some of the money they earn to help those less fortunate than themselves, a duty, compliance with which we can – or even have a duty to – enforce upon them? Or is that properly a matter of charity – something beyond the realm of the state? The three conceptions of justice we will look at shortly give different answers to these questions.

Justice can be the first virtue without being the only one. This is an instance of a quite general point that it is always useful to keep in mind. Different morally valuable political concepts – justice, liberty, equality, democracy – need not coincide completely. This is a hard thing for politicians to accept, since they tend to be reluctant to acknowledge that their preferred policies or positions might involve anything other than the complete and harmonious realization of all good things. You don't often find a politician being honest enough to say something like: 'I believe in social justice of type x. I accept that this involves significant restrictions of individual freedom, that it does not provide anything I could honestly call equality of opportunity, and that its realization requires substantial limitations on the scope of democratic decision-making. Nonetheless, here are my reasons for believing in it.' Why not? Because their opponents would make a big fuss about the loss of freedom, the lack of equality of opportunity and/ or the restriction on democracy – each of which would doubtless be described in terms much more confused and vague than they intended. Compared to real politicians – who have to worry about how their statements will be interpreted, twisted, used and abused rhetorically, and spun – political philosophers have it easy. They can say precisely what they mean, with a reasonable degree of confidence that they will be taken as meaning precisely what they say.

This point about conflicts between political values should not be misunderstood. Of course, our aim is indeed to achieve the best reconciliation possible – in the sense of coming up with an overall position which does the best job of giving proper weight to these differing values. Of course there are different conceptions of the various concepts in question, and which conception we favour may in part reflect our other value commitments, which will in turn influence our preferred conception of another concept. We may well have an overall vision about how society should be that informs the way we think about all of them. But none of this means that we should start by simply assuming that, since equality and liberty or justice and democracy are good things, we must be looking for a way of thinking about these concepts which avoids the possibility of conflict between them. On the contrary, clarity is best achieved by keeping concepts as distinct as possible, resisting the temptation to let them melt into one another.

The most common example of confusion on this issue concerns the idea of democracy, a concept with such positive connotations that it is typically stretched in all sorts of directions. Who will confess to not being a democrat? But democracy, at core, is to do with the people as a whole having the power to make decisions about the rules under which they are going to live. This, on the whole, is a good thing – for lots of reasons. Who is more likely to make good rules than those who have to obey them? Rules restrict people's freedom, but those restricted by rules they have themselves been involved in making retain a kind of freedom – at least when compared with those subject to rules made by others. It's fair – it treats citizens as political equals – if rules are made by citizens as a whole rather than by some subset of the population. It's good for people's characters and personalities that they should take an active role in the public life of their political communities. These are four, different, weighty reasons that do indeed make a very strong case for democracy. Part 5 will add more to the list. But even the weight of these combined does not mean that democracy is always a good thing, or that all good things must, because they are good, therefore be 'democratic'.

To think that a decision should be made democratically is to think that it should be made by the people as a whole. Do we really want all decisions to be made this way? Aren't some decisions better regarded as private, better left to individuals than to the political community? Imagine two societies. In one, there is a democratic vote on what religions people are to be permitted to practise. In the other, there is a constitution granting every individual the right to practise the religion of her choice. Which society is better? The second. Which is more democratic? I think the first. To be sure, some individual freedoms can be regarded as necessary for democracy itself. Freedom of association or freedom of expression are like this. If a society denies its members the right to say what they think, or to get together with others who agree with them, then we may well judge that it is denying them things that are needed for that society to be regarded as democratic. This is because of the connection between expression, association and political activity. So some constitutional rights may be necessary conditions of, not constraints on, democracy. But is freedom of religion like this? Suppose a society doesn't prevent would-be followers of a religion from putting the case for why they should be allowed to practise it, or from organizing with would-be coreligionists to advance their cause. It simply prevents them from practising it. Is there anything that should be called undemocratic about this? Or what about freedom of sexuality? One might well think freedom of sexuality to be a central human freedom. A society that allows its members to do what they like sexually – as long, of course, as they don't harm others – is, other things equal, better than one that doesn't. But I don't think we should say that it is also a more democratic society. In fact, we should say that it is less democratic. It removes an issue from the scope of democratic control.

If we judge that the individual has a right to freedom of religion, or of sexuality, then these freedoms can be regarded as central to social justice. A society that denies them treats its individual members unjustly – being willing to violate people's rights and to impose the will of the majority on a matter that should be left to the individual. There is, then, plenty of room for conflict between justice and democracy. Both are good things. We are ultimately going to be looking for the best balance between the different values that they embody. But we are not helped in thinking about the real issues by the misguided idea that the two concepts must coincide. On the contrary, we make intellectual progress by focusing precisely on the places where they come apart.

A society could be perfectly just – everybody is getting what they have a right to and all are acting dutifully towards one another – without its being a perfect society. Perhaps the vast majority of its members are bored (or, worse, not bored) couch potatoes, spending vast amounts of their time watching daytime TV. Justice is one dimension along which we can judge societies as better or worse than one another, but it is not the only one. It matters also how people live their lives within the social institutions that embody principles of justice – what they choose to do with their various rights and their just share of goods. Where things get interesting, of course, is where we think that justice and other good things are in some sense competing with one another. Then it really does matter whether we agree with Rawls about justice being the first virtue. There is a famous climactic scene on the big wheel in the classic movie *The Third Man*, where Orson Welles, as Harry Lime, sketches the relative merits of Switzerland and Florence under the Borgias. Florence was savage and violent – not much social justice there – and it gave us the Renaissance. Switzerland has been a model of peace, fair-mindedness and social solidarity – and it gave us the cuckoo clock. Lime's thought, of course, is that this is not coincidence. It's not simply that there are more good things than social justice, but, worse, that social justice is actually inimical to some good things. Justice, from this perspective, can start to seem a rather tedious, tame virtue. A virtue, to echo the German philosopher Friedrich Nietzsche (1844–1900), fit for slaves, not for people capable of actions nobler and more heroic than the petty, cowardly concern to treat one another justly.

The idea that justice might be inimical to excellence has other, less drastic, incarnations. Some defences of inequality appeal not to the idea that inequality is just, but to the claim that disproportionately concentrating resources in the hands of the few is a necessary precondition for intellectual or artistic progress. Alexis de Tocqueville (1805–59), the French aristocrat who wrote about democracy in America, thought that the system whereby estates were divided equally between sons rather than passing intact to the first, as happened in France, meant that America would necessarily produce fewer, perhaps no, great thinkers. Great thinking requires people with leisure and an aristocratic culture committed to the cultivation of the intellect so that, for example, children are not expected to pay their way but rather devote many years, perhaps their whole lives, to the acquisition of intellectually valuable but financially useless skills. America's commercial and democratic culture, though better in many respects, and, for Tocqueville, overall, was bound to lead to a kind of intellectual mediocrity. Similar arguments abound today. Is it right to spend large amounts of public money subsidizing cultural activities, such as opera, that tend disproportionately to be valued by the better off – especially if, as is the case with the UK's National Lottery, the money is disproportionately raised from those who are less well off? Can the British universities of Oxford and Cambridge justify the claim that the state should provide any of the extra resources required by their labour-intensive tutorial teaching methods – especially if it is children of the better off who are disproportionately likely to receive such an expensive education? We are surrounded by what, at least at first sight, are hard choices between social justice and other values.

Hayek v. social justice

According to Friedrich von Hayek (1899–1992), the very idea of social justice is a 'mirage', or the kind of confusion that philosophers call a 'category mistake'. Hayek, an Austrian, was Prime Minister Thatcher's favourite intellectual, and a major influence on the development of the New Right in Britain and the US during the 1970s and 1980s. In his view, the idea that 'society' is something that might be just or unjust involves a misunderstanding of the concept of justice. Justice is an attribute of action, a predicate of agents. A·person acts justly when she undertakes a just action. The aggregate distributions of resources that result from individuals interacting in the market are unintended by any individual agent, and therefore not susceptible of being judged just or unjust. The idea of 'social justice' involves a fundamental failure to see this point. 'Society', not being an agent, is not the kind of thing that can be just or unjust.

Hayek says other influential things too. He thinks any coercive redistribution by the state beyond the meeting of common basic needs involves an unjustifiable interference with individual liberty. The title of his most famous book, *The Road to Serfdom* (1944), conveys the key idea. For Hayek, the state's ambition to realize 'social justice' implies a centralized authority making people do things they might not want to do, interfering with their freedom to do what they like with their resources – and all this in the name of a conceptual confusion. Relatedly, Hayek thinks that state policies in the area of welfare and redistribution necessarily involve the state making judgements about the criteria that should govern distribution. Should goods be allocated on the basis of need or merit? If merit, what counts as merit? And so on. Hayek is a sceptic on these matters. He is doubtful that there are right answers to such questions and thinks that the only thing to do is to leave judgements of this kind to individuals. Finally, Hayek thinks that, just as long as the state doesn't stick its nose in and distort the process, individuals interacting freely will produce a 'catallaxy' or spontaneous order that crystallizes the information and wisdom dispersed in their individual heads. The free market represents such a catallaxy – with the price signal supplying knowledge of a kind in principle unavailable to any central planner, and guiding individuals towards economic activity conducive to the general good. This critique of the planned, socialist economy – a variant of the Scottish economist and philosopher Adam Smith's (1723–90) 'invisible hand' defence of the market – means that, for Hayek, attempts to plan the economy, or to redistribute resources in pursuit of particular distributive goals, are not just invasive of individual freedom, they also amount to inefficient distortions of market processes which, left to themselves, would tend, in the long run, to benefit everybody.

These are all big and controversial claims – too big to discuss here. But it is worth saying something about Hayek's distinctive rejection of social justice as a mirage. To begin with, even if it were true that nobody intended the overall distribution of resources that results from the market, it doesn't follow that nobody is responsible for it. People can be responsible for outcomes they don't intend. Think of the man who fails to check his brakes and, as a result, runs over somebody. He didn't intend to run anybody over, but, because he could reasonably have been expected to have checked his brakes, he is responsible for having done so. He is negligent, culpably negligent. Now Hayek would say that there is no agent in the distributive case who can be held responsible, even in the sense of being negligent. But is that right? Surely we, as political actors, are capable of coming together and deciding that we are not prepared to permit certain kinds of distributive outcome – say that some members of our society, through no fault of their own, will live in poverty and without access to education for their children. If we accept that this is a matter of justice, not something that should be left to individual charity, then each individual is responsible for ensuring that she does her fair share of contributing to the prevention of that outcome, by agitating politically and by bearing her share of the financial cost involved in its prevention. What matters is not whether anybody intends the injustice, but whether anybody is responsible for the fact that it exists. When governments devise their economic policies, they have a good sense of the distributive outcomes that will result. If they devise, and citizens vote for, policies that can reasonably be expected to produce distributions that include avoidable and unjustified inequalities, then, whatever their intention, they are responsible for the existence of those inequalities. If those inequalities are unjust, then the act of voting for them is an unjust act. Hayek's attempt to sever the link between individual agency and aggregate distributive outcomes fails. He misses the fact that individuals can act politically, in concert with others, to prevent outcomes that, as individuals, may indeed be beyond their control.

Rawls: justice as fairness

John Rawls wrote two big books – *A Theory of Justice* (1971), followed by *Political Liberalism* (1993). These have a combined length of more than 1,000 pages and goodness knows how many forestsworth of commentary and criticism they have jointly generated. A lot of attention has focused on whether and how Rawls changed his position between the two books, so answering the question 'What does Rawls really think?' is far from straightforward. In this section, concentrating on the first (though using elements of the second where that helps), I want to give the merest introductory sketch of what all the fuss has been about. More of Rawls's position will unfold as I compare it with the two other conceptions of justice – entitlement and desert – that come afterwards. (I will discuss *Political Liberalism* in part 4.)

The ideas at the heart of Rawls's theory of justice, which he calls justice as fairness, are the original position and the veil of ignorance. Rawls believes that the way to find out which principles of justice are fair is to think about what principles would be chosen by people who do not know how they are going to be affected by them. He thus imagines people choosing principles in an original position, behind a veil of ignorance. This is a thought experiment. The idea is to help us think about what would happen if people deprived of all knowledge that might serve to distinguish them from one another – how clever they are, whether they are Christian, Muslim or atheist – were to get together and decide how they wanted their society to be organized. Justice, for Rawls, should be understood as that which would emerge as the content of a hypothetical contract or agreement arrived at by people deprived of the kind of knowledge that would otherwise make the agreement unfair. The intuitive idea is the link between fairness and ignorance. If I don't know which piece of cake I'm going to get, I'm more likely to cut fairly than if I do. Depriving people of particularizing knowledge means that they will choose fair principles rather than allowing that knowledge to bias the choice of principles in their own interests.

There are two kinds of thing that the parties to this hypothetical contract don't know. First, they are ignorant of their talents – their natural endowments – and their social position. They don't know whether they are bright or dim, or born into a wealthy or a poor family. Second, they don't know their conception of the good. They don't know what they believe about what makes life valuable or what is worthwhile (art, sport, watching daytime TV), whether they are religious or not (or, if they are, which religion they believe in), and so on. But there are some things they do know. Most importantly, they know that they have what Rawls calls 'the capacity to frame, revise and pursue a conception of the good'. Indeed, they regard this capacity as one of the most important things about them and are very concerned to protect it, and provide conditions for its exercise, when they engage in the process of deciding what principles should regulate their society. And they know that, to exercise that capacity, they need certain all-purpose goods, which Rawls calls 'primary goods': liberties, opportunities, powers, income and wealth, self-respect.

The original position, then, is a device of representation. It is a way of representing particular claims about how we should think about justice. Rawls's idea is that it models fair conditions by abstracting from people's natural endowments and social (class) position, and from their particular conceptions of the good. It models conditions under which people solely regarded as free and equal are to agree what he calls fair terms of social cooperation. Society, for Rawls, should be understood as a fair scheme of cooperation between free and equal citizens, and the original position models or represents that understanding.

One way of thinking about what is happening in Rawls's theory is that he is attempting to model – to capture by means of a thought experiment – what kinds of reasoning are and are not acceptable when it comes to thinking about justice. Suppose you met someone who favoured low tax rates and minimal welfare provision. You ask her why, and she says that, as a very talented businesswoman with children at expensive private schools, she and they would be better off in such a society. She might well be right about that. But it's hard to see how she could seriously present these reasons as having anything to do with justice – at least not if justice has anything to do with fairness. (There are other kinds of reason she could give which would, but we'll come to those later.) Doesn't she think about all the untalented people, or children whose parents cannot afford to send them to private schools? Doesn't it occur to her that she is lucky to be talented, that she might just as well have been born untalented, and that justice is about seeing things impartially, or from everybody's point of view? The Rawlsian way to do this is to imagine what distributive principles you would have reason to endorse if you didn't know who you were, thereby thinking of yourself and your fellow citizens as equals.

So ignorance about talents and social background models the sense in which people are conceived as equal. It is ignorance of their conception of the good that models the sense in which people are conceived as free. For Rawls, reasons arising from conceptions of the good should be kept out of the process of thinking about justice because allowing them in would imply not respecting people's freedom, spelled out as their capacity to frame, revise and pursue their own conception of the good. Suppose you are a Christian, the kind of wholehearted Christian who believes yours to be the one true faith. You might think that it would be a good idea for the state officially to endorse Christianity: to give it favoured status in schools, to allow only Christians to hold certain public offices, to protect it and not other religions from blasphemy. But, for Rawls, this would be to bias the state, which is the collective power of free and equal citizens, in a particular direction, and that would be unfair to non-Christians. The only way to treat all citizens fairly is for the state not to take a view on how people should lead their lives (the same applies to art, or daytime TV), respecting their freedom – their capacity to choose how they live for themselves. This restriction on the kind of reasoning that may legitimately be invoked when thinking about justice is modelled, in the original position, by people's ignorance of their conception of the good.

So what principles does Rawls think people behind the veil of ignorance would choose? These:

1   Each person is to have an equal right to the most extensive total system of basic liberties compatible with a similar system of liberty for all.
2   Social and economic inequalities are to be arranged so that they are both (a) to the greatest benefit of the least advantaged, and (b) attached to offices and positions open to all under conditions of fair equality of opportunity.

(1) is the principle of equal basic liberties. This has priority over (2) which is concerned with social and economic inequalities and itself has two parts: (b), the principle of fair equality of opportunity, which has priority over (a), the difference principle. (It is mysterious why – and rather irritating that – Rawls lists these last two principles in reverse order. Perhaps he wants to keep his readers on their toes.) Taken together these mean that a just society will, first and most important, give each of its members the same set of basic liberties or rights – freedom of expression, of religion, of association, of occupation, etc. Then, if there are social and economic inequalities, it will make sure that all citizens enjoy equality of opportunity in the process by which they come to achieve (and avoid) the unequally rewarded positions. Finally, it will only allow such inequalities at all if they tend, over time, to maximize the position of the worst-off members of society.

Would people in the original position really choose these principles? Many critics say that they wouldn't. In particular, a lot of attention has focused on Rawls's assumption – essential to the difference principle – that they would behave as if they were risk-averse, concerned to make the worst-off position as good as possible (or, in Rawls-speak, to 'maximin' – to maximize the minimum) for fear that they might end up in it themselves. But why should they be quite so pessimistic? Wouldn't it be more rational to choose principles that would maximize the average position, perhaps subject to some 'floor' level beneath which they would indeed not want to take the risk of sinking? (Empirical simulations of the original position suggest that this is in fact what real people do choose.) Rawls has offered various defences of 'maximin' thinking, though he has tended to back off from the initial suggestion that this would be the technically 'rational' way for them to proceed given the uncertainty they face. One argument – which invokes what he calls 'the strains of commitment' – goes roughly as follows: 'It matters that all those living in a society endorse it in a way that means they will be committed to it – rather than seeking to change things. If the difference principle is in operation, those who are at the bottom of the pile will know that the rules are working to ensure that they are as well off as they could be. So even they will be committed to the society.' (One obvious problem with this move is that somebody could accept that those who are worst off are as well off as they can be without accepting that she should be one of the worst off. In that case, she may not have the kind of 'commitment' that Rawls is looking for.)

Another focus of objection is 'the priority of liberty' – Rawls's view that the parties to the hypothetical contract would not be prepared to trade off the basic liberties for the sake of economic gain. (The kind of 'priority' given to liberty is very strict. It's not just that liberty is given greater weight in any decision about trade-offs, it's that there can't be any trade-offs.) Here Rawls would appeal to his claim about the importance of people's capacity to frame, revise and pursue their conception of the good, and the way in which the basic liberties are essential to the exercise of that capacity. Would you be prepared to take the risk of not being allowed to say what you believed, or of not being allowed to associate with whom you liked, or of being forced to practise a religion you thought was nonsense, in return for more money? Your answer will probably depend on how poor you would expect to be without the extra. If the choice were liberty or food, we would all choose food. Rawls accepts this, explicitly acknowledging his assumption that everybody in society has reached a certain threshold of economic well-being. Only once we have reached that level do the basic liberties acquire their clear priority. (This in turn raises the question of how universally – to what range of societies – Rawls thinks that his theory applies. That's a big and difficult one that would take us too far off the current track.)

It is the last principle, the difference principle, that has attracted most attention in debates about distributive justice. How could inequalities tend to maximize the position of the worst off? Isn't the obvious way to do that to pay everybody the same? Rawls's thought is the familiar one that people may need incentives if they are to be motivated to work in those activities where they are going to be useful. Some inequality, so the argument goes, is necessary (sociologists might say 'functional') if the economy is going to be as productive as it might be. Without inequalities, people will have no incentive to do one job rather than another – hence no incentive to do the kind of work which it is most useful (for everybody else) that they do. Imagine all those brain surgeons and

dynamic entrepreneurs who would rather be poets. Without the
extra money that will induce them to forgo the pleasures of poetry,
the rest of us will be deprived of their surgical and entrepreneurial
skills. Generalize to the aggregate level and you have an inefficient,
stagnant economy which, because it pays everybody the same,
does not provide the kind of growth that benefits everybody –
including, over time, the worst off. This, so the argument goes,
is roughly what happened under state socialism in eastern Europe.

This justification of inequality is very widely accepted. It has
led some thinkers to conclude that there is no reason to worry
about inequalities at all. If what matters is the absolute position of
the worst-off members of society, then we should be prepared to
countenance any inequalities that improve that position. There
is, on this account, no need to 'mind the gap' between rich and
poor – our attention should focus solely on whether the economy
is organized in such a way that the poor are, over time, becoming better off. I will say more about this line of argument later
on, in Part 3 on equality. For now, it is worth pointing out that
Rawls's principle says only that inequalities are justified if they
serve to maximize the position of the worst off. It is quite consistent with this that, in fact, no inequalities are justified (because it
is not true that any are needed to maximize the advantage of the
worst off). We should (and will) think carefully about whether
they are needed, and if so, why. Notice also that the principle is
demanding: inequalities are justified only if they serve to maximize
the position of the worst off. The odd bit of 'trickle down' is not
enough to satisfy the principle. What matters is whether the worst
off are as well off as they could be, not whether they are better off
than they might have been.

Another major source of debate has been who is to count as the
'worst off'. Rawls initially suggested that we measure how well off
somebody is by seeing how many primary goods they have. Those
with least primary goods are the worst off. The problem with this
is that it pays no attention to the process by which those with
least came to have least. Suppose they are bone idle – people who
started out with a fair amount of resources but chose to consume
them rather than to work productively. After a couple of years
they have nothing left and are now, by Rawls's original measure,

the worst off. Does fairness really require the hardworking – and hence better-off – members of society to channel resources in their direction? Seeing the problem, Rawls amended his position to recognize that 'leisure' might be included in the index of primary goods. We will return to this issue when we look at justice as desert, and again in Part 3, when we consider whether those who are poor because they chose idleness really are worse off, all things considered, than those who chose to work hard and became rich.

To end this quick introduction to Rawls's position, a couple of thoughts about the 'contract' aspect of Rawls's argument. This can cause the kind of deep confusion that really gets in the way of understanding what he's up to. Rawls himself refers to the great tradition of social contract theory exemplified by the work of Thomas Hobbes (English, 1588–1679), John Locke (English, 1632–1704) and Jean-Jacques Rousseau (Swiss French, 1712–78). This is the tradition that thinks about social and political organization – law and state authority – as the outcome of an agreement between individuals who see that they will be better off under law than they would be in the state of nature. Or, rather, it thinks about it as if it were the outcome of such an agreement. It's not at all clear that any member of the tradition really believes that there was a moment in history when the state and law emerged as the result of a contractual agreement. The key idea is rather that it might have done; that, whatever its historical origins, it is in people's interests to submit to it – they should go along with it because they would have agreed to do so (because the alternative is the state of nature). On this interpretation, then, it is not just Rawls's contract that is hypothetical – the contract tradition as a whole is most plausibly understood as positing a hypothetical contract, the point being that that helps us think about what we can properly expect people to go along with (on the grounds that they would have agreed to given the chance).

A common objection to Rawls is that hypothetical contracts, unlike real ones, have no binding force. They are, so the joke goes, not worth the paper they're not written on. But this misunderstands the role of the contract in his argument. If somebody asks, 'Why should I go along with Rawls's principles of justice?' the answer is not, 'Because you agreed to, and are therefore under a contractual duty or obligation to do so.' That, as the objection observes, is not true. The answer is rather: 'Because you have a duty to act justly and Rawls has correctly identified what justice requires of you.' The hypothetical contract comes into the story only because it is, for Rawls, the right way to think about and identify what justice requires. If there were other, better, ways, then we should use them, and we would still be obliged to comply with the outcome. So it is not a contract argument in the everyday sense that people are bound to go along with the outcome because they agreed to it. The hypothetical contract is simply a device for thinking about what principles are indeed just, and it's because they're just that one is bound to comply with them, not because one agreed to them. (It's true that, for Rawls, the way to see that they are just is to see that we would have agreed to them under appropriate conditions, so it's not surprising readers get confused.)

The contractual aspect of the argument sometimes generates another misunderstanding. The normal way of thinking about a contract is as something voluntarily entered into by people pursuing their own interests, for mutual advantage, and Rawls talks about the motivation of the people in the original position in a way that suggests that he sees them as essentially self-interested (or at least what he calls 'mutually disinterested'). Each is concerned to end up as well off as possible, to protect her own interests. Her thought is: 'What principles are going to be best for me given that I don't know who I'm going to be?' All this is true. But that doesn't mean that Rawls's theory is one for people who are ultimately, or in any overall sense, egoistic or self-interested. It is a theory for people who see society as a fair scheme of cooperation, who care about treating their fellow citizens fairly, and who regard them as free and equal. That is why they will accept the original position – with its equalizing and impartializing veil of ignorance – as the right way to think about justice. Within the original position, people are indeed regarded as choosing principles by looking out for themselves, by thinking about how they, as individuals, will fare under them. But the moral content is already there by then. It is there in the way that the veil of ignorance is set up in the first place. The parties to the hypothetical contract look out for themselves, one might say, only after they have been deprived of all information that might enable them to look out for themselves.

One often reads that the liberal approach to justice – and to politics in general – assumes that people are basically self-interested or egoistic. This view used to be common in Marxist writings and is now most prevalent in communitarian and feminist circles. (I will examine it in more detail in Part 4, on community.) Certain aspects of Rawls's theory may have done something to encourage that misunderstanding. But it is a misunderstanding, and must be discarded before one can begin to see what Rawls is really about. Liberals like Rawls do care that individuals should be free to live the lives of their choice, but they care that all individuals should be free to do so and demand a fair distribution of resources for that reason. Moreover, the lives people choose can perfectly well include concern for others. It is hard to see what is self-interested about any of that.

Nozick: justice as entitlement

The American Robert Nozick (1938–2002) was Rawls's colleague in the philosophy department at Harvard, teaching alongside him when Rawls published *A Theory of Justice* in 1971. By 1974, Nozick had published his counterblast, *Anarchy, State and Utopia*, which is still the most coherent and systematic articulation of libertarian principles around, and one of the most fundamental critiques of Rawls's whole approach. For Nozick, justice is not about agreeing fair principles by imagining that we don't know how lucky or unlucky we have been in the natural or social lottery. It is about respecting people's right to self-ownership and their right to hold property, leaving them free to decide for themselves what they do with what is theirs. The proper role of the state, for Nozick, is not to meddle with the distribution of resources so as to produce some ideally 'fair' distribution. That would involve unjustified intrusions into people's legitimate holdings of private property. Its role should rather be limited to that of protecting people from such intrusions by others. Where Rawls is a 'left liberal' (or an

'egalitarian liberal') advocating a substantially redistributive welfare
state, Nozick is a 'right liberal' (or 'libertarian'), committed to the
idea of self-ownership and arguing for a laissez-faire 'nightwatchman' state. Like Hayek, his views – or at least versions of them as
filtered through various think-tanks and policy units – were influential in the development of the New Right.

Nozick attributes to Rawls, and objects to, the view that we can
regard goods as 'manna from heaven'. Were it the case that we had
woken up one morning to discover that the world was suddenly
full of things that people wanted, then it might be appropriate to
adopt Rawls's or similar principles to distribute them. In that case,
after all, why should anybody get more than anybody else? But that
is not how goods came into the world. They are made by people.
They are the result of individual people's work, sometimes in
cooperation with others. People create things by combining their
own abilities and efforts with the natural world, entering into voluntary agreements with one another for the mutually advantageous
exchange of such abilities and efforts, and the things that they
thereby create are theirs. They are not like manna from heaven,
unowned and up for distribution in accordance with fair principles.
They come into the world already owned, by the people who
produced them (or by those who have paid for the labour of those
who produced them).

Rawls objects to utilitarianism because it fails to take seriously
the separateness of persons. Maximizing overall happiness is a
mistaken goal partly because there is no overall person to enjoy
that overall happiness. There are just lots of separate people, and it
would be wrong to make some unhappy for the sake of creating
more happiness in some others. This thought underlies the idea
of the contract, whereby principles have to be agreeable to each
individual considered separately – which Rawls thinks will rule out
principles aimed simply at maximizing overall utility (or overall
anything else). What if I am one of the people made unhappy for
the sake of other people's happiness? But Nozick thinks that Rawls
does not take the separateness of persons seriously enough. Rawls
does not see that we are individual, separate people, each with her
own talents and attributes, which belong to her and her alone, and
which may not be used to benefit others without her consent. She

can choose voluntarily to give the fruits of her labour to others, but the state acts wrongly, failing to respect her separateness, when it forces her to give up some of those fruits to others. Nozick, then, opposes all redistributive taxation. If the wealthy are to give to the poor, they must do so voluntarily, not because the state forces them to.

In Nozick's view, people can do what they like with what is theirs. And there are three kinds of thing that might be theirs: (a) their selves – their bodies, brain cells, etc.; (b) the natural world – land, minerals, etc.; and (c) the things people make by applying themselves to the natural world – cars, food, computers, etc. I'll say something about the idea of self-ownership – that my limbs and brain cells are mine to do what I like with – shortly. And once people own bits of the world, and own themselves, it's easy to see how they might be thought to own what they produce by bringing them together. So let's start by seeing how Nozick thinks bits of the natural world might come to be owned by people. He identifies three ways in which people can acquire a legitimate property holding (or entitlement): initial acquisition, voluntary transfer and rectification.

Initial acquisition refers to the case whereby somebody comes to appropriate – to make their own property – previously unowned bits of the world. Imagine people settling for the first time an uninhabited continent. In Nozick's view, the land and natural resources of that continent do not belong to anybody, and may legitimately be acquired by individuals on a first-come–first-served basis, as long as nobody is made worse off by their doing so. (This is Nozick's variant on Locke's famous claim – in his *Second Treatise of Government* (1689) – that people may appropriate property just as long as 'enough and as good' is left for others.) This view has come under substantial and sustained criticism, and it would be fair to say that most political theorists think that Nozick's account of initial acquisition is inadequate. What exactly does one have to do to make previously unowned property one's own: walk round it, draw a circle on a map, put a fence round it? How do we decide whether others are being made worse off? They're clearly worse off in the sense that they are no longer able to appropriate that bit of land. And, in any case, who says that the continent was unowned – up for grabs – in the first place? Maybe it, and all the natural world, is jointly owned by all of us, in which case anybody wanting to use any of it needs permission from the rest of us. If the world were collectively or jointly owned, then it might look appropriate for us to get together and decide, collectively, how we want to use and distribute it – perhaps in accordance with Rawls's or other distributive principles.

For Nozick, however, the world is initially unowned and comes to be the private property of individuals through legitimate acts of initial acquisition. That is the first way to acquire property. The second way is by being given it by somebody who, by owning it herself, has the right to give it to you. Once somebody owns anything, she can do what she likes with it, including, of course, giving it to whomever she likes, on whatever terms may be voluntarily agreed between them. This, for Nozick, is what happens in the market. I own my labour. You own some land (which you acquired, let's suppose, by an act of initial acquisition). We enter into a voluntary agreement whereby I sell – or lease you – the use of my labour for a certain price, thereby coming to own some money, which I can in turn do what I want with. So those of us who missed out on the initial acquisition stage – who came into the world when everything had already been snaffled up – shouldn't worry too much. We own ourselves and are therefore in a position to lease ourselves to others. If we're lucky, the selves we own may command a high price in the market, in which case we can lease ourselves for lots of money and ourselves come to own substantial amounts of property.

So the history of the world should be one of legitimate acts of initial acquisition followed by legitimate transfers of property, through acts of voluntary exchange, the result being the just outcome that people own exactly what is theirs and nothing else. But Nozick knows that it hasn't really been like that. He knows that the history of the world is actually one of unjust, involuntary transfers, whereby those with better weapons have forced those weaker than themselves to give up what – in his view – was rightfully theirs. The most familiar examples of this would be the way that white settlers treated the native populations of North America or Australia, but world history has really been one long sequence of such unjust transfers. Nozick's third principle – the third way whereby one can come to have an entitlement over property – is meant to deal with this. It is the principle of rectification, which holds that unjust transfers may be rectified by compensating transfers that themselves create entitlements. In practice, of course, as Nozick is well aware, the difficulties raised by this idea of rectification are enormous. There is no way that we can identify who would own what if there had been no unjust appropriations, hence no way of rectifying properly. At one point Nozick suggests that the best thing to do might be to give everybody, as a starting point, equal amounts of property – that might at least be a closer approximation to a just set of property holdings than the vast and structural inequalities (inequalities between different ethnic groups, for example) that have been built upon those unjust acts of appropriation.

It would be a mistake, then, to see Nozick as an apologist for the status quo. He can perfectly well insist that existing inequalities are unjust, precisely because they have not come about in accordance with his three principles. That said, what is really significant about his position is that, on his view, vast and structural inequalities could be just. People own themselves, but the selves they own are going to be worth vastly different amounts to others. Some will be born strong, healthy and with high levels of natural ability. Others may be born weak, ill and without even the potential to develop those attributes that others are going to be willing to pay for in the market. Some will be born to wealthy parents who can spend on education and bequeath their wealth to their children, and so on down the generations, with more and more advantage accruing all the time. Others may be born to parents in poverty, with no means of helping their children get a start in life. Nozick thinks that this is bad luck – he might even concede that it is unfair – but it is not unjust. As long as people's property rights are respected, which means no coercive state action except that which is necessary for the protection of property rights (the nightwatchman or minimal state), whatever distribution results, however unequal it may be, is just. People can, of course, give voluntarily to those less fortunate than themselves. Nozick may well think that they ought to do so. But there is no justice claim involved – and no justification for coercive state action directed against the better off. Justice is simply about respecting people's property rights, about leaving people free to do what they like with what is theirs.

Nozick describes his three principles as 'historical' and 'unpatterned'. A summary slogan would be: 'From each as she chooses, to each as she is chosen.' The contrast is with 'end-state' and 'patterned' principles – principles that prescribe a particular state that must be realized (such as that inequalities are benefiting the worst off) or require distributions in accordance with a particular pattern (such as 'to each according to her need', or 'to each according to her deserts'). On Nozick's view, what matters is that people have stuff that is justly theirs, and whatever distribution results from voluntary exchanges between them is necessarily just. Whether somebody has a justice claim to something depends solely on the chain of events that led to them having it. Inequality could be just, equality could be just. That depends simply on what it is that people choose to do with their property.

One way that Nozick formulates his objection to the redistributive state is that it uses some people as means to other people's ends. He thereby leans on the thought famously formulated by the German philosopher Immanuel Kant (1724–1804) that morality requires us to treat others not as means to our own or other people's ends, but as ends in themselves. Treating people as means seems like a fairly accurate description of what is involved when the state coercively redistributes resources from some to others. Not all taxation, of course, is used for redistributive purposes. Some of it pays for street lights, and the police, and defence. Some pays for a public education and healthcare system from which those who are taxed themselves benefit. But some of it does involve involuntary transfers from some to others. When we tax people on their income, part of what we are doing is using their productive abilities, which they might otherwise use solely for themselves, to help others. They may not be forced to work, or to do any particular kind of work – so Nozick's claim that taxation is akin to forced labour looks a bit over the top. But, if they do work, we are using them – some proportion of the exercise of their abilities and efforts – as means to other people's ends. Though true, it's not obvious that this is an objection. It might be wrong to treat people solely as means (which is what Kant actually said) – to be willing to enslave them and generally make their lives a misery for the sake of others. That might indeed fail to take seriously the separateness of persons, each of whom has her own life to live. But, if some people are lucky enough to be productive, and others unlucky enough not to be, one might think it justified to use the former to help the latter – even if they have not consented to that use. That will partly depend on whether, or in what sense, people own themselves, of which more shortly.

Another core Nozickian thought is the idea that 'liberty upsets patterns'. Nozick's objection to patterned principles of justice – those holding that the justice of a distribution depends on whether or not it conforms to a particular pattern – is that the preservation of justice will inevitably involve restrictions, in his view unjustified restrictions, on people's liberty. This is the point illustrated by his famous 'Wilt Chamberlain example'. Wilt Chamberlain was, in 1974, a very high-earning basketball player in the USA, the Tiger Woods of his time and place. Nozick thinks that, if people are willing to pay a lot of money to see him play (and assuming the money they are willing to pay is money to which they are themselves entitled), then he is entitled to the money. The clever bit about the Wilt Chamberlain example is that Nozick allows us to imagine starting with whatever distribution of resources we like. Suppose we start with an equal distribution of resources. All members of society have exactly the same amount of money. Now some people so enjoy watching Wilt Chamberlain play basketball that they are willing to pay a bit extra to see him in action. So his club, as well as charging the normal ticket price, asks for an extra 25 cents specifically for Wilt. Millions of people watch him during a season, and he ends up a very wealthy man. There is no longer an equal distribution of resources, but nothing objectionable has taken place. People have simply freely chosen what they want to do with what is theirs. The general lesson is that liberty upsets patterns. If the initial distribution was just – whatever pattern it conformed to – then whatever emerges from voluntary exchanges must also be just. Any alternative conception of justice restricts people's freedom to do what they like with their just share of resources.

In its own terms, the Wilt Chamberlain example is very effective. If people really own property in such a way that it is theirs to do what they like with, then that must include it being theirs to give to others. If they want to give it to somebody else, like Wilt, with the explicit condition that it should thereby belong to him in the same way that it belonged to them (i.e., so that he could do what he liked with it), then it must be illegitimate for the state to come along and take any of it away for the sake of others. So anybody who wants to challenge the conclusion – that vast inequality could be just and that the state would be acting wrongly if it engaged in any kind of redistributive taxation – must challenge the premise. She must deny that anybody ever owns things in the sense that Nozick requires. The force of the Wilt Chamberlain example comes from Nozick's saying that the initial distribution of resources can be whatever one likes – and showing that vast inequality may result even from an equal distribution. But this involves a sleight of hand. For Nozick assumes that the initial distribution, whatever it is, must be a distribution of full or absolute property rights: 'full or absolute' in the sense that they imply that people can do whatever they like with their property. If this were granted, the rest would indeed follow. Lots of the critical literature on Nozick's view is concerned to challenge the idea that we can ever have that kind of ownership claim over property. Ownership is a complicated idea. I can have the right to use my work room without having the right to bequeath it to my children. I can have the right to use the office's shared photocopier without having the right to sell that right to others. If people have absolute rights over what they produce, why can't parents sell their children into slavery? Nozick, it is widely thought, needs to do more to establish that property rights of the kind his argument presupposes are valid.

What about ownership of the self? Surely people at least own their own bodies – including their natural talents – in this 'full, absolute' sense? On this issue Nozick contrasts clearly with Rawls. Remember that, for Rawls, the original position models the idea that people as citizens are free and equal, and the idea that they are equal is partly captured by their ignorance of their natural abilities. This represents Rawls's view that the possession of talents is 'arbitrary from a moral point of view'. It is just luck whether one is born less or more strong, or clever, and so it would be unfair for people to be worse or better off than one another on that basis. At one point, Rawls says that his conception of justice treats people's natural talents as 'common assets'. It is easy to see why Nozick would object to this apparent failure to take seriously the separateness of persons, and the idea that people own themselves. Nozick doesn't deny that people's possession of natural talents (like the social class of the family into which they are born) is a matter of luck. But that is neither here nor there. Even if it is luck, people nevertheless own themselves.

Most people accept some kind of self-ownership thesis. To test your intuitions, imagine how you would feel if the state argued as follows: 'It is just luck that some people are born with two good eyes, and others with none. To create a fairer distribution of eyes, we have decided to hold a lottery which will identify in random fashion some individuals who will be required to give up one of their good eyes to those who have none.' Most people, while accepting that the distribution of eyes is unfair, would nonetheless insist that their own eyes belong to them in a way that would make the state's proposal illegitimate. 'Look. These things are mine, they are part of me. If I want to give one of them to somebody who needs it more than me, then I can do so. Maybe I should. But the choice as to what I do must be mine, because the eyes are.' Those who endorse redistributive taxation while rejecting the coercive redistribution of body parts – probably the vast majority of the population – agree with Nozick about self-ownership, but deny that ownership of the self implies ownership, in the same full sense, of the things – goods, money – we create by using ourselves. People generally believe that forcible redistribution of body parts would involve a violation of their selves – would violate their integrity as people – in a way that forcible redistribution of things made by using those body parts does not. (Applying pressure to the pro-self-ownership intuition, imagine a natural disaster that leaves many injured and needing blood. Voluntary donations aren't enough. Is it obvious that the state would be wrong to set up a programme of compulsory blood donation?)

Rawls agrees with some aspects of self-ownership. Even though who has what body is 'morally arbitrary', we still have a right to bodily integrity, and an area of personal freedom within which we must be immune from intervention. In Rawls's view, for example, the individual must be free to do the job of her choice. The mere fact that I could be a brilliant surgeon, and would best serve my fellow citizens by becoming one, does not justify the rest of you in ganging together to force me in that direction. This, for Rawls, has more to do with the importance of the individual's capacity to frame, revise and pursue her own conception of the good than with a right to self-ownership in Nozick's sense. Still, it is important to see that Rawls's claim about moral arbitrariness still leaves room to accommodate some of the widely shared intuitions that Nozick tries to capture in his notion of self-ownership. The big difference between them is that Nozick wants to use those intuitions in a way that extends ownership of the self to include ownership of the products made by the self.

Popular opinion: justice as desert

It's important to see that Nozick does not claim that Wilt Chamberlain deserves the money he gets. To care about people getting what they deserve would be to go along with a patterned distributive principle of precisely the kind that Nozick doesn't like. The only reason Chamberlain has a justice claim to it – is entitled to it – is because his fans were entitled to their individual 25 cents and they freely chose to give that money to him. Whether he is deserving or undeserving is neither here nor there. If basketball fans for some bizarre reason decided to pay a bit extra to see some completely hopeless player, that player would still be entitled to whatever extra they paid.

Apart from wanting to get Nozick right, getting this clear matters because it helps us see how those who defend market outcomes on justice grounds tend very commonly, and completely illegitimately, to run together what are in fact quite different arguments. One argument holds that the market is essential to individual freedom or to respecting people's self-ownership. Forced redistribution of resources away from the outcome resulting from individual exchange violates people's freedom to do what they like with what is theirs. (I'll say more about this argument in Part 2, on liberty.) Another, quite distinct, argument claims that the market gives people what they deserve. Talented, hardworking people deserve more than untalented, feckless ones, and the market makes sure that they get it. These justifications may coincide, in particular cases, but defenders of the market shouldn't slide from one to the other without being aware that they may not.

So Nozick is not offering a defence of market outcomes that appeals to the idea of justice as desert. Rawls, too, from a completely different direction, is hostile to the idea that those whose productive activities can command a high price in the market deserve the money others are willing to pay them. In Rawls's case, this is essentially because luck plays too great a role in determining how much people can sell their productive activity for. The distribution of natural ability is 'arbitrary from a moral point of view', so those blessed with lots of the abilities that others are willing to pay for cannot claim to deserve greater rewards than those who are not. Rawls is thus hostile to what might be called 'conventional desert claims', claims such as: 'Usain Bolt deserves to earn more than Jean Mason because Bolt is a hugely talented sprinter who gives great pleasure to millions around the world and is thereby able to sell his labour for a very high price, whereas Mason is a social worker.'

Such claims are indeed 'conventional' in the sense that most people endorse them. We know that popular opinion is on Bolt's side. It may not think that Bolt deserves as much as he gets, but on the whole it is sympathetic to the idea that those who can do (and do do) things others are willing to pay for deserve to be better off than those who don't (even if the only reason why they don't is because they can't). We thus have the interesting situation that the two most influential political theorists on social justice – Rawls and Nozick – disagree with each other about whether it's just that Bolt gets what he does. (Rawls says it isn't, Nozick says it is – indeed Nozick thinks that he shouldn't even pay any redistributive tax on it.) But they agree with each other that achieving social justice is not about making sure that people get the value of their productive activity on the grounds that they deserve it. (Rawls because of the 'moral arbitrariness' objection, Nozick because distributing according to desert is a patterned principle.) And, in agreeing this, they both disagree with popular opinion, which is largely sympathetic to conventional desert claims of this kind. Political philosophers are, on this issue, significantly out of step with the woman in the street.

To clarify our thinking about desert, let's distinguish three positions, which I'll call the 'conventional' view, the 'mixed' view and the 'extreme' view. The conventional view holds that one person can deserve to earn less or more than another even if this is due to factors that are beyond their control. Suppose that Jean Mason works as hard being a social worker as Usain Bolt does being a sprinter. She worked just as hard at school and college, acquiring the skills she uses as a social worker, as Bolt did acquiring his current skills. Her job now is at least as demanding – in terms of the effort it requires of her (emotionally demanding, long hours, short holidays) – as his is. The difference between their earnings cannot be attributed to any difference in their efforts, either past or current. Most people think that, in this case, Bolt deserves to earn more than Mason. Not because he currently works harder, or worked harder to get where he is, but simply because his having been blessed with exceptional sprinting ability enables him to do something that is more valuable – at least as measured by other people's willingness to pay – than what she is able to do. It's not her fault that she can't do what Bolt does, and Bolt can take no credit for the fact that he can and she can't. He's just lucky. Even in this case, the 'conventional' view holds that he deserves to be better off than her.

Contrast this with the 'extreme' view. This says that people do not deserve to earn less or more than one another even if they are exerting – or have in the past exerted – different amounts of effort. Somebody who works hard does not deserve to earn more than somebody who does not. What could possibly justify such a view? Answer: how hard somebody works is itself something beyond their control. People's character and psychological make-up are a function of their genetic constitution and their childhood socialization. Some are born with a will to succeed, or to try hard. Others have that attitude instilled in them by their parents or other formative influences from an early age. Some are not so lucky. Why should those who have the good luck to be the kind of person who works hard deserve to earn more than those who have the bad luck not to be?

The 'conventional' view accepts the idea that someone might deserve less or more than others for deploying skills and abilities that she is simply lucky to have or unlucky not to have. The 'extreme' view thinks that luck undermines differential desert claims and, because it thinks that effort is itself a function of luck, denies even that those who work hard deserve to earn more than those who do not. The 'mixed' view is the halfway house position. People don't deserve to be rewarded differently for things (or 'circumstances') that are genuinely beyond their control, like being born clever or stupid, or into a wealthy or poor family. But they do deserve to be rewarded differently for things that are genuinely a matter of choice – which include things like how hard you work, or what job, from those available to you, you choose to do. Rawls is right to think that it's unfair for anyone to be better or worse off than others simply as a result of how they do in the natural and social lottery, but wrong if he thinks that people's choices should also make no difference to how well off they are.

Rawls is sometimes presented as holding the extreme view. He is not altogether clear on this point, but a plausible reading of what he says would have him acknowledging a role for free will, not claiming that every supposed choice an individual makes is actually determined by genetics and socialization. He believes rather that the choices people make about their level of effort are so influenced by factors beyond their control that it would be unfair to reward them simply in proportion to that effort. 'The idea of rewarding desert is impracticable', as he puts it, because it is impossible, in practice, to disentangle choices in the appropriate sense (i.e., choices uninfluenced by morally arbitrary characteristics) from the arbitrary characteristics that tend to influence them.

This seems plausible. Even if one believes that people do make choices for which they are responsible, and can deserve less or more than others on the basis of those choices, it is going to be very difficult to separate out anybody's current earnings into (a) that part due to factors for which they can be held responsible and which they thus deserve and (b) that part due to factors for which they cannot be held responsible and thus do not deserve. An important consideration here is that the abilities that adults possess reflect, to a great extent, how hard they tried when they were children. Some adult abilities reflect natural talent. But what isn't natural talent mainly results from people's habits as children. Some kids try hard, don't give up after the first attempt, develop the capacity to make what Rawls call a 'conscientious effort'. Some don't. But it is surely implausible to think that children are responsible for choices such as these. Their characters as children depend – when not on their genes – on their parents, their teachers and other influences over which they have little or no control. It may be that, as adults, we are capable of making responsible choices about what to do with our abilities – and can be said to deserve greater or lesser rewards depending on the choices we make. But the very abilities we have as adults – where they result from choices at all – result largely from choices we have made as children, and for which we cannot be held responsible.

The most important thing to keep in mind, however, is that the market makes virtually no attempt to disentangle these various components of people's marketable skills. I say 'virtually' because two identically skilled people will tend to earn less or more than one another depending on how hard they work. But the marginal return to that marginal effort is trivial compared to the return to the skills they possess, and the market couldn't care less how they came to have those identical skills. Perhaps one was born lucky – high levels of natural ability, wealthy parents hence good education – while the other is less naturally gifted, and has had to struggle to better herself despite an unhelpful school. The market doesn't care. It is blind to distinctions of the kind I have been outlining here. It rewards people as a function of their ability to satisfy the preferences of others (actually, to satisfy the preferences of those others who have the money to pay to have their preferences satisfied). It pays no attention to the process by which people come to have that ability.

Even someone, like Rawls, sceptical about conventional desert claims might think that there are some things that you can indeed deserve on the basis of attributes that you are just lucky to have.

Suppose one thought that Doris Lessing deserved the Nobel Prize for literature. That judgement need have nothing to do with any view one might hold about how she became able to write those novels – whether through effort or natural ability or propitious upbringing. Even if there were minimal effort involved – she just happened to have been born with a gift for writing and an unusually propitious upbringing – one could still say that she deserved the Nobel Prize. But that is because the Nobel Prize is awarded to the person who wrote the best literature. Since Lessing did that, she deserves the prize. So even the sceptic about conventional desert claims is likely to acknowledge that there are some contexts in which they are valid. The disagreement between the sceptic and the person who defends the market as giving people what they deserve turns, it seems, not on whether any conventional desert claims are valid, but on their proper scope. The sceptic says: 'Why should some people have more resources to devote to their life plans than others just because they are luckier than those others? Sure. If somebody wants to offer a prize for the best writer, then the best writer deserves to win it – however lucky she is to be the best writer. But the money people get from their jobs is not like a prize. It is too important to be left to chance.' The thoroughgoing sceptic might even say that Lessing deserved to be called the Nobel Laureate but did not deserve the money. Why should she have all that extra money to spend on her life just because she happens to be a great novelist? On this view, conventional desert claims extend to symbolic rewards, like prizes, but not to rewards like money.

Like many concepts in this area, the term 'desert' is sometimes used rather loosely. In line with my commitment to drawing nitpicking (but clarifying) distinctions, let me end by explaining how the idea of desert that I've been talking about here differs from other ideas that are sometimes formulated using the word 'desert'.

First, there is a difference between desert and 'legitimate expectation'. Imagine an institutional structure, a firm or the market economy as a whole, in which, as a matter of fact, people are rewarded unequally depending on their possession of certain qualifications. We might then say that somebody who acquired those qualifications 'deserves' the reward just because the institutions

were set up in such a way that the person acquiring the qualifica-
tion has a legitimate expectation that, by acquiring the qualifica-
tion, they would receive the reward. This is sometimes called an
'institutional' conception of desert. The important thing to see is
that it is a completely separate question whether the institutions
should have been set up the way they are in the first place. We
can perfectly well say: 'Since we are operating within a system
that typically rewards people with good money if they get an
MBA, and she has made various choices that have resulted in her
getting an MBA on the basis of that assumption, her expectation
that she should get good money is legitimate. In that limited sense,
she "deserves" to get good money. Nonetheless, a system which
rewards people with MBAs more than those without – indeed any
system which pays people differently depending on their ability
to pass exams of any kind – is fundamentally unjust, and certainly
doesn't give people what they really deserve.' It is easy to formulate claims about legitimate expectations in 'desert' terms. Indeed,
there's nothing wrong with doing so – as long as one is clear that
somebody can have a legitimate expectation of (hence 'deserve'
in an institutional sense) a reward that they do not really deserve
(because institutions are set up unjustly and do not reward people
in accordance with their 'actual' or 'brute' or 'preinstitutional'
deserts).

Second, some people use the term 'desert' when they are talking
about compensation or equalization. Suppose I think people whose
work is dangerous, stressful, dirty, boring or inappropriately stig-
matized should, other things equal, earn more than people whose
work is safe, comfortable, interesting, healthy or prestigious. I
might well say that they deserve to earn more. There's nothing
wrong with this kind of desert claim as long as it is clear how it
differs from the kind I was discussing above. That kind was specifically to do with the issue of whether people might deserve less
or more than others on the basis of their various attributes, and to
what extent responsibility for those attributes was relevant. What
we are talking about now uses a desert claim essentially as an equalizing claim. We can think of it in terms of the idea of 'compensating differentials'. In order to ensure overall or net equality between
different people, we take into account the different characteristics

of their work − interestingness, prestige, danger, etc. − and try to compensate for anything that would otherwise take them above or below some norm.

Again, there's no real problem using the term 'desert' in this kind of case. It's important, though, to see that is unlikely to justify the claim that Usain Bolt deserves to earn more than Jean Mason. It is completely implausible to think that the inequalities generated by the market in our society can be justified by appeal to the idea of desert as compensating differentials. (Some economists and political theorists think that the inequalities generated by an idealized perfect market could be. In that case the money people earned − the price for the job − would reflect nothing other than the net balance of advantages and disadvantages involved in doing their job. Employers would then have to pay more to get people to do unpleasant work than pleasant work − whereas the reverse is often the case at the moment.)

The third and last thought to be distinguished here can be, but need not be, related to this idea of compensating differentials. This is the idea that it is justified for some people to earn more than others because there will be bad consequences if they were not to do so. Sometimes this is formulated in terms of the idea of desert. Suppose we ask: 'Do brain surgeons deserve to earn more than nurses?' Somebody might reply: 'Yes, they do. Because if we didn't pay brain surgeons more than nurses nobody would want to be a brain surgeon. Since it's clearly important that some people are brain surgeons, they deserve to get more money just so that we can make sure that some people choose that job.' This is a claim about incentives − about the need to induce people to do socially useful tasks and the justifiability of paying them more if that is the only or best way to get them to do those tasks. Does it have anything to do with desert?

Not as it stands. It is not, in itself, anything to do with the relative deserts of brain surgeons and nurses. It is simply a consequentialist observation, an observation about consequences, about what would happen if we didn't pay them more. As it stands, we don't know why, to get brain surgeons, we need to pay them more than nurses. Perhaps it's because potential brain surgeons are more selfish than nurses and, realizing the value of their work to society, are prepared to hold the rest of us hostage, blackmailing us into paying them the extra. If that were the case, we would hardly want to say that they deserved that extra. (Any more than we would say that kidnappers who will only release a hostage if we pay them a ransom 'deserve' the money – even if we think we are justified in paying it to them.)

It can, however, be turned into a desert claim – at least a desert claim of the 'compensating differentials' kind. If we ask why we need to pay brain surgeons more than nurses if people are going to choose a career in brain surgery, the answer might be that they have high levels of responsibility and stress, or that they need to undergo many years of training – forgoing money they could be earning in other jobs and going through the arduous process of learning skills that most people don't need to worry about. So if we pay them above the average wage, to get them to do the job, this is just a compensating differential – money they 'deserve' given all the negative aspects of the job. The thought, now, is not simply that we have to give them extra money in order to get them to do the job – which is consistent with the blackmail scenario. It is that they actually deserve the extra, deserve it in the sense that it compensates for all the stress, long hours, training or whatever, and so provides the necessary inducement for them to take up brain surgery. Otherwise they'd be worse off, all things considered, than nurses. Construed this way, this is a genuine justice claim, and one that can be allowed appeal to the concept of 'desert' – even if it is a different conception of desert from the main one I've discussed. (Of course, such a claim could well be contentious. The kind of university education that some would present as investment, to be compensated for by higher pay, might well be enjoyable and valuable in itself. Just because someone tells us that something is a cost deserving compensation doesn't mean that we have to agree with them.)

Social justice v. global justice

This chapter is called 'social justice' and everything in it so far has taken it for granted that the thing we care about being just, or unjust, is society. But many of my students are more concerned about injustice across the globe as a whole. That's not because they think their own societies can afford to be complacent on the justice front. But in a world where millions die every year for lack of basic nutrition and medical care, and multinational corporations reap huge profits from the work of millions more earning subsistence wages, it is the inequalities between societies that seem more blatantly unjust than those within them. Whether affluent societies have organized things to benefit their least advantaged members, or whether those members get paid what they deserve, can indeed seem rather trivial from the global perspective. Political philosophers have been devoting increasing attention to the wider picture, extending their thinking beyond the domestic context and considering what distributive principles should apply at the international level.

A key issue – perhaps the key issue – is whether we should think about global justice as something like social justice writ large. Perhaps principles devised for individual societies should simply be extended in their scope to compass humanity as a whole. If it matters that all members of society enjoy fair equality of opportunity (as per Rawls's principle 2(b) – see above, p. 25), doesn't it also matter that all human beings enjoy it too? If so, then justice requires that the malnourished children among the world's bottom billion should have the same chances as those born to the richest parents in the richest countries. Rather than inequalities being just only if they serve to maximize the position of the least advantaged in a society (as per Rawls's principle 2(a)), why shouldn't they be required maximally to benefit the least advantaged on the planet? (This would be the 'global difference principle'.) If social justice involves people getting what they deserve, why not think of 'people' as all human beings, irrespective of geography or nationality, and think about how far the world falls short of realizing that principle? According to so-called cosmopolitans, the idea that all human beings are fundamentally equal means that their nationality, or which society they are a member of, should not make a difference to what they can claim from others as a matter of justice.

The alternative view insists that social justice and global justice really are different things. Members of a society have duties to one another that they do not have to members of other societies.

Those who share a nationality, or belong to the same state, are in a particular kind of association – a distinctive relationship with particular others – that makes a difference as far as justice is concerned. Maybe all are owed some duties of justice simply because they are human beings. The concept of human rights is often used to capture that idea. Perhaps, for example, it is unjust when those in some countries are denied access to the necessities of life while those in others have far more than they need. Perhaps we have duties not to harm or exploit people, wherever they may live. But, on this view, the principles that apply across borders are less demanding than those that apply within them.

In contemporary political debate, some version of the second position tends to be taken for granted. The UK government currently devotes 0.7 per cent of GDP to foreign aid and any politician who urged an increase would immediately find herself on the defensive. That's partly because of doubts about the efficacy of international 'handouts'. As always, issues of philosophical principle and matters of empirical fact are intertwined when we make judgements about what to do. But, as the language of 'aid' and 'handout' suggests, it also reflects the widespread view that global redistribution is a matter of charity, not justice. It's not only that people think they owe more to their compatriots than they do to foreigners. Even where the aim is merely to relieve life-threatening deprivation – and nothing like global equality of opportunity or the global difference principle – most people do not think they are under an enforceable duty to give up much of what they have to help those who live in other countries. Since even those philosophers who reject cosmopolitanism usually hold that we do have some duties to help people all over the world enjoy basic human rights, including the right to subsistence, this is yet another example of the mismatch between philosophy and public opinion. Compared to the status quo, even a relatively undemanding take on global justice would be radical in its implications.

That said, there is still a big difference between the two views, and although the second is much more commonly held, I'm sure some readers will feel a strong pull in the cosmopolitan direction. After all, if we are approaching the issue from a purely philosophical perspective, putting aside for now practical questions of what's feasible (including what those in affluent countries can be expected to vote for), the idea that duties of justice are owed to people as such, simply because of their humanity and without regard to geography, has a good deal going for it. We may know, as a matter of psychology, that we tend to favour those we identify with, just as we tend to favour members of our family. But it's tempting quickly to dismiss that kind of thinking as failing to achieve a properly moral, impartial, perspective – one that recognizes the fundamental equality of all human beings. That temptation should be resisted. Even if you do end up endorsing a cosmopolitan perspective, it's better to do that having carefully considered the case for the alternative. So it's worth having a sense of the various theories defending the claim that the demands of justice are different at home and abroad.

Common to all such theories is the idea that the kind of association we have with others is relevant to what we owe them justice-wise. There may be some very basic justice claims that all have against all. But distributive justice – principles that apply to the distribution of benefits and burdens, or how much people should have compared to one another – applies only among those in particular modes of relationship. Where the theories differ is over what kind of association or relationship is the relevant one. If you've been reading carefully you may have noticed that I started this section talking about 'society', slid to 'nationality', slipped in 'state', added in 'countries' and 'borders', and ended up with 'compatriots/foreigners' and 'home/abroad'. I also referred to 'those we identify with'. These can refer to different things. They involve different sets of people and different ideas about why we owe more to some than to others.

One starting point sees distributive justice as concerned specifically with the fair distribution of the fruits of social cooperation. If our conception of a 'society' is of individuals cooperating with one another for their mutual advantage, then it makes sense to think of distributive justice as concerned with distributing the benefits and burdens of that cooperation. Those who are not members of the cooperative scheme that is 'society' do not have the same kind of claims to fair shares because they are not involved in producing, or bearing the costs of producing, the good things that are to be distributed. But in today's globalized economy, with high levels of economic interdependence between members of different countries, it's implausible to suppose that the people with whom we are cooperating to produce those fruits are only our fellow nationals or members of the same state as us. So if that's the idea, then it looks as if the demands of distributive justice are going to extend way beyond my fellow citizens or fellow nationals.

A second approach focuses on the relationship between those who share a state – fellow citizens living together under the same coercive apparatus. That seems to correspond more closely to the way we conventionally divide people into 'us' and 'them', and it's certainly the way that our states encourage us to think about things. Within this kind of view, some philosophers emphasize the way in which compliance with a system of laws itself contributes to our mutual advantage. A fair share of the benefits and burdens of social cooperation is what we should get in return for our compliance. This is a variant of the previous perspective, but adds in the idea that submission to coercion through law is part of the cooperative package. Another angle sees citizenship as relevant to distributive justice because there is something special about being jointly authors of the laws by which we coerce one another. Not only are fellow citizens subject to the decisions they jointly make, those laws are made in their name. People participating in that form of association should not be subject to arbitrary inequalities – they owe one another a justification of any inequalities that exist between them – so principles of distributive justice apply within states in a way that they do not beyond state borders.

A further reason to take states seriously when it comes to global justice appeals to the value of sovereignty or collective self-determination. Cosmopolitans who claim that the same distributive principles should apply to all human beings seem to be denying that different states may make different judgements about how they want to allocate resources among their members. But it's not crazy to think that, as long as their collective decisions can be regarded as legitimate, and as long as their decisions respect human rights, the members of a state should be free to decide that for themselves. (It's a big question what counts as 'legitimate'. We won't get to 'democracy' until Part 5, so I can't go into that here.)

Still, the idea that a just world would consist of people divided into a number of different, legitimate, states – perhaps with different histories and cultural norms – with each state making its own distributive decisions, should have some intuitive appeal. From this perspective, global justice is not about applying the same distributive principles to each individual human being. It's more about making sure that the collectives (Rawls calls them 'peoples') in each individual state are provided with the just background conditions within which they can exercise the right to decide such matters for themselves.

A third way of resisting cosmopolitanism appeals to the relationship of shared nationality. At first sight, 'shared citizenship' and 'shared nationality' may seem like the same thing. That's because we tend to think of the world as divided into discrete nation-states, in which the distinctively political association of the state is shared by those who are members of a group with the same national (historical, linguistic, ethnic or cultural) identity. But even where nation and state do coincide – so we are putting to one side multinational states and stateless nations – we can still ask whether it's the statehood or the nationhood that is doing the work. Suppose I have an intuitive but vague feeling that I owe my compatriots more than I owe foreigners but I'm not sure why. One way to make progress is to work out whether it comes from a sense that those with whom I share a political relationship have special claims on me, or from a sense that I have particular duties to those with whom I share an identity based on history and culture? (I'll say more about this distinction towards the end of Part 4 (pp. 171–82).) While philosophers tend to answer in terms of the former, along the lines outlined above, my guess is that it's the latter that lies beneath much popular anti-cosmopolitanism.

Cosmopolitans are doubtful about these various attempts to defend the idea that we owe more to our fellow citizens/nationals than to other human beings. But notice that their position is quite compatible with thinking that we don't actually owe our fellow human beings very much. A libertarian like Nozick, for example, might hold that we have no duty of justice to do anything to help the world's poor (just as we have no such duty to help the poor in our own society). Our duties, on this kind of view, are negative

– they are duties not to do things to others (murder, torture, rob, etc.) Generally, we might say, what is morally required of us is simply that we not harm others. Those attracted to that kind of view will need to think hard about what counts as harm, and should consider the various ways in which the global economic order – regulated by things like the World Trade Organization – might be regarded as harming members of poor countries. For example, the philosopher Thomas Pogge (b. 1953) argues that wealthy countries benefit from a range of international arrangements that encourage corruption among elites and thus contribute directly to the continuation of global poverty. Even if there are no duties positively to aid those in need, the global affluent might still be acting unjustly simply by colluding in, and benefiting from, a global system that harms the global poor.

Conclusion

Each of the conceptions of social justice that we have looked at can be thought of as presenting a different justification of inequality. Hayek thinks that the whole idea of seeking social justice involves a philosophical mistake, so that inequality doesn't really need justification in the first place. Rawls holds that inequalities are justified if they conform to the principles that would have been chosen in the original position, most controversially the difference principle which holds that inequalities must serve, over time, maximally to promote the well-being of the least advantaged members of society. Nozick rejects this kind of thinking in favour of a principle of self-ownership that leaves people free to do what they like with property that is theirs – a principle that could justify extreme inequality. All three of these thinkers reject the popular view that people deserve differently depending on their productive contribution.

It is very common to find people defending the justice of the kinds of inequality we see in our society by appealing to some mish-mash of these different ideas. That is the reason carefully to distinguish between them. How could it be just that Usain Bolt, or Bill Gates, or any corporate lawyer should earn more than a social worker, or a schoolteacher, or somebody who is involuntarily unemployed? Does the question involve a category mistake? Is it because their earning more – and that much more – serves, over time, to help the poor? Is it because they own their talents and whatever people are willing to give them for exercising them? Is it because they are in some way more deserving? These justifications can, in special circumstances, coincide – but they won't always do so. Those who would defend the justice of existing inequalities – or anything like them – need to think hard about which way they want to jump when they come apart. And both defenders and critics of those inequalities need a reply to the charge of parochialism. Perhaps it's the world as a whole, not any particular society within it, that should really be the subject of distributive justice.

Further reading

Matthew Clayton and Andrew Williams (eds.), *Social Justice* (Blackwell 2003) is an excellent collection. Harry Brighouse's *Justice* (Polity 2004) and Tom Campbell's *Justice* (3rd edn, Macmillan 2010) are both good textbooks. Cecile Fabre's *Justice in a Changing World* (Polity 2007) nicely focuses on international, intergenerational and multicultural issues.

On Hayek, the key work is *The Mirage of Social Justice* (Routledge & Kegan Paul), first published in 1976, and incorporated as volume 2 of his *Law, Legislation and Liberty* in 1982. 'The Atavism of Social Justice', in his *New Essays in Philosophy, Politics and Economics* (Routledge & Kegan Paul 1978) is short and to the point. John Gray's *Hayek on Liberty* (2nd edn, Blackwell 1986) and Chandran Kukathas's *Hayek and Modern Liberalism* (Oxford University Press 1989) are the two best critical accounts of Hayek's work as a whole.

Rawls's *Justice as Fairness: A Restatement* (Harvard University Press 2001) is the user-friendly version of his theory. From the mountain of secondary literature, and in increasing order of length and complexity, it would be worth trying the introduction to Stephen Mulhall and Adam Swift's *Liberals and Communitarians* (2nd edn, Blackwell 1996), Thomas Pogge's *John Rawls: His Life and Theory of Justice* (Oxford University Press 2007) and Samuel Freeman's *Rawls* (Routledge 2007).

Nozick's *Anarchy, State and Utopia* (Blackwell 1974) is an entertaining read (as political philosophy goes); the middle section on distributive justice is the most relevant. The best critical commentary is Jonathan Wolff's *Property, Justice and the Minimal State* (Polity 1991).

What Do We Deserve? (Oxford University Press 1999), edited by Louis P. Pojman and Owen McLeod, is a good collection on desert. Chapters 7–9 of David Miller's *Principles of Social Justice* (Harvard University Press 2001) defend the view that the market can (though it currently doesn't) give people what they deserve. Chapter 8 of Gordon Marshall et al.'s *Against the Odds? Social Class and Social Justice in Industrial Societies* (Oxford University Press 1997) is more sceptical.

At the more accessible end of the scale, Brian Barry's *Why Social Justice Matters* (Polity 2005) is a thought-provoking polemic and Michael Sandel's *Justice: What's the Right Thing To Do?* (Penguin 2010) brilliantly illuminates a wide range of topical issues via some of the great moral and political philosophers.

Readers interested in global justice will find many good things in Thom Brooks's (ed.) *The Global Justice Reader* (Wiley-Blackwell 2008), while Jon Mandle's *Global Justice* (Polity 2006) is more than a good textbook. Thomas Pogge's important argument is most fully developed in his *World Poverty and Human Rights: Cosmopolitan Responsibilities and Reforms* (2nd edn, Polity Press 2008).

Part 2

Liberty

If Rawls's *A Theory of Justice* is the most influential book of contemporary political philosophy, Isaiah Berlin's 'Two Concepts of Liberty' is the most influential single essay. (It was his inaugural lecture as Professor of Social and Political Theory at Oxford, in 1958.) This is the essay which, as mentioned in the Preface, Tony Blair wrote to him about. In it, Berlin (1909–97) draws a famous distinction between 'negative' and 'positive' concepts of liberty, and argues that the latter should be seen as a wrong turning. So wrong, in fact, that totalitarian states like Nazi Germany and the USSR invoked the concept to justify their regimes. If the most blatant enemies of liberty could persuade themselves that they were its true friends, something very peculiar must have happened.

Berlin's essay is a brilliant account of just what did happen: of how two ways of thinking about liberty, which started out very close to one another, gradually drifted apart and became polar opposites. It is an insightful, stimulating and plausible tracing of a hugely important development in the history of ideas. It is not, however, as clear as it might be. Berlin draws the distinction between negative and positive liberty in a variety of different ways, and argues simultaneously what are actually significantly different points. So it is not surprising that the reader can be left confused about just what he is and isn't saying. Here I try to sort out some of the confusion. In so doing, I will explain why Blair was standing up for 'positive liberty', which Berlin regarded as a dangerous notion, ripe for perversion into the official ideology of a totalitarian state. It's not because Blair is a closet dictator. The answer is less exciting than that. It's because Berlin uses 'positive freedom' to mean a number of different things, only some of which have totalitarian tendencies. The kind of 'positive freedom' Blair was defending – and which plays a key role in centre-left thinking across Europe and North America – is not the kind that led to, or was endorsed by, Hitler or Stalin.

As well as clarifying the distinction between negative and positive liberty, this part of the book covers two other issues. First, it explores the connections between freedom, property and the free market. There is a kind of right-wing argument that defends private property and the free market by appeal to the value of individual freedom. Nozick's conception of justice as entitlement, discussed in Part 1, is a good example of this. There is more than a hint of it in Hayek too. Since this line of argument is important in mainstream political debate – low tax rates are often defended on freedom grounds – it is worth careful consideration. Finally, it looks at the idea of positive freedom that Blair was not defending – the kind that Berlin thinks leads to totalitarianism. By making a few distinctions, we can better see whether even this kind of 'positive' liberty is quite as dangerous as Berlin thinks.

Two concepts of liberty?

Most readers of Berlin's essay come away with the idea that the difference between negative and positive liberty is that between 'freedom from' and 'freedom to'. Advocates of negative liberty, they think, believe that freedom is essentially to do with being free from things (constraints, obstacles or interference), whereas advocates of positive liberty hold that it is rather to do with being free to do things. (There is no difference worth worrying about between 'liberty' and 'freedom', so I use the two interchangeably.)

This is a mistake. If there is a distinction between negative and positive liberty it is not this one. The 'freedom from' v. 'freedom to' distinction is a red herring. The way to see this is to notice that all freedoms are both freedoms 'from' and freedoms 'to'. Take any liberty you like, it will be both a freedom from and a freedom to. Take, for example, the kind of freedom much beloved of advocates of negative liberty (the kind Berlin likes): the individual's religious freedom. Is this freedom 'from' – freedom from the state telling you what religion you can practise? Or is it freedom 'to' – freedom to practise the religion of your choice? Take the kind of freedom that might be endorsed by advocates of a more positive conception of freedom (the kind that Berlin doesn't like): freedom as rational self-direction. Is this freedom 'to' – freedom to do the rational thing, or to act in accordance with your rational self? Or is it freedom 'from' – freedom from emotion, or ignorance or desire, or whatever else might prevent you from acting rationally?

In a well-known critique of Berlin's essay, the American philosopher Gerald MacCallum (1925–87) argued that Berlin was wrong to think that there are two concepts of liberty, and very wrong if he thought that there was any difference between 'freedom from' and 'freedom to'. According to MacCallum, all claims about freedom have the following form:

x is (is not) free from *y* to do (not do, become, not become) *z*

Freedom is a triadic relation. It necessarily involves reference to three things: *x*, the agent or subject of freedom; *y*, the constraint or interference or obstacle; and *z*, the goal or end. Whatever claim about freedom you have in mind, it will contain – explicitly or implicitly – the idea of an agent being free from something to do or become something. What people who disagree about liberty disagree about is what counts as an *x*, what counts as a *y* and what counts as a *z*.

For MacCallum, Berlin's talk about there being two concepts of liberty is doubly confusing. In the first place, there is only one concept, the one outlined in the triadic formula. People disagree not in their views about the concept of liberty but in their views about conceptions of it. Conceptions differ because there are

2

Liberty

differences of opinion about what should be regarded as an agent, a constraint and a goal. Now this is consistent with there being two conceptions of liberty. If there were just two ways of filling out MacCallum's formula, then we might sensibly say that there were two conceptions of liberty – and we could rescue Berlin simply by substituting 'conception' wherever he says 'concept'. But there aren't just two ways of filling out the formula. There are lots of different ways, and any attempt to divide them into two categories or types – as Berlin does – is likely to be unhelpful. It can be useful to divide them into categories. There are interesting ways of grouping different conceptions, as we shall see. But trying to fit them into just two boxes – called 'negative' and 'positive' – is too crude.

On this view, if we want to think about the differences between conceptions of freedom, we should focus on how they regard the agent, what they regard as constraints on that agent and what they regard as that agent's goals or ends. That is the way precisely and carefully to identify what is going on in debates about freedom. And, having identified the different views available, we can start to think about which conception we ourselves favour. Some issues concern the agent. Is the agent the empirical individual that we observe? Or is it her rational or 'higher' or 'moral' self? Or is it a collective or group, such as a nation or class? Others are about what counts as a constraint. Is it only intentional or deliberate interference by others? Can one be made unfree by one's own desires (such as one's desire for a cigarette)? Does poverty restrict freedom? Still others have to do with goals. Is somebody unfree just when they are prevented from doing what they want to do? Or what they might want to do? Or from whatever would amount to true self-realization for them? These are the difficult and important issues raised by Berlin's essay. The next section aims to bring them into focus.

Three distinctions between conceptions of liberty

I've suggested that it is not helpful to divide conceptions of freedom into 'freedom from' and 'freedom to'. The three distinctions outlined below are (I hope) helpful. Each of these is mentioned by Berlin as part of the 'negative' v. 'positive' distinction but, because they are different, his running them together gets in the way of a clear understanding of what is going on. In particular, we'll see that he labels as 'positive freedom' what are really three quite different conceptions. This will help us understand how Blair could endorse something he called positive freedom while not taking even the first step on the road to totalitarianism.

1 Effective freedom v. formal freedom

The difference between effective and formal freedom is the difference between having the power or capacity to act in a certain way and the mere absence of interference. The fact that nobody is preventing you from doing something does not necessarily mean that you can actually do it. Are you free to do it – because nobody is stopping you? Or unfree – because you are not able to do it?

Consider whether all British citizens are free to go on holiday to the Bahamas. Those answering 'yes' might say: 'There is no law against British citizens going on holiday there. Compare Britain with a country – Totalitaria – that denies its citizens the right to go anywhere on holiday. The citizens of Totalitaria are not free to go on holiday to the Bahamas, because there is a law preventing them from doing so. But Britain has no such law, so its citizens do have the freedom in question.' Those answering 'no' might respond: 'It is true that there is no law preventing British citizens from going on holiday to the Bahamas. But it is a cruel joke to pretend that all citizens are thereby free to do so. Those citizens living in poverty, with barely enough money to get through the week, are obviously not free to go on such a holiday. They may have the formal freedom – in the narrow legalistic sense that nobody is actually preventing them from doing so – but they do not have the effective freedom.'

This is the debate about freedom with most relevance to contemporary politics. Very roughly, the right argues that freedom is essentially about not being interfered with by others, so freedom is best promoted by a state that does as little as possible and a laissez-faire free-market economy, while the left claims that there is more to freedom than not being interfered with. People's real or effective (or, sometimes, 'positive') freedom can be promoted not just by leaving them alone, but by putting them in a position to do things they would not otherwise be able to do. The right wants to limit the role of the state – perhaps all the way down to the 'night-watchman' role advocated by Nozick (as discussed in Part 1). The left claims that a more active, interventionist, redistributive and 'enabling' state can be justified on freedom grounds. According to the left, the right is wedded to a simplistic 'negative' view of freedom, whereas the left sees freedom in a more 'positive' way. It is this 'positive' conception of freedom that Blair was seeking to defend.

This distinction can, of course, be expressed in terms of MacCallum's triadic relation. Those endorsing this variant of the 'positive' view think that poverty, or lack of resources, counts as a constraint on freedom – as a y in his formula. Whereas those endorsing the 'negative' view think that only deliberate interference by others (for example, by laws prohibiting particular actions) counts as such a constraint. The suggestion by the left is that the right has an unreasonably restricted view of what counts as interference. Giving people money increases their effective freedom. So too does giving them education or healthcare. With education and in good health, they are free to take advantage of opportunities that would otherwise not really be available to them. They might be formally available. But, for some people, government action is needed to make the freedom to take advantage of them real or effective.

This conception of freedom as effective – rather than formal – freedom is one of the things that Berlin calls 'positive' freedom, and one of the things that he warns against. We should not, according to him, confuse freedom with 'the conditions of its exercise'. On this view, all British citizens are free to go on holiday to the Bahamas. Some have the conditions to exercise that freedom, whereas others do not. If we endorse a conception of effective freedom, we are confusing freedom, which should really be understood in terms of the 'negative' idea of non-interference by others, with other values like equality or justice. Berlin is here warning against the optimistic thought that all good things necessarily coincide. Even if equality or justice requires redistribution of resources from some to others, we shouldn't claim that such redistribution promotes freedom also. The state may be right to interfere in people's lives in the name of justice or equality, but it is dangerously misleading to claim that that action can be justified by appeal to the value of freedom. Berlin is right that one should generally be careful to keep one's concepts distinct, rather than letting them blur into a fuzzy mess. But it doesn't follow that people living in poverty are free to go on holiday to the Bahamas, lacking merely the conditions needed to exercise that freedom.

Now I'm going to complicate things. Everything I've said about it so far has assumed that the distinction between formal and effective freedom is indeed a real distinction. It is certainly one that plays a role in political argument. But let's press at it to see what is really going on. The contrast, in the example, is between Totalitaria, whose citizens are actually not allowed to go on holiday, and Britain, where all citizens are allowed to go but some don't have the money. In the former, there is a law that stops people going. In the latter, it's their lack of resources. Both sides to the dispute I outlined would accept this description of the situation. What they disagree about is what counts as a constraint on freedom. But is this actually the right way to describe the situation?

Think about what happens, in Britain, when somebody with no money tries to go on holiday to the Bahamas. She walks or hitches a lift to the airport, she tries to board the plane, she is stopped at the gate because she doesn't have a ticket (and can't afford to buy one, even though, let's suppose, there are empty seats), she persists in trying to get on board – she really wants this holiday – and eventually, after a struggle, she is arrested by the security guards or airport police. What is it that is preventing her from going on holiday? It is the law. The law that says that people must have a valid ticket before they can fly. Totalitaria has a law that prevents any citizen from going on holiday. Britain has a law that prevents any citizen who does not have a ticket from doing so. So what actually stops our poor person is not simply her lack of money, but that in combination with the law of the land, as enforced by the police. This is deliberate interference by others – just like the interference in

Totalitaria. We have set up the rules for our society in such a way that those without the money to pay for a ticket (or to get one by some other means) are not allowed to go on the holiday.

These may well be the right rules. I'm not suggesting that anybody who wants to should be able to get on any plane (nor even that exotic holidays should be distributed randomly, by ballot, so that people's chances of getting one have nothing to do with how much money they have). The law restricting the freedom of those without the means to get a ticket may well be a justified law, and the restriction of freedom it implies may well be a justified restriction. The point of the example is very specific. It is simply to bring out the fact that the kind of constraint on freedom in question is the law backed up by the coercive power of the state – just like the kind of constraint on freedom in Totalitaria. Having money gives you the legal right to do things that you would not otherwise have the right to (i.e., be free to) do: get bread if you're hungry, a roof over your head if you lack shelter. We may be right to have the laws about private property and money that we do. But we should acknowledge that such laws imply deliberate restriction by the state (in a democratic state, by the people as a whole) of people's choices about how they live their lives. They are, in that sense, 'formal' restrictions on people's freedom.

This doesn't mean that the distinction between formal and effective freedom is completely useless – another red herring like 'freedom from' and 'freedom to'. Unlike the 'from' v. 'to' distinction, there really is something at stake between those who hold the different views. If the last three paragraphs are right, then the way those views are sometimes characterized (restriction as law v. restriction as lack of resources) can be misleading. But those who do and do not think redistribution can be justified in the name of freedom do still disagree, and disagree about something important. It helps to discuss what they're disagreeing about. Remember too that the formal v. effective distinction does not always have something to do with money and law. Think about somebody who is very ill, and cannot pursue her preferred career without medical treatment. If freedom were merely absence of interference by others, we would have to say that she is free to pursue that career – she simply lacks the effective capacity (here health) to do it.

Armed with the distinction between formal and effective freedom, we could, if we wanted, say that while nobody is preventing her from pursuing that career, so she is formally free to do so, she will not have the effective freedom to pursue it unless she is given the medical treatment. Here is a different kind of example where the distinction between formal and effective freedom looks capable of doing some work, and where the state might be thought able to act to promote the effective freedom of some of its citizens (in this case by providing medical care). It's different because the restriction on effective freedom – the y of MacCallum's formula – is not lack of money (and hence law, a deliberate creation precisely designed to stop people doing things), but poor health.

2 Freedom as autonomy v. freedom as doing what one wants

The second distinction is completely different from the first but also gets called the distinction between negative and positive liberty. This is the difference between freedom as autonomy and freedom as doing what one wants. Autonomy, literally, means 'self-rule' or 'self-law' ('auto' as in 'auto-mobile' – a car that goes by itself; 'nomy' as in 'astro-nomy' – a science concerned to discover the rules or laws governing the stars). The thought behind this distinction is that somebody could be doing what she wanted without really ruling (or being in control of, or governing) herself. She would then have negative freedom – nobody is interfering with her – but would she have positive freedom? Would she have the kind of freedom that consists of being in control of one's life?

It should be clear how this differs from the previous distinction. Nothing in my discussion of formal and effective freedom called into question the idea that freedom has to do with lack of constraint on people's doing (or being able to do) what they want (or might want). If we give resources to the poor in order to increase their effective freedom, we are enabling them to do things they want (or might want) to do but would otherwise not be able to do. We do not add the further thought: 'OK, now they're able to do more of what they might want to do. But are they really in control of their lives? Are they really living an autonomous life rather than simply going along with whatever desires they happen to find themselves having?' Freedom as autonomy is more controversial than freedom as effective power or capacity to act. Why? Because it involves the thought that a person could be doing what she wants to do but, because her wants don't satisfy some further condition – the condition that would make those wants autonomous – she is not really free. Many people, including Berlin, think that this is a dangerous idea. It is this, according to Berlin, that eventually led to the perverse situation whereby totalitarian regimes justified their rule in the name of freedom.

Before seeing why, let's stick with the distinction between effective freedom and freedom as autonomy. Think about what the state is doing for people when it provides education to those who would not otherwise receive it. An educated person might be regarded as more free than an uneducated person in two quite different ways. First, she will have more options available to her. Someone who can read, or programme a computer, is effectively free to do things – such as get jobs that involve reading or computer programming – that someone who does not have those skills is not effectively free to do. By teaching her, the state is increasing her effective freedom – her freedom to do things she might want to do. In that sense, giving her education is like giving her money. But there is a second aspect to education that is not like money, and that is intimately related to freedom as autonomy. Someone who has been taught relevant information, and been taught to process it, to think for herself, to consider consequences, to evaluate different courses of action, is more autonomous, more in charge of her own life, than somebody who has not. This is so quite independently of the fact that education also increases the range of options available to her. We might think of education as coming in two parts: the part that increases your effective freedom, opening doors that would not otherwise be open to you, and the part that makes you more autonomous, telling you what doors there are and putting you in a better position to decide which of the open doors you really do want to walk through.

As well as helping get clear on the difference between effective freedom and freedom as autonomy, the education example also suggests that freedom as autonomy doesn't have to be scary. If part of having autonomy is simply being able to think clearly and make informed judgements about what one wants, then it may seem hard to see what Berlin is worried about, hard to see where the totalitarian menace comes in. It is certainly important to see that autonomy can be understood in a relatively innocuous way. Indeed, I will end this part of the book by outlining various other ways in which freedom as autonomy need not be as dangerous as Berlin thinks. But, to see what concerns Berlin, the concept of autonomy needs to be related to the idea – most systematically developed by Kant – that we can think of each person as divided into two distinct 'selves'. An 'ideal', or 'inner', or 'higher', or 'rational', or 'true', or 'transcendental', or 'noumenal' or 'moral' self, and an 'empirical', or 'lower', or 'irrational', or 'emotional', or 'phenomenal' or 'base' self. Autonomy is achieved when the first of these selves – let's use the term 'higher self' from now on – is in control of the 'lower self'. If you act in accordance with mere desire or emotion, then you are not really in control. You are acting, in Kant-speak, heteronomously ('hetero' = 'other', as in 'hetero-sexual'). If you've ever felt torn because you want to do something but something inside you – your higher self – tells you that you shouldn't (smoke? try to sleep with your best friend's boyfriend?), then you'll have some understanding of this idea. And if you've ever gone against that inner voice, and felt yourself to be less free than you would have been if you'd been able to do what it said, then you – like Kant – think that there is more to freedom than doing what you want. Where this idea gets dangerous, of course, is when somebody else claims to know better than you what is the 'rational' or 'higher' thing for you to do. That's when somebody else (such as the state) may be tempted to come along and say: 'You think you want A. But that is only what your heteronomous self wants. What your true self wants is B. So I'm going to give you B. This may feel like a restriction on your freedom, but it won't be really. Actually, by getting you to do what your true self really wants, I'm making you more free.' The most famous phrase in Rousseau's most famous work *The Social Contract* (1762) talks about people being 'forced to be free'. A phrase which nicely captures the paradox (and danger) in this line of thought.

Of the various different things that he calls 'positive liberty', this is the one that Berlin is most interested in and concerned about. It is this 'divided self' perspective that is central to the tradition in the history of political ideas which he charts so brilliantly, the tradition which begins with Rousseau and moves on through German philosophical Idealism – Kant (1724–1804), Fichte (1762–1814), Hegel (1770–1831) and Marx (1818–83) – to the totalitarian doctrines of national socialism and state communism. Today, with the Cold War over, the idea that human beings have some higher or true purpose which justifies a state forcing them to live their lives a certain way – and thereby puts them on the path to true freedom – is most frequently associated with religious doctrines. One thinks of the Taliban in Afghanistan, convinced of their fundamentalist version of Islam and ready to deny women, and of course religious dissidents, all kinds of conventional freedoms. Berlin was essentially aiming at secular doctrines hostile to the kind of freedom he cared about. But, as when Locke and other key figures in the liberal tradition developed their arguments, his more obvious enemy today would be intolerant state religion.

One development within this way of thinking about positive freedom was particularly important. What one finds elements of in Rousseau's 'general will', and which is completely explicit by the time one reaches Hegel, Fichte and Marx, is not just the positing of a higher self 'inside' the individual but also the positing of a collective 'higher' self. For Fichte, this was the nation (he was a major influence on Nazism). For Marx, it was the proletariat – which represents, for him, true humanity as a whole. The individual's higher self is that element within her which puts the interest of the collective above her own individual interests. Not only, then, is the true subject of freedom something other than the empirical self – with her actual desires, beliefs and emotions; it becomes, in these theorists, something other than the individual. And once we think of freedom as something that is achieved by the collective – by the nation or class or race – when it achieves its true purpose (world domination, communism), then it becomes even easier to denigrate the freedom of empirical individuals to do what they happen to want to do.

This is the story that Berlin cares most about, and it correctly identifies a profound difference between conceptions of liberty. That's why, if I had my way, I would insist that the term 'positive liberty' should be restricted to this idea of freedom as autonomy. Using that term also to describe the two other ideas I've laid out does Berlin and us no favours. Clearly one could agree with Tony Blair that freedom should mean effective (and not merely formal) freedom, while disagreeing with Kant – let alone his collectivist descendants – that freedom consists in rational self-direction or living in accordance with the one true faith (rather than doing what one wants). To evaluate claims about freedom properly, we need first carefully to distinguish and identify them. Then we can take them one at a time and be clear about what is at stake in each case.

As MacCallum's formula implies, the differences I've been talking about concern what counts as an agent x, a constraint y, and a goal z. Is freedom essentially a matter of empirical individuals (x) being free from interference by other empirical individuals (y) to act on their wants (z)? (In his *Leviathan* (1651), Thomas Hobbes said: 'A free man is he that . . . is not hindered to do what he hath the will to do.') Is it a matter of higher selves being free from desire or emotion or ignorance to act rationally or achieve self-realization? Or of a nation achieving freedom from domination by an imperial power to determine its own laws? There are many different ways of specifying the conception of freedom as autonomy, so we should think of this conception as a family of more specific conceptions. On some views, like Kant's, freedom consists in acting morally. On other, more Romantic, views, it consists in the true expression of the self. It may be identified with a life spent in accordance with the one true faith. What all these have in common is a notion of agency (x) which allows that there can be internal constraints on freedom – that freedom can be limited by inner factors (such as desires), not just the interference of external others.

3 Freedom as political participation v. freedom beginning where politics ends

A third way in which Berlin draws the distinction between positive and negative freedom contrasts those who see freedom as being achieved through political activity with those who see freedom as being essentially to do with that sphere of activity which is left to the private individual. This variant of 'positive freedom' holds that one achieves true freedom through political participation in the state, through taking part in collective self-government, through being involved in making the laws under which one lives. The contrast is with the more conventional view that the laws are the rules that determine what the individual is and is not free to do.

This version of positive freedom can clearly overlap with a 'freedom as autonomy' conception. Suppose we identify freedom with true self-realization. Add to this the thought that human beings achieve true self-realization through political activity, and one will conclude that freedom is achieved through political activity. Aristotle thought that 'man is a political animal', by which he partly meant that what is special about human beings – what distinguishes them from other animals – is their capacity to come together collectively to deliberate and decide how they are going to organize their society. Classical republicanism, on traditional interpretations, held just this view of freedom. For republicans, political participation is the true end of man, the privileged locus of the good life for human beings, and thus the way to real freedom. (For American readers, I should say that the kind of 'republicanism' I'm talking about has nothing to do with membership of the Republican Party; for Brits, that it does have something to do with opposition to the monarchy.) This republican view is, of course, very different from the more commonsensical liberal view that freedom is to do with people being left to live their lives as they think best. In contemporary terminology, this kind of republicanism would be seen as too 'perfectionist' – or insufficiently neutral between rival accounts of what is the good life for human beings – to justify state policy in its name. (The difference between perfectionist and neutralist views about what the state can do will be explained in Part 4, on community.)

'Freedom as political participation' can overlap with 'freedom as autonomy' in a different way also. Suppose we think that there have to be laws – if only because the alternative is the state of nature – and we accept that what laws do is restrict people's freedom. A good question is: how can people live under law yet still be free? (This was Rousseau's question.) There are two different kinds of answer to this. The first, and more obvious, answer is that law itself promotes freedom. The law can restrict people's freedom in the name of promoting their freedom. For example, the law against murder prevents me murdering – thereby restricting my freedom – but it also prevents me being murdered – thereby promoting my freedom. One strand of thought underlying the social contract tradition is that it makes sense for people to sacrifice their freedom to do whatever they like (such as murder one another) for the sake of freedom under law, which, on the whole, is more worth having. This is the conventional liberal account of the role of the state. On this account, the kind of freedom promoted by law is negative liberty (such as the freedom not to be murdered). This link between law and liberty says nothing about who makes the law. My freedom not to be murdered may be protected by law even if that law was decided by a dictator.

The second, more interesting – and distinctively republican – answer reminds us that autonomy means 'self-rule'. Rousseau says that the most important kind of freedom consists in obedience to a law we give ourselves. How can we live under law but yet be free? Second answer: we can do that if we live under laws we have given to ourselves. That is why there is a kind of freedom achieved by citizens of a democracy, participating in the making of the law, that is not achieved by subjects of a dictator (however much freedom of the more conventional, negative, kind that dictator grants to those subjects). Even those who are outvoted – and so are forced to comply with laws they do not themselves favour – are free in the sense that they are equal members of a self-governing collective rather than subject to law dictated by others. This is freedom as non-domination. The slave of a liberal master may find that she is free to do all kinds of things that the slave of an authoritarian one is not free to do. But she is still not her own master. She is subject to the will of another. However much her owner may care about and look after her, if he makes the decisions, she does not enjoy freedom as non-domination. In MacCallum's terms, this kind of freedom is freedom of a citizen (x) from domination by others (y) to make the rules she is to live under (z).

So far, I've distinguished two ways of spelling out republican freedom; two ways in which political participation might be

regarded as crucial to freedom, both of which can be put in terms
of freedom as autonomy. One involves the idea of 'self-realization
through politics'. The other involves 'freedom as living under
laws you've made for yourself'. There is, I'm afraid to say, a third
account of the republican position. This holds that the kind of
freedom republicans are interested in is neither the controversial
and metaphysically dodgy 'freedom as self-realization via politics',
nor freedom as non-domination. On this third account, the kind
of freedom republicans care about is boring old negative freedom,
the individual's freedom from interference by others. Political participation is crucial to freedom not because freedom is achieved in
the very act of participation, nor because participation in making
the laws one is to live by means that one is not subject to the will
of another, but because participation is the most effective means
of protecting it. On this account, participation is instrumental to
freedom, not intrinsic to it. If liberals and republicans disagree
about anything, they disagree not about the good life for human
beings, nor what counts as freedom. They disagree simply about
whether, or to what extent, an active, engaged, politically aware
citizenry is necessary for the secure protection of negative liberty.

The instrumental republican argument runs roughly as follows.
Suppose we care about negative liberty. Now it is perfectly possible
to imagine a very liberal dictator, one who cares about the negative
freedom of his subjects and makes laws that are maximally conducive
to its protection. The people aren't involved in making the laws – so
they don't have freedom on the 'freedom as participation' or 'freedom
as non-domination' views – but they do have as much freedom from
interference by others as they could possibly have. Does the conceiv-
ability of a liberal dictator mean that those who care about negative
liberty should favour dictatorship as the best way to make the laws?
Of course not. Why not? Because even though the people in the
society may enjoy lots of negative liberty, that liberty is hardly robust
or secure or resilient. Their enjoying it depends solely on the good
will of the dictator. If he changes his mind, or is succeeded in power
by his illiberal son, then their liberty will just disappear. What system
for making the laws makes it most likely that individuals will enjoy
negative freedom? Under what system is their negative liberty most
resilient (or secure or robust)? Answer: a self-governing republic, in

which all citizens are actively engaged in politics. Citizens must be actively engaged in politics, and imbued with a strong spirit of civic duty, because that is the surest way for them to protect their freedom from interference by others. There is something paradoxical about this view. (Quentin Skinner (b. 1940), the English political theorist who proposes this interpretation and is sympathetic to the view, calls one of his articles 'The Paradoxes of Political Liberty.') For the better protection of their own freedom, it may be necessary for citizens to accept that they have duties to do things that they would not otherwise choose to do: vote, keep in touch with political affairs, be prepared to die for their country (to protect it from invasion by illiberal external powers). If they don't accept it, it may be justified for the state to impose compliance with the duty on them. In Australia, citizens are legally obliged to vote. Part of the justification for this restriction of their freedom − they aren't free not to vote (at least not without paying a fine) − is that it encourages them to keep in touch with politics, and thereby helps to protect their own, negative, freedom.

Freedom, private property, the market and redistribution

A lot of political argument involves debate about private property, the market and redistributive taxation. The concept of freedom often plays a pivotal role in such debate. In this section I'm going to set out five positions that one might take on this issue. By keeping clear on the differences between them, the reader will, I hope, be better placed to think about which position she agrees with, and about why she disagrees with the others.

1 Justified redistributive taxation does not infringe the freedom of those who are taxed because their claims to the property in question cannot be established in the first place

This is the position argued for by the American philosopher Ronald Dworkin (1931–2013), who is the other leading egalitarian liberal, alongside Rawls. He says that when we take property from those whose claim to it is not justified, we shouldn't think of ourselves as restricting their freedom at all. This is because judgements about what counts as a restriction of freedom depend upon judgements about what property rights are justified in the first place. Essentially the opposite view is put forward by the Canadian philosopher G. A. Cohen (1941–2009), who believes that my freedom is restricted whenever someone interferes with my actions, whether or not I have a right to perform them and whether or not my obstructor has a right to interfere with me. Dworkin thinks that the question of whether an action is a restriction on freedom, and whether it's justified, boil down to the same thing. Cohen thinks that they are different.

Suppose we decided that Queen Elizabeth II could not, after all, justify her claim to own 'her' estate at Balmoral, and we decided instead either to take it into common ownership or to divide it up into a number of small plots which were then given to previously propertyless Scots. Would we thereby be restricting the queen's freedom? She would no longer be, as she was before, free to go wherever she liked on that land, or free to decide who else could cultivate, or walk on, it. So in this sense it seems right to say, with Cohen, that this kind of redistribution, even when justified, does indeed restrict freedom. Of course, whether the queen does indeed have a property right to the Balmoral estate is crucial to the question of whether we would be justified in taking it away from her. This is not an argument trying to show that there should be no such thing as private property, or that redistribution (even of large estates) is justified. The point is simply that, even if it were justified, we should acknowledge that we are restricting the freedom of those from whom we are taking it.

Others take a similar line to Dworkin. In his *Second Treatise of Government*, Locke said 'that ill deserves the name of confinement which hedges us in only from bogs and precipices'. In contemporary language: 'If somebody puts up a fence to stop us wandering into quicksand or falling off a cliff, then we shouldn't call that a restriction on our freedom.' (In MacCallum's terms, 'we shouldn't regard that fence as a *γ*'.) I think it makes things clearer if one acknowledges, what is surely the case, that the fence does restrict people's freedom but that this might well be a justified restriction.

To see this, think about the contrast between a fence that actually prevents people walking in a certain direction and a notice that warns people about the dangers but leaves them 'free' to walk where they like.

Notice the overlap between these approaches to freedom and the variant of positive freedom that identifies it with autonomy. Locke's thought is that, since nobody in her right mind would want to walk into quicksand or fall off the edge of a cliff, preventing her from doing so is not really interfering with her freedom. This makes sense if one thinks that freedom consists in doing what one would do if one were in one's right mind. Dworkin's thought is that, since the super-rich do not have a right to all their property in the first place, taking some of it away from them is not really interfering with their freedom. This makes sense if one thinks that freedom consists in doing what one has a right to do, or is morally justified in doing. I'll say something about this overlap later on. For now, it is worth pointing out that Dworkin and Locke are both working with what some call 'moralized' definitions of freedom, a conception that ties judgements about 'freedom' to moral judgements about what people should (and should not) be free to do. Against both of them, Cohen wants to separate judgements about when somebody is and is not free to do something from the question of what people should (and should not) be free to do. First, we look and see what people are and are not free to do. Then, we think about whether what we have seen is justified, and, if not, what would be.

The distinction between moralized and non-moralized conceptions of freedom can help our thinking about the kind of libertarian claim we came across in our discussion of Nozick's view of justice as entitlement. Part 1 discussed the suggestion that those who value freedom must believe in private property rights and should oppose redistributive taxation. Of course, few in real politics object to all redistributive taxation. But it is true that many on the right think that the value of freedom necessarily supports minimal redistribution from market outcomes. They think that, if such redistribution is to be justified, it must be on grounds other than freedom (equality, justice, public order). So it is worth looking at how this argument is supposed to work.

It is true that those who have private property are free to do things that they would not be free to do if they did not have it. Think about the queen walking around Balmoral, or the wealthy person who owns a fleet of aeroplanes and can fly to the Bahamas whenever she likes. But what about those who do not have private property? To them, the fact that the queen owns the hills at Balmoral constitutes a restriction on their freedom to walk around those hills. The fact that somebody else owns the planes and will let others fly to the Bahamas only if they pay the fare constitutes a restriction on their freedom to go to the Bahamas. Libertarians say that they care about freedom, and argue for private property rights on freedom grounds. But they don't seem to care about, or even notice, the unfreedom implied by the existence of private property rights.

What explains libertarians' blindness to the unfreedom implied by their preferred arrangements? The best explanation is to see them as working with a moralized conception of freedom. Their view is that private property does not restrict the freedom of those without it as long as one can justify preventing them from doing what they might otherwise do. On this view, we should not think that those prevented from walking on the Balmoral hills are deprived of freedom, because the queen's property right to her estate justifies that constraint. To take the estate away from the queen, however, would involve an interference with her freedom, precisely because it is rightfully hers. This suggests that the libertarian view is, ultimately, a view about the legitimacy of property rights. Where they appeal to freedom, it is to a conception that makes judgements about what does and does not count as a restriction of freedom depend on judgements about the legitimacy of particular property rights. In that sense, the term 'libertarian'– with its appropriation of the word 'liberty' – is misleading. Those working with a non-moralized conception of liberty are going to notice the lack of freedom, in a libertarian society, suffered by all who are prevented from doing what they might otherwise do by the very fact that property is privately owned. Such people might advocate the abolition, or redistribution, of private property in the name of freedom, and are likely to resent the suggestion that they are enemies of freedom.

2 Even if justified redistribution does restrict the freedom of those who are taxed, and whether or not it increases the freedom of those who benefit, it makes them better off in other ways and can be justified on these non-freedom grounds

Before going on to explore the suggestion that the redistribution of property might be justified in the name of freedom, it's worth pointing out that it might also, or alternatively, be justified in the name of other values. Even if we think that redistribution does reduce the freedom of those who are taxed, this reduction needn't itself be justified on freedom grounds. We shouldn't think that freedom can only be restricted for the sake of freedom. It might be justified because it promotes equality, or justice, or social order, or utility, or any of a number of other values.

This point is generalizable. Think about legislation making it compulsory to wear seat belts. One could perfectly sensibly think all of the following: (a) this is good legislation; (b) it restricts people's freedom; (c) it does not also promote people's freedom. Locke, presumably, would want to say that, since they are protecting us from worse evils, seat belts should not really be thought of as restrictions on freedom ('That ill deserves the name of confinement which dramatically decreases the likelihood of our dying in a car crash'). But this looks like an implausible and unnecessary addition to what is already a perfectly coherent position. Of course we might try to argue that seat belts actually promote the freedom of those forced to wear them. Because a fully rational self would choose to wear them and freedom consists in doing what a fully rational self would choose to do. Because people almost universally recognize that they are better off wearing seat belts and welcome laws that help them get into the habit of doing something they actually want to do anyway. Or because anything that helps protect people from death must be thought of as promoting their freedom. (How free are the dead?) But these look like unnecessarily controversial or misleading claims. Why not simply say that the legislation is justified because it makes people better off than they would otherwise be, even though it does this by restricting their freedom? This, of course, involves the claim that people don't always freely and spontaneously choose to do what will make them better off

— in that sense the legislation is paternalistic. It implies that some, like parents in relation to their children, know what is good for people better than the people do themselves. But this looks more plausible than claiming that the legislation promotes their freedom.

3 Redistribution reduces the effective freedom of those who are taxed, but is justified because it makes for more effective freedom overall

As I suggested above, it is the appeal to effective freedom that tends to do most work in the kind of freedom-based justification of redistribution most common in contemporary political argument from the left and centre-left. Think of all that talk about the 'enabling state'. Since the idea of effective freedom should be clear by now, let's focus here on the distinctively quantitative aspect of this claim.

Why might redistributive taxation be thought to increase the total amount of effective freedom? One answer might be that taking, say, £10,000 from a very well-off person and giving £500 each to 20 different poor people means that there is a net increase (of 19) in the number of people who are free to do things they were not previously free to do. Here the idea that redistribution produces more effective freedom depends on the thought that it makes more people better off, in terms of effective freedom. Another thought pointing in the same direction notices that the state can spend the money it raises in taxes on goods that are available to many – perhaps all – citizens at once. Leaving the £10,000 with the rich individual may leave her free to do things she wouldn't be able to do without it, but spending that money on high-quality TV, or on public healthcare, may produce extra options (and hence effective freedoms) for many.

A second answer might be that taking £500 from a rich person and giving it to a single poor person counts as a net increase in effective freedom, because the marginal £500 is worth more to the poor than to the rich. Here the thought is not that more people have more effective freedom, but that money yields diminishing marginal returns of effective freedom. This answer looks a bit suspicious. One might agree that the marginal £500 is worth more to the poor than to the rich, and think that a good reason for redistributing. But is it worth more to them because it gives them more effective freedom? Isn't it rather because what it gives them the effective freedom to do is more valuable or important? Being free to eat healthy food, or to watch television, is doubtless more important than being free to buy that extra bottle of champagne. But that isn't enough to show that depriving somebody of the freedom to buy the champagne involves a smaller reduction in their freedom than that which is gained by those enabled to eat healthy food.

Comparisons of amounts of freedom are famously hazardous. Luckily they are also probably worth avoiding, because amounts of freedom are not that important. What matters is not how much freedom people have, but what it is that people are and are not free to do, and whether the restrictions that society places on people's freedom are justified. Adapting an example from the Canadian philosopher Charles Taylor (b. 1931), compare Britain and Afghanistan. In Britain, people have freedom of religion but there are lots of traffic lights. In Afghanistan, there are very few traffic lights but people do not have freedom of religion. Suppose we don't know anything else about the two countries. Which gives its members most freedom? Well, in Britain one is constantly having one's freedom restricted by traffic lights. But in Afghanistan there is only one thing one cannot do: practise the religion one believes in. So in purely quantitative terms Britain looks as if it restricts the freedom of its citizens more than does Afghanistan. Taylor thinks that this conclusion is absurd. He thinks it is obvious that Britain gives it citizens more freedom than does Afghanistan. Taylor believes that this shows that, when we make comparisons of freedom, we cannot avoid making judgements about the value of what it is people are and are not free to do. This may be right if we are asked to compare societies, or even individuals, in terms of their overall 'freedom'. It does seem that judgements about that are going to find it hard to avoid some qualitative, and not merely quantitative, input. (One might bite the bullet and describe Britain as a society in which people's freedom is more restricted than it is in Afghanistan, but that would surely be misleading.) But the lesson might be that claims about 'overall freedom' are a

red herring. There are some actions that Britons are not free to
perform, and others that Afghans are not free to perform. What
matters is not 'Who has most freedom overall?', but 'What are the
actions that are restricted in each country?', and 'Is their restriction
justified?'.

*4 Private property rights and market relations encourage people
to misconceive their real interests and hence render them
heteronomous and unfree*

None of the positions discussed so far invokes 'positive' freedom
in its controversial – 'freedom as autonomy'– sense. Though some
appeal to the distinction between formal and effective freedom,
none is concerned with anything other than the actions that people
might want to perform. There is no mention of autonomy, or the
kind of higher or rational or inner self that might lead us to claim
that somebody was unfree even though she was doing what she
wanted to do. Freedom is understood as the absence of interference with actions that people want or might want to do. There are,
however, other arguments, particularly in the Marxist or radical
left tradition, that would put the case not merely for redistribution
but, rather, for the abolition of private property and transcendence
of market relations altogether, in terms of this more speculative and
controversial conception of freedom as autonomy.

  For example, some Marxists claim that the very existence of an
economy based on private property and market exchange leads
people to misconceive their 'real interests', fostering a conception
of themselves as 'possessive individualists' or 'materialist consum-
ers' that takes them away from a proper understanding of the true
essence of what it is to be a human being. True self-realization
for human beings does not consist in the acquisition of private
property through exchange with others. Only people alienated
from their true selves, misled by bourgeois ideology, the function
of which is to legitimate and stabilize capitalism, could fail to see
that true self-realization for human beings consists in cooperative
or communal activity with other human beings; in production for
use, rather than exchange; in distribution according to need, rather

than according to productive input. If true freedom consists in this kind of self-realization, and capitalist societies encourage a stunting and distorted conception of what it is to be a human being, then such societies lead to the kind of heteronomy that stands in the way of freedom. A free human being is someone who is free of all that distorting ideology and the institutions that embody and promote it. So true freedom consists in rejecting private property and markets as embodying an alienated and distorted understanding of what it is to be human.

5 Freedom = autonomy, autonomy = rationality, rationality = morality, morality = justice, justice = redistribution, therefore the person who recognizes her duty to redistribute her resources is herself freer than the person who doesn't recognize that duty

This (last) position is a variant on the 'freedom as autonomy' idea. Here, though, the argument does not run through the idea that true freedom consists in self-realization, with a thickly specified conception of what self-realization requires. Rather, it goes via the claim that the truly free (i.e., autonomous) person is someone who is acting rationally, hence morally. Suppose acting morally implies redistribution from rich to poor. (Perhaps this is for reasons concerning what would be a justified distribution of freedoms in a more conventional, negative sense.) This leads to the conclusion that the rich themselves are more free in giving their money to the poor than they would be by holding on to it for themselves. They may have less freedom understood as 'range of options available to one without interference', but they have more freedom understood as 'action in accordance with one's higher (= moral) self'. If we assume that there is only one morally correct (or rational) way to act – an assumption I'll question in the next section – then we have the paradox that freedom consists in doing just that thing and nothing else. Freedom as obedience indeed. Obedience to the moral law.

This suggests one more move. Suppose we think that the queen's claim to the Balmoral hills cannot be justified, and that a justifiable distribution of property would involve her giving them up for public use, or for allocation to those more needy than herself. The position we're considering here holds that she herself achieves real freedom by seeing and acting on this moral insight (even though she also loses the freedom to walk around the estate without worrying about bumping into strangers). It's not just that those who now have access to the hills are free to do things they were not previously free to do – though that's true too. It's that she herself achieves freedom, in the important, 'real' sense, through her action of giving up her own – less important – freedoms. But suppose she doesn't see or act on this insight. She persists in her mistaken belief that her claim to the estate is justified. If we take it off her nonetheless – on the perfectly reasonable grounds that it wasn't hers in the first place – can we still claim that we are promoting her freedom? After all, we are only getting her to do what her moral self would do if it were in control, unimpeded by whatever it is – ideological illusion, unreflective traditionalism – that prevents her from seeing what her moral duties really are. Here, of course, we have the suggestion that those who fail correctly to identify the 'general will' for their community – a concept that translates roughly into Kant's moral law – should not think of the coercion that compels them to comply with that will as something inimical to their freedom. Rather, they are being 'forced to be free'. This is just the train of thought that Berlin disliked so much.

Resisting the totalitarian menace

This setting out of various positions on the relation between freedom, private property, the market and redistribution ended up with a couple that invoked positive freedom in the sense that Berlin, and many others, regard as leading us down the slippery slope to totalitarianism. It is this prospect of the totalitarian menace that drives Berlin to defend negative liberty – freedom from interference by others – as the best way to specify the concept of liberty. In this last section, I want to draw a few distinctions that might lead us to wonder whether this particular 'positive' conception of freedom – freedom as autonomy – is really as dangerous as Berlin suggests. We don't want to throw the baby out with the bathwater. We may not like totalitarianism, but that doesn't mean we have to reject any and every conception of freedom as autonomy. My interpretation of Tony Blair's letter to Berlin suggested that the variant of positive freedom that he was trying to defend was 'effective freedom', which would fit with centre-left talk about the enabling state, and involves no controversial claims about higher or true selves. That's why Blair was, on this score at least, cleared of the charge of being a closet dictator. Here I point out seven ways in which he could, if he had wanted, have made some of those controversial claims yet still steer clear of the totalitarian menace.

1 Promoting people's autonomy can involve just providing information and helping them think for themselves

When first introducing the contrast between 'freedom as autonomy' and 'freedom as doing what one wants', I used the example of education. As well as increasing people's effective freedom, by opening doors that would otherwise remain closed to them, education gives people a sense of what their options are and the likely outcome of any action they might take. This is the information-giving aspect of education. It also teaches them to think – to evaluate the different options available to them, to process and reflect upon the information they have. This is the aspect of education that promotes rational reflection. Imagine two people. Penny wants to be a doctor because she thinks that doctors have an exciting life and get paid lots of money. She decided to be a doctor at a very early age because she saw a TV programme featuring a glamorous female doctor and has not considered any other possible careers. She has no idea about what it's really like to be a doctor, and doesn't know how much they actually earn. Claire also wants to be a doctor. She has gathered a great deal of information. She knows what is involved, the chances of her succeeding, what the life is really like, how much she is likely to earn. She has thought carefully about her various options and decided that, on balance and all things considered, medicine is the thing for her. So Penny and Claire both want to be doctors. Suppose they both act on this desire. Are they both acting equally freely? Isn't Claire more autonomous, more in charge of her life, and in that sense more free, because her desire has emerged from rational deliberation based on good information?

Autonomy is here being taken in a fairly weak and uncontroversial sense. People who can think properly, and have appropriate relevant information, are more autonomous than those who can't or don't. Does this way of thinking about autonomy involve any idea of a divided self, or of internal obstacles? Well, if we think Claire is more free than Penny, presumably that's because we think that her desire to be a doctor is somehow more rational, or truer to her authentic self, than is Penny's. Penny is at the mercy of her irrational beliefs. Her desire, though hers, is less truly hers than is Claire's. This may not be her fault. She may not have been provided with the relevant information, nor taught how to think clearly about the information she has got. But it does seem that her ignorance and lack of deliberative capacity stand as obstacles to her genuine self-realization, to her being genuinely in charge of her life. Her true self may or may not want to be a doctor. Perhaps, having been taught to think sensibly and provided with full information, she would still want to be one. That desire would be truer to her real self than is the one she happens to have. Freedom would consist in acting on the desires she would have if she were more rational and better informed. Her ignorance, and her lack of capacity to engage in rational deliberation, do indeed seem like inner obstacles to her freedom.

This way of thinking about autonomy does, then, posit some idea of freedom as 'rational self-direction' and absence of inner constraints. So it does belong with the views that Berlin dislikes so much. But it is surely an innocuous variant of this family of conceptions. We are a very long way indeed from any fear that the state will come along and force people to be free. Children are indeed forced to go to school and this is usually justified precisely on the plausible grounds that it will increase their freedom as autonomy (as well as their 'freedom as effective options') later on. If being taught about the world, and learning how to think about it, promotes autonomy, then autonomy needn't be such a dangerous idea after all.

2 To recognize that there can be internal obstacles to freedom is not to say that anybody other than the agent herself is the best judge of when they exist

The conventional negative conception of freedom holds that somebody is free to do something just as long as nobody else is stopping her, as long as she could do it if she wanted to. This view rejects the idea that there can be internal obstacles to freedom. But, as Charles Taylor argues, it seems undeniable that we do experience such obstacles. Imagine somebody who really wants to be a politician but is so terrified of public speaking that she cannot pursue this goal. Other people may not be preventing her from becoming a politician, but her fear – an internal obstacle – surely is. Sometimes, indeed, we may experience our desires themselves as obstacles, the overcoming of which is freedom, the acting on which is unfreedom. Imagine a would-be explorer whose desire to sleep in a comfortable bed prevents her ever carrying out any expeditions. Or somebody who wants to do the morally right thing but finds herself yielding to temptation. Or somebody who wants to do well in her exams but finds herself unable to resist her urge to go out drinking every night. Or somebody who really wants to give up cigarettes but finds her desire for nicotine too strong. Such people experience true freedom when the desires of their 'autonomous' or 'higher' selves overcome the desires of their 'heteronomous' or 'lower' selves.

In cases like this, we are thinking of the self as divided into two parts. Freedom is achieved when the 'true' or 'higher' part is in control of the 'false' or 'lower' part. Now it is a very good question how we know which part is which, and who is the best judge of that. What makes these examples plausible is the fact that, in each case, the individual herself is making that judgement. So one obvious way to resist the slide towards totalitarianism is to insist that, though there can be internal obstacles to freedom, it is always and necessarily the individual who is the best judge of what is to count as what. That should be enough to prevent the state justifying its coercion by appeal to the claim that, because it knows what people 'really' want better than they do themselves, its coercion is really forcing people to be free.

It's worth pointing out what this position does not involve. Somebody can be the best judge of something without being always and necessarily right about it. I don't think that I always correctly identify what I really want. Sometimes, for example, I persuade myself that I want (really want) something, when it turns out, with hindsight and a greater degree of self-awareness, that my judgement was biased or distorted, that some kind of self-deception, or at least lack of self-knowledge, had been getting in the way of my forming an accurate judgement. But though I have to accept that even I can be wrong, I don't have to accept that anybody else is in a better position than me to judge correctly. Of course, if I believed that somebody else knew me better than I did myself, then I might also believe that she could be a better judge. But I don't have to believe that, and, most relevant to the political issues we are discussing, I certainly don't have to believe that the state is in that position.

3 To recognize that there can be internal obstacles to freedom is not to identify freedom with rationality

The idea that there can be internal obstacles to freedom is often associated with the thought that the true or higher self is the rational self. This is clearest in Kant, for whom the autonomous self is indeed the rational (and moral) self, and what that self is free from is empirical desire and impulse. (Kant was so hostile to wants and desires that he is sometimes interpreted as holding that somebody who wants to do the morally right thing is acting less morally than somebody who doesn't want to but does so out of duty, that duty being recognized by her rational self.) The idea that there is a 'right answer' about what an autonomous person would choose obviously gets a lot of support from the identification of autonomy with rationality. Once the issue of what makes people free turns into that of what it is rational for them to do, then it looks as if the way is open for debate about what is indeed rational for people. And in that debate it might seem that the individual does not occupy a particularly privileged position.

But consider the examples given in the previous section. These were all supposed to be cases where it is plausible to acknowledge internal obstacles to freedom, but none of them required that what was impeded was the exercise of a person's rationality. It's true that the would-be politician suffering from a fear of public speaking is plausibly regarded as having an irrational phobia, but we can regard her as constrained by that without knowing whether wanting to become a politician is a rational thing for her to want. It's true also that we may be inclined to see someone who studies for her exams as more rational than someone who goes out every night, and someone who wants to give up smoking as more rational than someone who doesn't. But the examples don't depend on that. We could, for example, imagine a student who really wanted to go out drinking and who experienced her 'conscience' as an irrational urge inculcated by repressive socialization, hence as a constraint on the freedom of her autonomous self. I might really want to go and watch Oxford United (or the Milwaukee Brewers) play, and regard my desire for warmth and comfort as a constraint on the pursuit of that true purpose of mine. But those who have watched them would agree that it is hard to describe watching United or the Brewers as a rational way to spend an afternoon.

One way of thinking about this – developed by the American philosopher Harry Frankfurt (b. 1929) – is to make a distinction between 'first-order' and 'second-order' desires. First-order desires are desires for things like a comfortable bed, or being an explorer, doing well in exams, or going out drinking. These desires, as we all know, can conflict. A good way of thinking about such conflicts is the idea that we also have second-order desires, which are desires about our first-order desires: they are desires to have or not have other desires. Take our would-be explorer. Does she really want to be an explorer and get rid of her pathetic desire for a comfortable bed? Or is what she really wants to sleep in a comfortable bed untroubled by romantic yearnings for exploration? To answer that question, she must look to her second-order desires. Those will tell her whether or not she is being prevented from doing what she really wants by a desire that she does not really want. Another way of putting a similar point is to talk, as Taylor does, about 'strong evaluation'. We do not just have 'brute' desires that we assess solely in terms of their strength or force. We are also capable of evaluating our desires, of judging them more or less worthy or appropriate, of identifying with or disowning them. This, perhaps, is something that distinguishes us from other animals. Unlike theirs, our desires are not simply less or more intense than one another. We can reflect on them – identify with some, repudiate others – and it is this capacity to discriminate between desires that allows us to regard some as constraints on, or obstacles to, our freedom, which is achieved when we act on our 'real' or 'authentic' ones. To think that desires can be obstacles to freedom, then, we don't need to posit freedom as rationality. We need only the idea that less significant desires can get in the way of the realization of more significant ones. The issue of who is the best judge will then be formulated in terms of who is best able to judge which of a person's desires are more 'significant'.

4 To identify freedom with rationality is not to claim that the same thing is rational for each person

Though we do not have to, we might after all want to make some kind of connection between autonomy (and hence, on this conception, freedom) and rationality. Somebody doing the rational thing is doing what they most have reason to do, and it is not absurd to think that somebody doing that is more free than somebody who is acting irrationally. And, though again we do not have to, we might believe that the individual is not necessarily the best judge of what is rational for her – at least not in areas where others have access to superior information or are better able to process information available to all. After all, most of us believe that parents are better judges of what is and is not rational for their children than those children are themselves. Might not the same apply, even if only to a limited extent, in the case of at least some adults? If we made both these assumptions, rejecting the chances to get off the slippery slope offered by the two previous headings, would we then be committed to going all the way to totalitarianism?

The answer is no. Berlin typically identifies doctrines of positive freedom with what he calls 'monism' – the view that there is one harmonious and correct system of values that tells us how we should live. Berlin thinks, by contrast, that there are many different values that conflict with one another. What he objects to, primarily, are theories that claim correctly to have identified the right way for people to live, and then force them to live that way in the name of their own freedom. But even if we do identify freedom with rationality, we don't have to accept monism in this sense. We can think that different ways to live are rational for different people, so that a state helps its members towards freedom not by getting them all to live the same way, but by doing what it can to help them to live in ways that are rational for them, as the individuals they are. There might be particular areas of life where what is rational is the same for all people (drive around without getting killed, avoid drug addiction). So there might be a limited common core of things it is rational for all people to do and not to do (comply with traffic lights, avoid getting addicted). On the view under discussion, the state could make us do and not do those in the name of our own freedom. But these need not go anywhere near as far as the kind of extensive monistic claims typically associated with totalitarianism. On the contrary, we are likely to end up with a pluralistic, liberal state in which individuals are basically left to decide for themselves what is rational for them.

5 To identify freedom with rationality is not to claim that there is a single thing that is rational for any individual

We don't, then, need to assume that there is a single way of life that is rational for all people. But nor must we assume that there is a single way of life that is rational for any individual person. Think about your own life. It may be that there are some ways to live your life that would be clearly irrational. Given my abilities, it would have been clearly irrational for me to pursue the life of a professional footballer. Given my interests, it would have been irrational for me to become a gardener. But that doesn't show that there is only one life-plan that would be rational for me. Maybe my decision to try to be an academic was no more or less rational than would have been my decision to try to become an actor. Perhaps reason can help us decide between some ways of life, but that doesn't mean it can help us decide between all of them, narrowing the options down to a single right answer for each of us. Perhaps, to use the current terminology, some different ways of life are simply 'incommensurable': not capable of being compared in terms of a metric that would allow us to choose between them on the basis of reason.

If that is right, then the idea that one is only truly free when doing what is rational looks even further from the totalitarian menace. Not only are different ways of life rational for different people, but different ways of life may be equally rational for the same person! Of course, the state might still claim that there are some ways of life that would be irrational for anybody, and seek to promote the freedom of its citizens by preventing (or at least discouraging) them from living those ways. Some ways of life are evil; some are empty or worthless. Nobody has any reason to pursue those, and so the state is promoting the freedom of its citizens when it discourages or prevents people from doing so. But the image of a state leaving citizens free to choose how to live, and choosing from the array of options that their own reason has identified as equally rational for them, is a very long way indeed from the kind of totalitarian state that Berlin regards as the consequence of accepting a doctrine of positive liberty.

6 To identify what would be rational for a person does not necessarily justify interfering with their irrational action

The last two points are supposed to reassure those who dislike the state's interfering in individuals' lives in the name of 'freedom as rationality'. Different things may be rational for different people. Different things may be rational for the same person. So even a state that believes itself justified in helping its citizens to choose rational lives, because that is what true freedom consists in, can be pluralistic, not the monistic totalitarian state that Berlin fears. But there is another way of avoiding the slippery slope. This consists in noticing that even if we could identify what would be rational for a person to do, it doesn't automatically follow that we can justify interfering to get her to do the rational thing.

Suppose you have a friend who uses drugs that are potentially addictive. You know her well enough to know that this is irrational for her. (She hasn't made a careful, reflective judgement about her choice to use drugs. She uses them, let's say, because that is the norm among a group of friends that she wants to be popular with, but you know her well enough to judge that her wanting to be popular results from irrationally low self-esteem and that drugs won't help her become more popular.) Even if you are completely confident in your judgement that she is acting irrationally, it doesn't follow that you would be justified in using force to prevent her from taking them. You might, of course, be justified in trying to get her to sit down and think about what she is doing. You might even be morally required to do that. But doing what one can to get people to see for themselves what is and is not rational for them is quite different from forcing them to do that which is rational. The latter involves a lack of respect, a failure to respect the value of her living her life in her own (irrational) way. It involves, we might say, an unjustified restriction on the individual's freedom to choose for herself.

If we did say that, then we would not, of course, be using a conception of 'freedom as autonomy as rationality'. And we would want to know why the restriction is unjustified – why people should be free to choose irrationally. The notion of 'respect' is part of one answer. The idea that people's living a life they themselves have chosen is necessary for that life to be valuable for them is another. (This builds on Locke's suggestion, in his *Letter on Toleration* (1689), that forcing non-believers into church does them no good – even if every word of the religious doctrine being forced on them is true.) John Stuart Mill's *On Liberty* (1859) provides a number of different answers. Recall, from Part 1, Rawls regarding a person's capacity to frame, revise and pursue a conception of the good as the most morally significant capacity she has. Freedom matters, on these liberal views, because of the importance of individuals being able to live lives they believe in – rather than those foisted on them by others. We will explore these arguments further in Part 4. In this context, the important point is simple: somebody can know better than another what would be rational for that other without being justified in using all available means to get her to do it.

*7 Interference aimed at getting people to act rationally might be justi-
fied while acknowledging that it does involve a restriction on freedom
and without claiming that it is justified on freedom grounds*

So far the discussion has been wholly couched in freedom terms.
But, as noted in the case of private property, we should remember
that things don't have to be argued this way. Recall the discussion of seat belts. Freedom-restricting legislation might be justified simply on the grounds that it makes those restricted better off
than they would otherwise be – and 'better off' in terms that have
nothing to do with freedom. Discussions of positive freedom, and
of the state interference it has been invoked by some to justify, can
lead us to forget that freedom is only one value among many. As
always, what matters, ultimately, is whether, all things considered,
the state's action is justified.

Conclusion

The concept of liberty is used in many different ways, with different theorists and traditions invoking quite different conceptions of
it. This leads to quite understandable confusion, confusion that is
not dispelled by Berlin's famous essay. It is not helpful to divide
conceptions into two kinds, because doing that requires lumping
together conceptions that are importantly different. At its worst,
it leads to the really misleading idea that the distinction between
'freedom from' and 'freedom to' captures a crucial fault line, when
it fact it captures nothing at all. MacCallum's suggestion – 'x is free
from y to do (become) z'– is a better means to clarity. Armed with
this, we can be precise in our freedom claims and get on with the
important business of deciding who should be free from what to
do or become what.

Much political debate invoking the concept of freedom has
focused on issues to do with property and redistribution. During
the 1970s and 1980s, the right appropriated the concept of freedom
for its own purposes. To believe in freedom meant to favour the
free market, and to want the state to do as little as possible, leaving

Part 3

Equality

Equality is more controversial than justice – even social justice – or liberty. Many reject equality. Egalitarians, it is said, endorse the politics of envy, foster a culture of dependence in which individuals nannied by the state lose all sense of responsibility, and show wilful ignorance of the functional requirements of a modern, dynamic economy operating in a global marketplace. Equality is regarded, even by its former friends, as an outdated ideal. Politically, 'equality' is bad news, out of touch with the individualistic, aspirational values of today's voters. In the US, current debate is about whether inheritance tax should start to kick in on estates worth less than $5 million. British politicians who support increasing the share of tax paid by the wealthy are immediately accused of reviving 'class war'. Redistributive taxation, taxing the better off to help the worse off, is done almost secretly – 'stealth tax', not 'wealth tax'. Even those who still believe in it frame their objectives in other terms: 'Opportunity for the many, not the few.'

All this is at the level of popular political rhetoric. But equality has been given a hard time by political philosophers too. Valuing equality, they argue, is a mistake. What matters is not that people have equal shares of good things. Nor is it even that people have equal opportunity for (or access to) good things. What matters, if we think about it, is that everybody has enough, or that those who have least have as much as possible, or that people who most need things take priority. To care about equality is to care that people have the same amount as each other, which looks like a peculiar thing to care about. After all, a possible world in which people have equal amounts is one in which nobody has anything.

In the discourse of today's electoral politics, redistributive taxation has got itself a bad name, is carried out somewhat surreptitiously (where it is carried out at all), and, when it does reach the surface, is presented in terms that make scant reference to equality. Meanwhile political philosophers are increasingly abandoning equality as a political ideal. Against this background, it is important to see that the philosophers' arguments against equality are not necessarily arguments against redistributive taxation. Someone who rejects equality can care passionately that resources should be transferred from the rich to the poor. Rejecting equality, in this sense, means rejecting a particular reason that might be offered to justify the redistribution. One can, then, approve of the fact that redistributive policies are presented as aiming not at equality but at other goals while having no sympathy with politicians' reluctance to argue the case for redistribution. It is perfectly coherent to reject equality at the philosophical level, as a fundamental ideal, while arguing that, for other reasons, resources should be more equally distributed – perhaps much more equally distributed – than they are at present.

But it is also important to distinguish between philosophical and practical arguments. Philosophical objections to equality, which point to the oddness of focusing on equal shares, are quite different from practical objections that oppose redistribution because of its alleged consequences. Suppose I care above all else that the poorest members of society should be as well off as they can. I could still oppose a more sharply progressive tax-and-transfer system. Why? Because I might believe that the result of such a policy would be effects on economic productivity serious enough to reduce the size of the pie, and hence the size of the smallest piece, in the long run. People doubtful about redistribution – as a matter of policy – could doubt purely on practical, empirical grounds, while being no less committed to the goal of helping the disadvantaged. As always in politics, one must keep clear on the distinction between means and ends. The kind of political philosophy discussed in this book clarifies concepts and arguments, enabling the more precise identification of goals that a society might seek to achieve. Which policies will best realize those goals is a further and separate question.

The egalitarian plateau

Political philosophers have recently given equality a hard time. But almost everybody – including almost all political philosophers – believes in equality in some sense. With the exception of a few racists, contemporary politics, and political philosophy, is carried out on what the Canadian philosopher Will Kymlicka (b. 1962) has called an 'egalitarian plateau'. Nearly all agree with the principle that members of a political community should be treated as equals, that the state should treat its citizens with equal concern and respect. What they disagree about is what 'treatment as an equal' amounts to. For libertarians such as Nozick, as we saw in Part 1, treating people as equals means respecting their property rights, including their right to self-ownership, equally; not using some as means to others' ends. This may produce vast inequalities of money, but, for Nozick, that is not the kind of equality that matters. Some think that treatment as an equal requires equality of opportunity. No prejudice, based on race or gender, creating barriers to individuals' efforts to better themselves. (I will discuss different conceptions of equality of opportunity shortly.) Others take it to imply a much more equal distribution of income and wealth. And so on.

This is a strange state of affairs. Equality has recently been subjected to fundamental criticisms by political philosophers, yet contemporary political philosophy takes place on an 'egalitarian plateau'. Few believe in equality, but everybody agrees about the importance of 'treatment as equals', disagreeing only about how to interpret this claim. How can this be? The answer is that 'the state should treat all its citizens with equal concern and respect' is not a claim about equality as a distributive ideal (which is the way it is understood by those rejecting it). What it really says is that all citizens have the same right to be treated with concern and respect – and that the respect and concern with which they should be treated depends solely on their status as citizens (and not on their race, gender, religion, how clever or rich they are, or whatever). Principles like this are not designed to make distributions more equal, but to encourage recognition that the well-being of all citizens counts. As we will see shortly, recognizing that all citizens have an equal right to concern and respect may, on some views, have implications for the kinds of distribution of goods that are acceptable – including perhaps implications for the kinds of inequality that are permitted – but the fundamental or underlying principle is not that of equality as a distributive ideal.

It is, however, that of people relating to one another – and hence the state relating to them all – as equals. Those who think that the value of equality is essentially concerned with the distribution of goods are sometimes criticized for failing to recognize the importance of equality in social relationships. What those who care about equality (should) really object to, on this account, is not the fact that people have unequal amounts of anything material, but that relations between them are hierarchical, conceived as relations between superiors and inferiors. Unequal social relations lead to oppression – marginalization, exploitation, exclusion, domination – which typically leads to inequalities in the distribution of goods. But it is the oppression and inequality in social relations that is the fundamental problem. Historically, egalitarian political movements have challenged the idea that some people – whites, men, aristocrats – are better than others, and asserted the equal value of all human beings, and the importance of their relating to one another as equal members of a community. Today, groups such as ethnic minorities, gays and lesbians and the disabled seek not so much equal amounts of goods as equality of status or recognition. Even if the idea that the state should 'treat people as equals' is not about equality as a distributive ideal, it still reflects a commitment to relationships characterized by equality rather than hierarchy.

It is surely true that we still live in a society characterized by oppressive (exclusionary, exploitative, etc.) social relationships – between genders, ethnic groups, those of differing sexualities or physical abilities, and so on. Nonetheless, most of my discussion will be concerned with equality specifically as a distributive idea. This is for two reasons. First, I don't know any political philosophers who defend unequal and oppressive social relationships. It's true that some claim that the approaches of others too often neglect, or perhaps unwittingly contribute to, such relationships. It's also true that some have done much to bring them to our attention, to illuminate the way in which they work, and to identify what kinds of political action might remedy them. But, in terms of the kind of argument I am interested in, that isn't where the action has been. Second, and more importantly, what is bad about unequal and oppressive social relationships is, presumably, that they are bad for those on the wrong end of them. Translate this into talk about their effects on people's well-being – how well or badly off they are, all things considered – and it looks as if we can immediately start talking in distributive terms, with 'well-being' as the stuff we care about the distribution of. I may give disproportionate attention to inequality with respect to obvious and individualistic goods like money, but many of the points made could be generalized to include other factors relevant to the distribution of human well-being, such as the quality of people's relationships with others.

Back to the idea of 'treatment as equals'. This formula can be interpreted in a variety of different ways, yielding less or more radical distributive implications. By way of example, consider two uncontroversial respects in which we think that the state should treat people as equals: equality before the law, and equality of citizenship. Equality before the law could just mean that the law applies to all people without exceptions: that there isn't one law for the rich and one law for the poor, or different laws depending on a person's status – property-holder, slave, or whatever. That would be a very thin or formal notion of equality before the law. But, by appealing to considerations such as those that might lead someone to prefer 'effective freedom' to 'formal freedom' (as discussed in Part 2), one could plausibly claim 'equality before the law' to imply more than that. It could be taken to mean that inequalities in the resources available to people should not affect their standing in relation to the legal process as a whole. A weak version of this would support legal aid: equality before the law requires that people's ability to go to law, or to put up a proper defence, should not be impeded by lack of resources. This is weak because it doesn't stop wealthy people spending as much as they like on their legal representation. It makes sure only that everybody has some basic threshold of resources available for legal purposes. A stronger view would hold that people shouldn't be allowed to spend their own resources on the legal process, on defending their claims or making claims against others, if that results in a very unequal input by litigants. There might, for example, be a limit on the amount that somebody could spend – say twice the amount supplied by legal aid. And the strongest view would hold that people should be able to devote only strictly equal amounts of resources. Only then would people really have equality before the law understood as equal access to the same quality of legal representation.

Similar moves apply in the case of equal citizenship. Formally, this might mean simply that all citizens have the right to vote, to stand for public office, and so on. But it could mean rather more. It could mean, for example, that all citizens have some kind of basic minimum or threshold level of those goods that are relevant to the proper performance of the role of citizen: education, freedom from poverty – those preoccupied with finding their next meal are not in a position to deliberate sensibly about the political issues facing their community – and so on. If citizenship is about informed input to the political process and you really do care that all citizens are able to exercise their citizenship rights, then you will be deeply concerned about those who are not in a position to do so. More strongly still, one may worry about the extent to which inequalities in private resources lead to inequalities in political influence. Politics in the US is increasingly about the ability of candidates to raise funds to buy air time for their TV commercials. Some object to this on the grounds that it violates the democratic principle of equality of citizenship. As with the legal case, one version would put a cap on the amount that individuals or parties could spend, in order to keep inequalities within acceptable limits. Another would insist on public funding of political campaigns, which could involve strict equality of financial input.

In both cases, then, principles demanding that all should be treated equally by the law, or as citizens, can be taken to have less or more stringent distributive implications. They can be treated purely formally, with no such implications at all, or they can be taken to require certain distributive arrangements. If the latter, these arrangements can in turn differ in terms of how much they are concerned with equality. Making sure that all citizens can read, write and are free from the kind of poverty that precludes political participation implies something – a lot – about the distribution of education and money. But it implies nothing about how equal that distribution should be. A concern that two opposing parties in a lawsuit should not be permitted to spend vastly unequal amounts of money on making their case shows some concern with relativities – with how much people can spend relative to one another – but no concern to achieve strict equality. At the egalitarian extreme, one might indeed hold that equality of citizenship would only truly be realized if people's private resources made no difference whatsoever to their political influence.

Some of these thoughts can be put in terms of the principles that 'like cases be treated alike', or that inequalities be justified by 'relevant reasons'. You and I may have vastly unequal amounts of money. Perhaps you are a brilliant entrepreneur who spotted a lucrative gap in the market, and perhaps this is a reason relevant to our having such unequal resources. It justifies the fact that you are much wealthier than I am. But that reason is, or should be, irrelevant to our (equal) standing as citizens. As citizens we are like cases, and, in matters relating to our common citizenship, we should be treated alike. This way of thinking about the issues clearly focuses attention on the question of what counts as a relevant reason, and it is an approach that has been most fully developed by the American philosopher Michael Walzer (b. 1935). Walzer argues for what he calls 'complex equality'. This is the idea that different goods belong to different distributive 'spheres', each of which has its own appropriate distributive principles. There is nothing wrong with the unequal distribution of money, as long as that inequality results from the right source – people's ability to make money in the market – and as long as money inequality doesn't influence (and distort) the distribution of goods belonging to other spheres, such as health, education or politics. What is objectionable, on this account, is not inequality as such, but inequalities that are not justified by relevant reasons. Rather than worrying about money inequality (and inequality with respect to commodities that are quite properly for sale in the market), we should concentrate on preventing the conversion of money into goods that are not, or should not be, marketable commodities – goods that should rather be distributed in accordance with their own, internal, sphere-specific, criteria. This 'spherical' argument isn't really an argument for equality. But, in appealing to the idea of sphere-specific relevant reasons, Walzer does rely on some of the intuitions that underlie these arguments about equality before the law and equality of citizenship.

Equality of opportunity

Can you imagine somebody saying they didn't think that people should have equality of opportunity? Even the most fervent anti-egalitarian is likely to say that of course she endorses that kind of equality. It's equality of something else – something more hostile to individual freedom, or more damaging to an efficient economy – that she opposes. Equality of opportunity is the acceptable face of equality, commanding support across the political spectrum. Does this mean that those of all political persuasions do actually agree on some fundamental value? Unfortunately not. The appearance of consensus is illusory. Instead, the term 'equality of opportunity' is used to mean a range of quite different and incompatible things. Real and important disagreement is concealed by an apparently uncontroversial form of words. Politicians sometimes like it when this happens. They can seem to be agreeing with everybody. Philosophers always hate it. They want to know precisely what people mean or believe, to dig down behind the innocuous veneer and expose the disagreement.

From the many different things that get called 'equality of opportunity', let's pick out three, which I'll call the 'minimal', the 'conventional' and the 'radical' conceptions. These terms are made up by me and don't refer to any well-known labels in the literature, so don't worry if they seem strange. (In case it helps, another philosopher calls them 'right-liberal', 'left-liberal' and 'socialist'.) (Generally, in my view – though be warned that this is somewhat controversial – and thinking as a philosopher not a politician, it doesn't matter what a position or argument is called. That is just a matter of words. What matters is its content. We philosophers spend a lot of time worrying about what words mean, but this is not because we care about what words are used to refer to what ideas. We have to work out how people are using the words they do so that we can see what they mean. Once we've done that, the words they use drop out of the picture. I'd be happy to call the three conceptions Tom, Dick and Harry – as long as we all knew what each of them meant. True, those names wouldn't be very helpful to the reader, since they don't give any clues about the content. True, once we had decided which conception we favoured we would probably want to make it sound attractive, which might well lead us back into the business of using the normally value-laden language of 'equality' and 'opportunity'. But, in principle, we could proceed with the business of analysing and assessing claims in this – and every other – area using any words, as long as we all knew what we all meant by them.)

What, then, is the content of what I'm calling the 'minimal' conception of equality of opportunity? This means simply that a person's race or gender or religion should not be allowed to affect their chances of being selected for a job, of getting a good education, and so on. When we talk about equal opportunities legislation, or admissions or hiring policies, it is this kind of attempt to combat prejudice or discrimination that we have in mind. On this view, race, gender or religion are – usually – reasons irrelevant to the question of who is the best person to do a particular job, or get a place at university. What matters is their skills, their potential, their relevant competences. The way to secure this kind of equality of opportunity is by careful monitoring and regulation of recruitment and promotion procedures in educational institutions and the labour market.

For most people, however, this is not enough. Those endorsing the 'conventional' conception hold that equality of opportunity requires more than that people's relevant competences – rather than the prejudices of others – determine whether or not they get the jobs or education they apply for. It matters also that all have an equal chance of acquiring those relevant competences. People's prospects in life should depend on their ability and effort, not on their social background. The fact that the poorest 50 per cent of its households supply only 7 per cent of its university students suggests that the UK does not give its children equality of opportunity in that sense. The fact that middle-class children are roughly three times more likely to get middle-class jobs than are working-class children, and roughly three times less likely to get working-class jobs, suggests that class background makes a difference to people's job prospects. (I say 'suggests' because it's possible that middle-class children are that much more likely to be clever and motivated. In that case these unequal probabilities would not reflect inequality of opportunity in the conventional sense. They would result rather from poor or working-class children not being clever enough, or working hard enough, to take advantage of their equal opportunities.) On the conventional view, coming from a poor family should not be relevant to one's chance of getting into university, or getting a good job. That should depend on a person's natural ability and the choices she makes, so the state is justified in levelling the playing-field.

Taking conventional equality of opportunity seriously may well demand extreme measures. (Remember we are not yet discussing the 'radical' conception!) A person's social background affects her prospects in so many different ways that removing its influence altogether is impossible, or achievable only by massively restricting parental freedom, almost certainly by abolishing the institution of the family. This shows that those who say that they believe in equality of opportunity of this second kind usually only think that they do. They may genuinely want to remove some of the mechanisms by which children's differing social backgrounds influence their life-chances. Perhaps they oppose private education, support universal grants for students and endorse policies aimed at giving disadvantaged children access to the kind of pre-school education that research has shown to be hugely important to their development. Presumably they accept that policies promoting this kind of equality of opportunity require a redistribution of resources – the disadvantaged themselves can hardly pay the cost of policies designed to give their children a more equal start in life. This is levelling the playing-field understood as making it more level. But it is not making it completely level. We know that children whose parents read them bedtime stories do better than those whose parents do not. But I don't know many people whose commitment to equality of opportunity leads them to wish to ban bedtime stories (or to support a law requiring parents to read to their children). As so often, a political ideal there are good reasons to support comes into conflict with other things that we value – here, the autonomy of the family. And many people say they want 'equality of opportunity' when what they really want – all things considered – is actually just less inequality of opportunity.

On the radical view, even the full-blooded pursuit of conventional equality of opportunity would still not be enough. Correcting for social disadvantage does not really yield equality of opportunity, because it leaves untouched natural or inborn disadvantage. People should have equal opportunities in the sense that their prospects are influenced neither by their social position nor by their position in the distribution of natural talents. Only in that case will different outcomes really reflect people's choices rather than unchosen differences in their circumstances. Only then will people have an equal chance of living the life of their choice, rather than having their set of feasible options determined by factors beyond their control. It's not enough for clever poor children to have the same opportunities as clever rich children. Equality of opportunity requires also that untalented children – whether rich or poor – should have the same opportunities as talented children. Not necessarily opportunities to do particular jobs. It would be odd to want the musically inept to have the same chance of becoming a concert pianist as the child prodigy. But opportunities to do particular jobs are not the same as opportunities to get the rewards usually associated with those jobs. Someone who endorses the radical conception of equality of opportunity can accept that the talented and the untalented should have unequal chances of getting particular jobs. What she rejects is the idea that they should have unequal chances of getting the same rewards.

Is the conventional position stable? Can it resist sliding into the radical view? Those who think not argue as follows. The reason to endorse the conventional conception of equality of opportunity, rather than just the minimal one, is that it is unfair that social disadvantage should hold people back. Why should some be born with a silver spoon in their mouth – on a well-trodden path from posh family to posh school to posh university to posh job – while others go to worse schools, and have to think hard about whether they can afford to stay on at school or go to university? And what makes it unfair is that, as far as children are concerned, it is just a matter of luck what kind of family they are born into. But if this is the reason, it seems hard to escape the Rawlsian thought (discussed extensively in Part 1) that it is also a matter of luck how clever people are. Those who think that we should seek to provide greater equality of opportunity between those from different backgrounds with similar levels of natural ability want a fair competition in which 'merit' alone, and not class background, produces the outcome. But if what makes that competition fairer is that it reduces the influence of 'morally arbitrary' factors – factors for which individuals are not responsible – we should be committed also to providing greater equality of opportunity between those with different levels of natural ability. After all, people aren't responsible for that either. (Part 1's discussion of desert is also relevant here.)

One way of resisting the radical version of equality of opportunity is to reject equality of opportunity altogether, perhaps by affirming a principle about self-ownership, like Nozick. Nozick is an honourable exception to my claim that everybody endorses equality of opportunity. Being a political philosopher, rather than a politician, he is ready to acknowledge that his libertarian theory of justice is in no' way concerned to ensure that people have equal opportunities of any kind. On his view, people can hire anybody they like, on whatever grounds, so he does not even endorse the minimal version. This amounts to getting off the train before it leaves the station and is unlikely to appeal to those who support the conventional conception.

The conventional conception would not slide into the radical one if it were argued for in a different way. Instead of claiming that we should compensate for social disadvantage on fairness grounds, we might seek to reduce – or eliminate – the influence of social background for a different reason. There is a kind of inefficiency that comes when clever children from poor families find it harder to get to university than not so clever children from better-off ones. In economic terms, this kind of inequality of opportunity implies a sub-optimal allocation of resources. The more level the playing-field, the less distortion or bias in the processes by which individuals are selected for education and jobs, the more efficient the conversion of human resources into marketable skills (and hence the production of things that other people want produced). Making things harder for children of disadvantaged families implies squandering a 'pool of ability' from which we could all benefit.

This argument has indeed been influential in making the case for state action to improve the opportunities of those who would otherwise be held back by their social circumstances. But it is a completely different argument. It tells us to worry about people having unequal chances due to social disadvantage only where and because their doing so is economically inefficient. The objection to inequality of opportunity is no longer that it is unfair to individuals. It is rather that it is wasteful for society. Because it neglects this justice-based aspect of the concern for equality of opportunity, those who endorse the conventional conception are unlikely to find it attractive. (Unless, that is, it is combined with the view that economic efficiency matters because it means that there will be more resources to devote to those who, through no fault of their own, are badly off. In that case the reason to make optimal use of the pool of ability is so that we can give most help to those who need it most. Conventional equality of opportunity is here valued instrumentally, as a means not an end, but what it is a means to might itself be a morally desirable – perhaps even a fair – outcome.)

Equality of opportunity, so innocuous on the surface, turns out to be highly controversial. Part of its attraction is precisely that it seems less demanding than equality of outcome. It seems to conflict less with other things we have reason to value. One often finds equality of outcome being rejected, while equality of opportunity is held up as obviously worthy of support. But even if this were right – at the level of fundamental principle – it would still be important to remember that the achievement of (greater) equality of opportunity might well require, or on some views even entail, (greater) equality with respect to outcomes. Let me end this section by exploring some of these.

Some ways in which equality of opportunity has implications for equality of outcome apply even on the conventional view. It is because children are born into households with unequal amounts of resources that they have unequal opportunities. Children of the advantaged have more and better opportunities than children of the disadvantaged precisely because they are children of the advantaged. So one way to equalize opportunities is to equalize starting-points. But a child's starting-point – say an affluent middle-class household in a neighbourhood with good schools – is a parent's outcome. This means that, if we really care about equalizing opportunities, we need to think about equalizing outcomes also. Some take this line of argument as showing the incoherence of equality of opportunity as an ideal. We start off by saying that we want people to have equal opportunities so that their outcomes reflect natural ability and choices rather than social circumstance. But in order for this to hold also for their children, we end up having to deny that they be permitted to achieve unequal outcomes. Moreover, the very thing that people often choose to employ their abilities for – the outcomes they might strive to achieve – is precisely the opportunity to give their children better opportunities than are available to others!

There is indeed a problem reconciling conventional equality of opportunity with respect for people's choices about what to do with their abilities. But that doesn't mean we have got the balance right. Even if parents started with equal opportunities and, because of differing abilities and choices, ended up unequal, it might still be justified, for the sake of equality of opportunity, to prevent some actions they might take to pass their advantages on to their children. Since we don't live in a society where it could plausibly be claimed that people's unequal positions have indeed arisen solely as a result of their abilities and choices, there is ample justification for some equalization of outcomes for the sake of greater equality of opportunity. We have already noted that policies aimed at levelling the playing-field by compensating children for their social disadvantage – such as the provision of free pre-schooling in deprived areas – cost money. That money can only come from those who have it. Taking money from those who have it to spend it on the education of those who do not is redistribution of resources. A more equal distribution of resources, as between those born into unequally advantaged social backgrounds, may be – surely will be – required for the sake of conventional equality of opportunity.

On the radical view, the connection between equality of opportunity and equality of outcome is much stronger. It is not so much that equalizing outcomes might be a necessary means to the equalization of opportunities. It is rather that, on that conception, the two kinds of equality amount to the same thing. To see why, remember that radical equality of opportunity seeks to correct for all unchosen disadvantages – natural as well as social. Where this is achieved, differences of outcome can only reflect genuine differences of taste and choice. (If those different outcomes reflect different talents or family background or tastes and choices for which people cannot be held responsible – perhaps because they were not fully informed about the consequences – then that means that people did not really have equal opportunity in the radical sense.) For example, some people may choose to work longer hours than others, thereby earning more money and ending up rich, while others may choose to take more leisure, earning just enough to stay alive and ending up poor. They will then be unequal with respect to money outcomes. But will they be unequal overall? No, they will have equal outcomes in terms of overall bundles of 'income plus leisure'. It looks as if there is inequality here, but really there have just been different choices. Generalizing, we can say that as long as people really are making a choice, and are fully informed about its consequences, equality of opportunity amounts to equality of outcome. Somebody who believes in equality of outcome has no reason to object to differences of outcome that result from equality of opportunity in the radical sense, because these differences aren't really inequalities. If they do indeed result solely from people's fully informed preferences and choices for which they are genuinely responsible, then they are not really unequal outcomes at all.

Gender equality

The previous section talked a lot about equality of opportunity between those born into different social classes (conventional), and between those born with different natural talents (radical). But it hardly mentioned another factor that many see as a crucial aspect of any egalitarian political agenda: equality of opportunity between those born male and those born female. (Ditto those born into different racial or ethnic groups, but I'm afraid lack of space means I'm going to continue to ignore them.) True, the minimal conception objects to gender discrimination at the point at which people are applying for jobs. But what about the more complex processes that lead many to regard the minimal conception as inadequate? Although the extent of the inequality differs massively across the globe, and although societies like the US and the UK have seen a substantial reduction in inequalities between men and women over the years, and although in some societies girls are now doing better than boys in educational terms, there is still a sizeable pay gap and women are significantly less likely to make it into top jobs. One might assume that feminists would want girls to enjoy equal chances with boys for employment and income.

Things are not that simple. As I mentioned earlier, some theorists who call themselves egalitarian reject this kind of focus on distributive issues, favouring a 'relational egalitarianism' that is more concerned with eliminating oppressive relationships. Feminists in this camp are likely to want an end to patriarchy (Greek *pater* = 'father', *arche* = 'rule') – moving beyond a social order in which men have authority over women who are subordinate to them. The problem is not that men and women have unequal chances of getting high-paying jobs. That's at best a rather trivial symptom of a much deeper concern. The problem is that men have had the power to structure all our social institutions – family, economy, polity – in ways that suit them. Indeed, the very way that we think of ourselves and others when it comes to gender – what it means to us to be a man or a woman, what kind of behaviour is and isn't appropriate – is a social construction that reflects millennia of male domination. (Some of this happens in the very process of learning language. The classic example here is that English contains many words for a sexually promiscuous woman, all with negative connotations, hardly any for a sexually promiscuous man, nearly all of them with positive connotations.) And for some, to worry about women's ability to compete for top jobs is already to adopt a distinctively male perspective (competitive, ambitious, self-interested) on what matters. Gender equality, on this view, involves a lot more than closing the pay gap.

I'd love to be able to cover all this in the few pages available. Instead, I'll try something more realistic. A frequent claim among feminist philosophers is that mainstream (or, as they sometimes say, 'malestream') political philosophy doesn't have the intellectual resources to accommodate or acknowledge their concerns. Sometimes this comes as a critique of liberal political philosophy in general: the capacities that liberals care so much about – autonomy, rationality – are distinctively male; what about caring and compassion? (I'll say a little about the communitarian aspect of that critique in Part 4.) But sometimes the focus is more specifically on the 'distributive paradigm'. The charge here is that we miss important features of our society that are bad for women if we frame the issue in distributive terms. I want to show how a suitably sophisticated understanding of equality of opportunity can address or incorporate at least some of the things that feminists are, rightly, concerned about.

Consider the distribution of opportunities for income. The data show that, on average, women earn considerably less than men. This is worse than it seems, as it leads to women becoming economically dependent on men, which in turn affects power relations within the family by increasing the cost of separation for women and making it more likely they will stay in an unhappy (or, worse, abusive) relationship. Men who have become the primary breadwinners, and who can exit at less financial cost to themselves, have more control over the terms of the relationship. To what extent can we think of this as evidence of any inequality of opportunity? When we are thinking about the contrast between rich children and poor children, it's natural to assume that they tend to end up with better and worse jobs and pay because they start in different places – they are born into families that yield unequal opportunities to develop the attributes rewarded by the labour market. But boys and girls do not start in different places: girls are no more likely to be born poor than are boys. Could it be, then, that the pay gap, and often-ensuing dependence relationships, have nothing to do with unequal opportunity and result rather from the different choices made by men and women? Maybe women are more likely to choose part-time work, or lower-paid full-time jobs, because they are more compatible with other things they want from life – like looking after children. If that's what is going on, then, as noted at the end of the previous section, what looks like an inequality of outcome might not be one after all.

In fact, it is well established that some of the pay gap persists even when we compare men and women doing equivalent jobs (hence the demand for 'equal pay for equal work'). There is evidence also that some employers are less likely to offer jobs to women than to similarly qualified men. So it can't all be put down to women making different choices. But we should question the suggestion that boys and girls start out in the same place in a more fundamental way. Much of the inequality may indeed be due to women and men making different choices about what kinds of job to do and how much to work at different stages in their lives. But the choices people make reflect both their preferences (what they want) and the options available to them (what they can have). It's the interaction between the two that generates the choices we observe. Different kinds of feminist emphasize different elements in that combination, but both can be regarded as ways in which women and men are differently, and unequally, 'placed' from the start.

One way to see this is to notice the way in which well-paid full-time jobs require workers who do not have to spend much of their time looking after children. The world of work is still a man's world in the sense that such jobs tend to take it for granted that somebody else is doing whatever childcare needs doing (and, perhaps, care of ageing parents). If we assume that women are more likely to be doing that caring work, and that's why they don't choose to go for those kinds of job, then we can see that men and women may both be choosing, but they are choosing from unequal opportunity sets. Men have the option of a full-time well-paid job and having their children cared for; women have to choose between the two, often going for the compromise of poorly paid and/or part-time work that is compatible with their caring responsibilities. Women are making their choices from a menu of options that has been structured by men for men.

This may seem too quick. Suppose women are indeed more likely to be doing the 'carework', and this explains why they are less likely to be in full-time well-paid jobs. Isn't that itself a choice? After all, nobody forces women to have children, and there is no law that says it must be the mother who cares for them if she does. To see whether women are really on the wrong end of an inequality of opportunity, we can't avoid the question of why it is that women tend to be the ones who do the childcare.

There are, crudely, two perspectives on that. On one view, women are naturally predisposed to want to look after their children in a way that men are not. Just as it's a matter of biology that women become pregnant, carry the child to term and go through childbirth, so is it that women have a natural instinct to care for the child thus produced. This is sometimes combined with the view that women are better at it than men, so there's an efficiency gain if women do it. We can think of this as a preference if we want, but it's not a preference they've chosen. It's one they have whether they want it or not.

On this analysis, it looks like a good question to ask: why should women end up worse off than men – in terms of income and economic dependency – simply because they find themselves, for reasons beyond their control, wanting different things from men and operating in a society that penalizes them for that fact? (Notice the overlap here with the radical conception of equality of opportunity set out in the previous section.) The same applies if women just happen to be better at it than men – why should they be worse off because of that? After all, it's not as if men don't want to have children. They're just less keen on (or less good at) actually looking after them! From this perspective a sensible gender-egalitarian reform would be to change the balance of economic rewards attaching to childcare (which women naturally want to do) and work outside the home (which is more congenial to men). Or, perhaps, to reconfigure well-paid jobs so that they can be done by those who also have domestic responsibilities.

The alternative perspective holds that there's no deep biological reason why women rather than men should want to look after children, or be better at it. If women do want to do it, then that's the expression not of a natural instinct but of a cultural expectation

– part of the way our society defines the social role of mother as opposed to father. A brother and sister may be born into the same family, but that family may itself have different expectations of them and provide different role models. This is most blatant in traditional religious families where gender roles are very well defined and affect the kind of education made available to children. In the extreme case, in cultures where girls are denied access to the skills needed to compete in the labour market, we can think of this as denying them even minimal equality of opportunity – there is straightforward gender discrimination in terms of access to education. (Here we touch on the conflict between equality of opportunity and parents' rights over their children's upbringing.) But gendered expectations can be less sharply defined than that and still be very real. And they are by no means confined to the family. In all sorts of ways, the wider society – peer groups, TV shows, films, adverts – quickly lets boys and girls know that they are not starting from the same place in terms of how they will be regarded, and treated, by others. (Such processes, of course, affect far more than attitudes to motherhood and childcare.) As far as others are concerned, their gender is part of who they are, and because of the interactive or 'relational' way in which people come to understand themselves, it very quickly becomes part of their identity. Who we are affects what we want – think about little boys' and girls' views about appropriate birthday presents to see how quickly this kicks in. So the very process by which our preferences are constructed is heavily influenced by gender norms and expectations.

On this view, when women disproportionately choose to look after children they are making those choices on the basis of preferences that are not 'natural' but have been formed in a particular, gendered, context. Many women choose jobs that are compatible with their desire to fulfil what gender expectations have encouraged them to regard as their – rather than men's – responsibilities to others. (Men's preferences are, of course, subject to similarly gendered influences, but these tend to work in the opposite direction. Men are pushed towards better-paid full-time work, sometimes involving long hours, which are feasible for those with children only because someone else is willing to take on a disproportionate share of domestic labour.) The question then is whether we should regard these processes by which preferences are formed and identities constructed as undermining equality of opportunity for women. One suggestion here is that someone who has to buck a social norm, or reject an aspect of their identity, in order to earn the same as a man actually faces a different opportunity set from him. A man can comply with gendered expectations and earn good money; a woman has to choose one or the other. The gender-egalitarian move here would be to challenge the norms that lead women to define themselves as caregivers, and to adjust male norms so that men are more likely to see themselves that way. Or, perhaps, to move the culture away from the idea that it is parents who should be doing so much looking after their children in the first place, promoting instead the merits of high-quality professional childcare. As you've probably noticed, both tacks are currently being pursued. (Another one, already familiar in many countries, is to give women a legal claim to some of the earnings that have accrued, or will accrue, to their children's fathers. This is partly intended to get at the problem of economic dependency which means that women don't have equal opportunity to exit a relationship. That looks like a sensible move on either analysis of the different choices.)

That was indeed putting it very crudely. Of course there are sophisticated accounts of why women tend to choose to care for children that combine both perspectives, and some that appeal to other considerations. And I certainly don't mean to suggest that everything feminists do or should want to say can be fully captured by talking about distributions. I haven't mentioned a whole set of issues around pornography and the objectification of women that are surely relevant to relational egalitarians. It's plausible that the prevalence of pornography encourages men (and women) to objectify women, to see them(selves) as sex objects. This will be inimical to relationships based on mutual respect, in which men and women treat each other as equals. One doesn't get very far in understanding that problem by talking about inequality in the distribution of opportunities to avoid being regarded as a sex object. Still, I hope I've at least done something to show how someone who cared about equality of opportunity might approach some key issues around gender.

Equality and relativities: should we mind the gap?

Equality has come under fire from political philosophers because it is necessarily concerned with comparisons and relativities. To care that people have equal amounts of any good is to care that they have amounts equal to those of one another. But why should we care about that? Why does it matter at all how much people have relative to one another?

Many of those who think that they believe in equality – including those who think that they believe not in complete equality but in greater equality – believe in it as a means, not as an end. They argue for a more equal distribution of resources and are frustrated by governments' unwillingness to make the case for redistributive taxation. But when you ask them why, they talk about the importance of relieving poverty, or of focusing resources on those who need them most, or of making sure that all members of a society are able to participate in its common life. (This last is the 'social inclusion' strand in centre-left thinking.) They do want a more equal distribution of resources, but only because that more equal distribution is, as it happens, the way to achieve these other goals. To be sure, they couch their thinking about these other goals in terms of people being equal in some fundamental sense. It's because all are morally equal that poverty, need and social exclusion are so unacceptable. But this use of 'equality' is the 'everybody counts equally' use mentioned earlier. What it really means is that all citizens – those in poverty as much as anybody else – should have their moral claims recognized and acted upon by government.

To see quite how odd valuing equality is, contrast the following two societies, X and Y. Both are made up of two classes, A and B. In society X, members of A and B both have nothing. In society Y, members of A have 99, while members of B have 100:

	A	B
X	0	0
Y	99	100

Which society would you – or any member of A and B – prefer to live in? Which society is the more equal?

The example is a useful stimulus to our anti-equality intuitions, but its message is weak. Equality is not the only thing we value. We also value people having something rather than nothing. Big deal. The interesting question is whether there is any reason to value equality at all. Is it of any moral importance whether people have equal – or not too unequal – amounts? Why do relativities matter?

Our intuition in the previous example may be influenced by the thought that those in society X have nothing whatsoever. They are, we might imagine, all starving to death. Perhaps it is affected by the size of the contrast between society X and society Y. 99 and 100 sound like a lot of stuff – certainly by comparison with 0. Perhaps it is influenced by the fact that 99 and 100 are very close. Society Y has some inequality but not much. More purely to identify what we think about equality, try a different example:

	A	B
X	20	20
Y	20	40

Now society X has complete equality between classes A and B, but everybody has 20. (Suppose – to get rid of the anti-starvation intuition – that 20 is enough to live on.) Society Y has inequality: class A has the same amount as it does in society X. But now it has only half as much as class B. In absolute terms, class A has the same level of advantage in both societies. But in society Y it is worse off than – is disadvantaged relative to – class B. To focus on the issue we're supposed to be thinking about, don't worry about where the stuff comes from – who made it, and whether they might not deserve or be entitled to it. Suppose that, in both societies, the amounts that the two classes have are completely a matter of luck. It's not that members of class B are cleverer or harder working or more prudent (nor even that they had cleverer or harder-working or more prudent parents) than members of class A. (In Nozick's terms – discussed in Part 1– we're talking 'manna from heaven'.) This is a 'brute' inequality – one that isn't justified on other grounds.

Which society do you prefer? If you think that society X is better in any respect, this might mean that you really do believe that equality is valuable. If you actually prefer X to Y, then you are willing to deprive members of class B in society Y of their relative advantage, making them worse off than they would otherwise be, and without benefiting members of class A, simply to prevent them having more than members of class A. You would waste – chuck away– those extra resources even though doing so would make some worse off and nobody better off. One can see why those who argue for equality are sometimes accused of engaging in the politics of envy.

This connection between equality and waste may strike a chord with parents of two or more children. It sometimes happened that there was some indivisible good (sitting in the front, the last sweet) that could go to one or other of my two, but with no obvious reason why one rather than the other should have it. They would prefer that neither of them should get it than that either of them should. They would rather I throw the thing away, or give it to some other child, than create an arbitrary inequality. Each would rather not have it than be better off than the other. Anticipated envy, spite and irrational guilt? Or sibling affection? (My kids were not moved by my attempts to introduce procedural equality, or equality of opportunity, by tossing a coin. They would rather throw the thing away than have an equal chance of getting it. This showed that they were silly – a conclusion supported by much other evidence. Fortunately for me, they were less hostile to the suggestion that they take it in turns, which proved a more successful non-wasteful egalitarian strategy.) Children are notoriously obsessed with equality and fairness, and Sigmund Freud (1856–1939), the Austrian founder of psychoanalysis, offers a fascinating – and somewhat disconcerting – account of the infantile roots of such ideals in his writings on group psychology. Roughly: our sense of justice develops as a reaction to early feelings of envy and jealousy. Discussion of his approach – which is sometimes taken to imply that people particularly obsessed with equality and the like were particularly envious infants – would, I'm relieved to say, take us too far off track.

I said that those thinking society X to be in any respect better than society Y might really believe that equality is valuable. But it might turn out that the reason why they prefer X to Y goes like this: 'It all depends on what we're measuring. Suppose the units we're talking about are resources. Members of A may be no worse off in Y than they would be in X in terms of resources, but they will be worse off in other ways. The very fact that members of B have more resources than they do is bad for members of A – even if it makes no difference to the amount of resources they have. So, reporting how many resources they have, and saying that they are no worse off in Y than in X, is misleading. All things considered, members of A are worse off in Y than they are in X. This has nothing to do with envy or spite, or cutting down the tall poppies for its own sake. The reason not to have resource inequality is that it makes things worse, in other ways, for those on the wrong end of it.'

Before we consider why or how resource inequality might be bad for those on the wrong end of it, notice that, if it has any force, this thought might apply even to choices between resource equality and alternatives where the worst-off class is better off, in resource terms, than it might otherwise be. Consider the following scenarios:

	A	B
X	20	20
Y	25	40

Now everybody is better off, in resource terms, in society Y than in society X. Class B is 100 per cent better off; class A is 25 per cent better off. If all we cared about were resources, we would surely have to prefer Y to X. But, if there is anything in the claim about inequality being bad for the worse off in other ways, it is possible that even in this case members of A might be better off in X than in Y.

This thought is particularly relevant to the 'trickle-down' defence of economic inequality. A standard argument holds that inequality is justified because it promotes economic growth, thereby benefiting even the poorest members of society. Rather than doing too much in the way of redistributing resources to those who have least, which involves taxing the most productive in a way that may impair their incentive to produce, we must understand that the real way to help the worst off is to promote economic growth. Even if their share of the overall pie remains the same, perhaps even if it gets smaller, the pie will be growing at such a rate that the absolute size of their piece will be growing. Witness how much better off, in absolute resource terms, those officially in 'poverty' are today than their counterparts were 20 years ago. Rather than 'minding the gap' between rich and poor, which is itself of no consequence, we should be looking at the absolute improvement in the position of the relatively disadvantaged.

Is the gap of no consequence? That is precisely what the person preferring X to Y denies. In her view, the gap is bad. Not bad in itself – not bad for some intangible metaphysical reason – but bad for the people in the society with the gap, or at least for those on the wrong side of it. The gap does matter because people's overall well-being is affected not just by the amount of economic resources they have, but also by the amount they have relative to others. We may be concerned solely to make the worst-off members of society as well off as they can be – and not at all interested in equalizing the extent to which people are well or badly off. But money isn't everything. Perhaps economic inequality does, over time, improve the economic situation of the worst off, as the trickle-down defence suggests. But that doesn't mean that economic inequality improves their position overall. It may make it worse. Suppose it does. In that case, if we are interested in maximizing the overall well-being of the least advantaged, we should indeed worry about the economic gap. In Rawlsian terms, there may be maximin-type reasons to care about economic inequality.

Why might this be? To explain, consider three aspects of well-being for which economic inequality might be absolutely bad: self-respect, health, and fraternity. (There are other candidates, but these should do as illustrations.)

Perhaps the problem is this. Self-respect is a crucial component of people's overall well-being. (Rawls says that it is the most important of his primary goods.) But a person's self-respect depends significantly on what she can do relative to others, partly because that influences how she is regarded by those others. For example, a society that denies citizenship rights to some of its members – women, those belonging to a particular ethnic group – is denying them the possibility of taking part in collective deliberation and, in so doing, publicly labelling them as inferior. Both aspects of the situation are likely to lead to a lack of self-respect, a negative self-image of those excluded. But people's capacity to take part in the common life of their community, and how they are regarded by others, both of which feed through into self-respect, depend not only on citizenship rights but also on their economic position relative to those others. If the economic gap is too big, those on the wrong end of it may find themselves excluded from activities participation in which is central to the way a society defines membership, and from which individuals derive self-respect. This kind of argument is what motivates the view that poverty should be defined in relative rather than absolute terms (e.g., less than half the median income). What matters is not just that all people have enough to eat, nor is well-being simply a function of absolute material advantage. It matters also that whatever people have is enough, relative to what others have, for them to participate in the shared life of the society, to be regarded as fellow members by others, and hence to be self-respecting members of the society. This does not, of course, require complete equality. But it may give us a reason to mind the gap.

For some, this talk about membership and self-respect may seem a bit nebulous. Disease and death sound rather more rigorous and measurable. In recent years, medical sociologists have come up with the fascinating finding that economic inequality is bad for the health of those at the bottom of the distribution. We have always known, of course, that there is a strong association between economic position and health. The poorer one is, the more likely one is to get ill, and die young, and the more likely one is to have children who get ill, and die young. This suggests that one way to improve the health of the poor would be to improve their economic position. But it does nothing to imply that inequality is bad for anybody's health. The research I have in mind has found, much more interestingly, that the health of those at the bottom of the social hierarchy is worse than those at the top just because they are worse off than those others. Controlling for absolute levels of material advantage – looking at societies with a wide range of levels of economic prosperity overall – it seems that those who have least compared to others in their own society are, for that very reason, likely to be more unhealthy. It is not clear why this should be the case. Is it that the existence of better-off others makes poor people more stressed and anxious, which in turn affects morbidity rates? Is it that those who have least are more likely to be subject to the authority of others, at work and in relation to state institutions, and lack of autonomy is bad for one's health? Whatever the precise mechanism by which it comes about, one can see how belief in this association between inequality and illness might lead someone to argue that the economic gap does matter after all.

Finally, and returning to the nebulous, there is the argument from fraternity or community. On this view, economic inequality is bad because – or to the extent that – it undermines fraternal relations between members of society. Even if inequality does promote growth, and does tend over time to increase everybody's economic position (including that of the least advantaged), it may also lead to a stratified and divided society whose members live in different places, pursue different lifestyles, send their children to different schools, and generally have little or no contact with one another. In such a society there will be no feeling of solidarity or community, of people being 'members one of another'. People may be richer than they would be in a more equal society, but they will lack a sense of togetherness or community that is also crucial for human well-being. This is different from the 'self-respect via participation' line of argument because the idea is not that inequality may exclude some people from mainstream society, with negative effects on their self-image. It is rather that a fragmented and divided society deprives all who live in it – rich as well as poor – of the good of fraternity. (The rich will, of course, be better off in other ways, but as far as 'living in a fraternal society' goes, they will be as badly off as those at the bottom.)

Because it invokes a more questionable conception of well-being, this third line of argument is (even) more controversial than the other two. One can deny that economic inequality affects people's self-respect, or health, but one is unlikely to deny that, if it did, that would be a bad thing. The value of 'living in a fraternal society', on the other hand, is much more disputable. It might make sense to sacrifice some of the poor's absolute economic advantage for the sake of self-respect, or health, but would we really prefer a society in which economic inequality was kept in check for the sake of fraternity – if the result were a society in which the poorest were poorer than they could otherwise be? (The answer might depend on the absolute economic level of the poorest. Research suggests that above a certain threshold more money doesn't make people any happier. Suppose what we really cared about was happiness. In that case, allowing inequality because it makes the poorest richer makes sense only while the worst off are below that threshold. Once they're above it, considerations of fraternity start to look more compelling.)

One more complication with this invocation of fraternity. We are considering how a concern to maximin, to maximize the absolute position of the worst off overall, might have implications for the economic relativities (equality) that we should be prepared to tolerate. In this context, it is worth pointing out that Rawls regards maximin thinking itself as an expression of fraternity. In a society governed by the difference principle, and known to be governed by it, all members of society understand that any economic inequality that exists does so precisely because it contributes to the well-being of the least advantaged. Suppose I am one of the poorest members of such a society, and I see others better off than me. In Rawls's view, it makes no sense for me to wish that they had less, or even to wish that I had some of what they have. The very fact that they have more than me must mean that, over time, I am going to be better off than I would otherwise be. If their having more than me didn't work to my advantage, they wouldn't have it in the first place. So when a society endorses and agrees to be regulated by the difference principle, it is institutionalizing the feeling of fraternity. Nobody wants to be better off than anybody else unless their being so is helpful to the worst off. I will return to the oddity in this view later on. How could somebody else being better off than me be helpful to me? If they really want to help me, why don't they just give me some of what they've got and I haven't? For now, the point is just that Rawls presents the difference principle as institutionalizing the value of fraternity. This doesn't challenge the

thought that economic inequality may be inimical to fraternal relations in a society – because of the stratification and fragmentation
I mentioned. But it does suggest that economic inequality doesn't
have to signal a lack of fraternity. Inequalities justified by the difference principle might be consistent with it.

Positional goods

There are some goods for which it might not make sense to think
in difference principle terms at all. For them, there may be no way
that inequality could tend to improve the position of the worst off.
These will be goods where the only way to give more to some is
to give less to others. In the case of money, it is of course true that,
at any particular moment in time, the way to optimize the position
of the poor would be to redistribute what the rich have up to the
point of equality. But this would be a rather short-term view. A
better way to help the poor in the long term could be to permit
those inequalities that serve to increase the size of the pie. There
might be some goods where this kind of thinking does not apply.

   Think about equality of opportunity in relation to the education system. Suppose some universities are better than others, and
consider the distribution of opportunities to get a place at one of
the better ones. Could an unequal distribution of those increase
the opportunities of those who have least opportunity? If middle-
class children have a better chance than those from working-class
homes, then the latter have a worse chance than the former. It is
hard to see how this inequality could improve the chances of the
working-class children. Because there is a competition for places,
one cannot give more to some without giving less to others, and
that inequality cannot lead to an increase in the amount available to
those who have less. No trickle-down – or pie-expansion – story
can be told in this case. The only way to improve the chances of
working-class children is to reduce the chances of their middle-
class counterparts. This is a problem for politicians, who don't
like to be seen to be making things worse for anybody. The great
thing about economic growth is that it allows politicians to fudge

distributive issues. While the pie is expanding, everybody can be getting better off. This may apply in some areas. But it does not apply in all.

We can, of course, expand the number of places in higher education. The US federal government did exactly this in the 1950s and 1960s, and more recently the UK government has followed suit. Though this may increase the chances of working-class children getting to university, it won't necessarily increase their chances of getting to university relative to the chances of middle-class children. (Remember, we're interested in equality of opportunity.) Perhaps the expansion will be disproportionately taken up by middle-class children. And it won't necessarily increase their chances of going to one of the better universities. But going to a better university – rather than just going to university at all – may be particularly important. Here's why.

Education is a funny good because it has both intrinsic and positional aspects. In some ways, education is valuable intrinsically, without reference to the amount of it that others have. My ability to understand Shakespeare, or to solve quadratic equations, is good for me irrespective of how many other people can do the same or better. But in other ways – particularly when it comes to thinking about the economic return to education in the labour market – what matters about education is one's position in the distribution of education, the amount one has relative to others. Education acts as a way of ranking people in the queue for better- or worse-rewarded jobs. So what counts is not really what one has actually learned, it is where one stands in the distribution.

Considered as an intrinsic good, it makes sense to prefer a 25:30 distribution to a 20:20 one. The least educated have an absolute level of education that is higher in the former than the latter, they have more of the intrinsically valuable good, and it looks perverse to prefer a society in which everybody has less. But looking at it from a positional perspective, 20:20 does not look so crazy. Perhaps it is better for people's class background to make no difference to their educational achievements, for there to be what I called 'conventional' equality of opportunity, than to have an education system in which there is inequality due to class background – even if working-class children do actually know more in absolute terms.

To the extent that education is valued positionally – so that what matters is not people's absolute level but how much they have relative to others – working-class children might rather compete for jobs on equal terms than know a bit more history or maths.

Apply this thought to the issue of private education. When those who can afford it send their children to elite private schools, they may be intending only to buy things that are valuable intrinsically – Latin, lacrosse, whatever. They could quite reasonably say that their children learning those things does nothing to harm those children who do not learn them. They might even add that, since they are paying their taxes towards state education but not taking up places, their act of going private is actually making those in state education better off than they would otherwise be. All this might be true if we think about education solely as an intrinsic good. But things look different when we consider the positional side to the story. Suppose those who can afford it going private does indeed release resources to the state sector, thereby making state education better than it would otherwise be. It doesn't follow that children at state schools are better off overall than they would be if elite private schools didn't exist. If going to such a school gives children a better education than is had by those going to a state school, it gives them positional advantage where it matters, in the competition for university places and jobs. So state-school children, even if they do know a bit more than they otherwise would, are still going to be worse off, relative to those who have been to the private schools.

This is why some people find private education more troubling than private healthcare. There is an argument that people opting out of the British public healthcare system, the National Health Service, improves – or at least doesn't worsen – the quality of care for those who remain in it (by shortening waiting lists, releasing resources, etc.). Whatever one thinks about that as an empirical claim, it is at least true in principle that somebody's getting better healthcare than me doesn't reduce the quality of the healthcare I am getting – and could even improve it. Unlike education, healthcare doesn't seem to have a positional aspect to it. (This is different from the issue of whether economic inequality is bad for people's health.) So, even though healthcare – being a matter of disease and life and death – is probably more important than is education, private education can seem more objectionable, to someone with egalitarian sympathies, than private healthcare. This is because somebody's getting a better education than me automatically makes my education worse – in positional terms – than it would otherwise be.

Insofar as goods have a positional aspect, then, the only way to make sure the worst off have as much as possible is to go for equality. We may be motivated by maximin thinking, but we will be led to equality as the only way to realize it. Trickle-down thinking doesn't apply.

Three positions that look egalitarian but aren't really

I've already said quite a lot about how precise or specific equality is. Here are three positions that might conventionally be regarded as 'egalitarian' but, on closer inspection, turn out not to be.

1 Utilitarianism (or any aggregative principle)

Utilitarianism is the view that what matters morally is utility, or happiness, and that the right action in any situation is that which maximizes the total amount of it there is. (The English utilitarian Jeremy Bentham (1748–1832) talked about 'the greatest happiness of the greatest number'.) The idea that what we should aim for is the maximization of overall utility might lead one to favour a more equal distribution of resources. But it will do this only on the assumption of diminishing marginal utility (i.e., that people get less utility from each extra unit of resource). It will only imply complete equality of resources if we assume equal diminishing marginal utility. An obvious way to increase the amount of utility around is to redistribute resources from those who are getting less utility from them to those who are going to get more utility from them. If it is true that the more resources you have the less utility you get from having more, then it will make sense, on utilitarian grounds, to take from those who have got a lot and give to those who have got less. This is a common intuition underlying the case for redistribution. A few million dollars must be worth less to Bill Gates than they would be to the thousands of people to whom they might be redistributed.

It should be clear that, in this case, any reduction in inequality is an accidental by-product. One way of seeing this is to talk, rather fantastically, about a man philosophers call the 'pleasure wizard'. He is simply superb at turning resources into utility, and goes on doing it at all levels of resources. If all we really cared about were total utility, then we would forget about equality and shove all available resources in his direction. This thought applies to all aggregative goals. To aim at maximizing the total amount of anything, is, by definition, to have only an incidental and instrumental interest in the distribution of that thing (here, utility), or of whatever it is that produces that thing (here, resources). You will go with whatever distribution achieves the overall maximum.

This is a point about aggregative v. distributive concerns. It is important to keep it distinct from a quite separate issue that standardly arises in discussions of equality and utility. The example of the pleasure wizard may persuade us that we should not be interested solely in the aggregate amount of utility. The obvious move is to become interested in the distribution of utility. Perhaps, we might think, we should organize things so that people have equal amounts of utility. This is a genuinely egalitarian position. What we care about equality of is utility. This isn't the place to go into the problems with this view, but here are a couple of clues. First, imagine the opposite of the pleasure wizard. Call him the miserable bottomless pit. Do we really want to go on taking resources – and utility – from normal, happy people up to the point where everybody else is as fed up as him? Second, what about expensive tastes? Suppose I get the same utility from beer and crisps that you get from champagne and caviar. Equalizing utility means you get more money than me, which seems counterintuitive. Our considered view may depend on whether you are responsible for your tastes. If not, then it would be harsh to condemn you to a life of unhappiness just because you had been brought up in such a way that you needed more resources than me to be happy. ('It's not my fault that Mummy and Daddy spoiled me so that I need champagne and caviar to be happy.') The view that what we should care about equalizing is resources, rather than the utility that people generate from those resources, supposes that people are responsible for their preferences. ('If you're less happy than me with your equal amount of money, tough, change what makes you happy.') This kind of issue has generated an 'equality of what?' debate in the academic literature. Suppose we care about distributive equality, what is it that we care about the equal distribution of? I don't have the space to go into it here, but suggest some further reading below.

2 Diminishing principles, priority to the worse off, and maximin

We often think that those who have less of something have a stronger claim to it than those who have more. This is what motivates the case for channelling resources to the least advantaged. But it has nothing to do with equality. Instead, it has to do with what the Israeli-British philosopher Joseph Raz (b. 1939) calls diminishing principles. These are principles where the strength of the reason to give someone a good depends on the degree to which they possess the property that qualifies them to have the good, and the more they have already got diminishes the reason to give them any more.

The hungrier a person is, the greater the reason to feed them. But once you have fed them they become less hungry, so there is less reason to give them more food. We give bread to the hungrier person not because of equality, but because her being more hungry means that she has a stronger or more urgent claim to the bread. The same might go for healthcare and money, and all kinds of other things. Diminishing principles may well lead us to redistribute goods from those whose claims are less to those whose claims are more urgent. But there is no thought here that equality matters. Raz thinks that reasons to do with diminishing principles, not reasons to do with equality, account for all our intuitions in favour of redistribution.

I can't explain it better than Raz himself:

> What makes us care about various inequalities is not the inequal-
> ity but the concern identified by the underlying principle. It is
> the hunger of the hungry, the need of the needy, the suffering of
> the ill, and so on. The fact that they are worse off in the relevant
> respect than their neighbour is relevant but it is relevant not as an
> independent evil of inequality. Its relevance is in showing that their
> hunger is greater, their need more pressing, their suffering more
> hurtful, and therefore our concern for the hungry, the needy, the
> suffering not our concern for equality is what makes us give them
> priority.

Comparisons matter, but only as a means of identifying who has
the strongest claim. We are not comparing people in order to
establish equality.

So far so good (I hope). But properly to understand the view
that philosophers call 'priority to the worse off' (or 'prioritarian-
ism'), we need one more distinction. Suppose it is indeed 'the
hunger of the hungry', rather than equality, that explains why we
(should) give them priority. The obvious way to understand this
is simply that the hungry will benefit more from food than the
well-fed will. It's better to give the food to the hungry because that
will have greater impact on their well-being, on how well off they
are. Now that is a sensible thought, and a good reason to give the
hungry priority when it comes to food. But it's not what the prioritarian has in mind. The prioritarian claim is not that we should
distribute goods in ways that favour the worse off because they will
benefit most. (That thought is a bit like the utilitarian view just
discussed.) The claim is that we should favour them simply because
they are worse off. The worse off people are, the more it matters
that their position be improved. The worse off should have priority even if they're not going to benefit more.

One last point under this heading. Rawls's difference principle
is often regarded as the flagship prioritarian view. Certainly his
claim that inequalities are justified only if they work over time to
benefit the least advantaged is a variant of, and was in large part
the inspiration for, the general idea that the worse off should have

priority. But it's worth keeping in mind quite how specific the difference principle is. It urges us to maximize the absolute position of the worst off. One could regard the claims of the worst off as particularly weighty without thinking they were that weighty. Suppose we had to choose between policies likely to lead to the following two societies, X and Y:

	A	B
X	50	100
Y	51	52

If all we cared about was maximizing the position of class A, then we would prefer Y, even though that makes it only slightly better off while also massively worsening the position of class B. This raises the same worries as the levelling-down objection. So it's important to see that the more general idea of 'priority to the worse off' leaves open the question of how much priority they should have. Taken literally, the difference principle gives the worst off absolute priority, which even those sympathetic to prioritarian thinking may find implausible.

3 Entitlement and sufficiency

'All our children have a right to a roof over their heads, three meals a day, decent healthcare, and an education that will prepare them to participate in the political life of their society and equip them with the skills they need to compete in the job market.' Claims like this are often made in the name of equality, and satisfying them may require a much more equal society than the one we live in. But, as I hope is clear by now, they have no distinctively egalitarian content. They are claims of the form: 'All Xs should have – perhaps have a right to – Y.'

We can connect this with the idea of sufficiency. What matters, it might be thought, is not that people have equal amounts of whatever is valuable, but that all have enough. As long as everybody has sufficient, the distribution – the fact that some have more than others – is not important. There is some threshold level that everybody should reach, but inequality as such is neither here nor there. This is like the diminishing principles approach insofar as it means that we have more reason to give things to those who have least. But it operates with a cut-off point. Rather than people's claims diminishing gradually, as a more or less smooth function of what they already have, this approach posits a sharp cut-off point or discontinuity, a level of adequacy which it is important to provide but beyond which distributions don't matter. (We could imagine a sophisticated mixed view which held that people have a right to sufficiency, so we have a duty to provide one another with that, but that there are other moral reasons to give them more, beyond that threshold level, in line with the idea of diminishing principles.)

Making sure everybody has sufficient, as a fundamental principle, may, of course, have implications for the equality of distributions. Perhaps giving everybody enough means taking from those who have more than enough. And it is important to see that people can agree in endorsing a sufficiency approach while disagreeing sharply over what counts as sufficient. For some, it might be 'enough' that everybody has shelter and basic subsistence. Others might have a much more demanding conception of sufficiency (such as that in the first sentence of this section). Clearly, these will have very different distributive implications. Going with a sufficiency view – rather than a genuinely egalitarian one – implies nothing about how 'radical' one is. One can endorse a radical conception of sufficiency. What matters, philosophically speaking, is how one conceives the goal. Is it to give people equal amounts of something, or to make sure each individual has (whatever one considers to be) sufficient? Moreover, recalling my discussion of whether we need to mind the gap, it might be that one's conception of what counts as sufficient has a more direct relation to issues of inequality. Suppose it were true that people could not have self-respect in a society with economic inequalities of a certain kind. The mere claim that everybody must have self-respect – building self-respect into one's notion of what is 'sufficient' – would be enough to rule out those inequalities.

Equality strikes back

Equality has been under the cosh, in this discussion and in the work of the political philosophers on which it reports. Let's end by looking at what can be said in its favour.

First, we must bear in mind that a looser notion of equality, not to do with equality as a distributive ideal, underlies these other non-egalitarian principles. The obvious case is Rawls's derivation of the difference principle. If we ask, 'Is Rawls an egalitarian?', the strict answer is 'No. He permits inequalities if they benefit the worst off and sees no intrinsic value in equality.' But recalling, from Part 1, how Rawls generates the difference principle, it is easy to see that the idea of people as equal to one another plays a central role in the argument. The original position, in which people behind a veil of ignorance choose principles to regulate the distribution of benefits and burdens in society, is presented by him as modelling the sense in which citizens are to be understood as free and equal. It is because we are all equal as citizens that justice requires us to think in ways that abstract from our differences in talent and social circumstance. Thinking that way, says Rawls, we will seek to maximize the worst-off position in society, choosing the difference principle rather than strict equality to govern the distribution of income and wealth. So, while it would be a mistake to describe Rawls as an egalitarian in the strict sense, it would be very misleading to suggest that he is not interested in equality of any kind. His theory takes people's equality as citizens as a fundamental premise. Something analogous applies in the case of all the other principles that look egalitarian but aren't really.

Second, even if it does make sense to prefer maximin to equality, or even if our reasons for giving money to the poor rather than the rich are not reasons of equality, we don't have to abandon our intuition that there is something wrong about inequalities due to circumstances beyond people's control. Assume that we have a proper all-things-considered measure of advantage that has taken into account reasons why the gap might matter. It may, on balance, be perverse to prefer 20:20 to 25:30, if that is the only choice available to us. Who would benefit from a decision to go for 20:20? But if the inequality between those who have 25 and those who have 30 has no independent justification – it's not, for example, the result of those with 30 having chosen to work harder, but is simply a matter of luck – we may well still feel that we are somehow preferring a situation that, though better overall, is worse in the particular respect that it is unfair. (Recall, from my discussion of radical equality of opportunity, that if the 25:30 gap were entirely due to people having made different choices about how hard to work, we might not want to regard it as an inequality at all. You cannot make a claim about the justifiability of inequality simply by looking at the distribution of particular goods at time *t*. You need also to know the process by which it came about. This is the way in which equality of outcome and equality of opportunity can come to be equivalent.)

Finally, let's explore the difference principle in more detail. Part 1 considered three conceptions of justice: Rawls's justice as fairness, Nozick's view based on self-ownership and entitlement, and a desert view. Those who are keen on equality think that they have good objections both to Nozickian libertarianism and to the kind of conventional desert claim that holds that people can deserve unequal rewards for exercising talents they are lucky to possess. But the difference principle, being closer in spirit, is more of a challenge. How could it make sense to prefer equality to maximin? Egalitarians can answer by turning the question round. 'OK', they say. 'Let's suppose we do care, not about equality, but about maximizing the absolute position of those who have least. We endorse the principle that justifies inequalities if they contribute to that goal. Now tell us how inequalities do, or even could, contribute to it?'

They know, of course, how someone invoking the difference principle to defend inequality will reply: 'Need for incentives . . . inequality crucial for economic growth . . . we have to produce before we can distribute . . . a bigger pie increases the size of everybody's slice . . . look what happened under state socialism.' This is familiar stuff. The fundamental idea is that, unless some are paid more than others, people will have no incentive to work in a productive rather than an unproductive activity – or even to work at all. Differential market prices of jobs perform the crucial function of providing the motivation for people to do jobs that other people want them to do. If everybody earned the same, the whole system would collapse into an inefficient mess. So inequality helps the worst off.

Notice, incidentally, that market prices would be important even if nobody were motivated by the desire for money. If the market is working properly, those prices aggregate people's preferences, telling us what it is that people – taken together – want. This is what economists call the 'signalling' function of the market. Even completely altruistic saints, concerned solely to do whatever others most want them to do, would need the price signal to tell them what that was. The market signal allocates resources – including human resources (people and their skills) – to their most productive use. This is, in principle, quite separate from the way the market distributes money to people. Joseph Carens (b. 1945) has devised an explicitly utopian system that separates the allocative from the distributive functions of the market: there is a price signal (so people know what is the most useful thing for them to do), but everybody earns the same (so people don't keep the money they would have earned in a real market). The assumption is that people's incentives are moral, not economic. They want to do whatever others want them to do, not for the money, but because those others want it.

Back to the real world, peopled by real people not egalitarian saints. As a description of that world, and a prediction about what would happen if we got rid of economic inequality, the familiar account seems fairly accurate. People are motivated by economic incentives, and without some inequality the system would collapse. But let's think about it not as a description of how people do behave, or a prediction about how they would behave in response to an absence of economic incentives, but as a justification of inequality. How does the justification work? It appeals to the fact that people are selfishly motivated by the desire for economic reward. More specifically, it assumes that people are not motivated to maximize the well-being of the least advantaged. If they were, they would do whatever job was, in the long run, most beneficial to the least advantaged without worrying about how much they would get paid for doing it. Something funny must be going on somewhere. There is something schizophrenic about an individual who claims simultaneously to be concerned about maximizing the advantage of the worst off and to require incentive payments to do what will in fact help them. 'Because I recognize, with Rawls, that it is completely a matter of luck who has what level of talent, I don't believe that I deserve to earn lots of money. I agree with him that inequalities are justified only if they help the worst off. But, if you want me to use my talents and become CEO of a large corporation, I'm afraid you're going to have pay me lots of money. Otherwise, I simply won't be induced to do the job.'

Those devising a tax policy must of course take into account the fact that people are indeed self-interested in this way. If we endorse the difference principle, we should set up whatever tax regime we believe will serve, over time, to maximize the position of the least advantaged. We must take people's motivations as they are, and do what we can to harness them so that they work in the right direction. This is a very difficult job, especially given the global labour market, whereby some can threaten simply to go elsewhere if they don't like the tax regime of any particular country. We should doubtless end up allowing people's incomes to vary widely, rather than imposing a tax regime which ensures that everybody ends up with the same. Perhaps the inequalities that characterize the UK or the USA today are justified given people's selfish motivations. But the question at issue is whether those motivations are themselves justified. If not, the incentives argument does not provide a genuinely thoroughgoing defence of inequality. It shows, at best, that inequality is a necessary evil. I may be justified in giving money to someone who has taken my child hostage. But it doesn't follow that the distribution of rewards after that transfer is a justified distribution.

We are very specifically considering the difference principle justification of inequality. It is not, in this context, a legitimate move to appeal to self-ownership or the kind of desert claim supported by public opinion. Many of those who command above-average salaries believe that they are justified on one or both of those grounds. In that case, the egalitarian response will be different (roughly: 'No, people don't own themselves in the sense required to justify that kind of economic inequality. No, luck plays too great a role for us to think that people deserve what they get in the market.') But we are talking about people who justify inequality precisely on the ground that it helps the worst off, not for either of those reasons. The alleged incoherence comes in asserting both that one endorses that justification and that one is oneself justified in receiving incentive payments.

From an egalitarian perspective, those who demand incentive payments are exploiting – blackmailing – the rest of us. 'We are talented people. The market tells us that the things we can make or do are very valuable to the rest of you. You want us to use our talents? OK, we will, but only if you pay us more than what other people are getting. Otherwise, no deal.' Because they have not themselves endorsed the difference principle, there is no incoherence here. Just extortion. Add in endorsement of the difference principle – 'We believe that inequalities are only justified if they help the worst off' – and we get incoherent extortion.

Even from this perspective, some kinds of inequalities might indeed be justified by someone who sincerely endorses the difference principle. Suppose being a brain surgeon, or CEO of a big corporation, is so stressful that the job can only be done well by people who have a jacuzzi and long holidays and the odd midweek round of golf. In that case, their getting those advantages may indeed help the worst off. Were I about to be operated on by a brain surgeon, I would hope she'd had a pleasant evening and slept well the night before. Some kinds of advantage may simply be functional requirements for the proper performance of the job. Perhaps the efficient organization of production in a factory or office requires some people to be able to tell others what to do. Perhaps, in order fully to fulfil their intellectual potential, academics need lots of autonomy, very long holidays and jobs for life (worth a try). These are not pure incentive payments. They are not external advantages that brain surgeons or supervisors or academics receive in order to induce them to do the job. They are, we are supposing, just what people need in order to do the job well in the first place. There's no incoherence in endorsing the difference principle and demanding these. If true, the reason for these inequalities is not that they benefit the person doing the job, but that they benefit the rest of us. Nobody is holding anybody to ransom.

Some things that might look like inequalities aren't really. Where work is particularly arduous, or stressful or unpleasant, higher pay is best regarded simply as the kind of 'compensating differential' that came up, in Part 1, in our discussion of desert. People who do unusually stressful jobs may commonly, and rightly, be held to 'deserve' higher pay than those who do not, but this is not a genuine desert claim, nor a justification of inequality. It is a counterbalancing equalizer, an attempt to secure equality all things considered. Similarly, it may be that some jobs require an extensive period of training, during which people earn little or nothing. In that case, some level of higher-than-average pay might be thought of as compensation for the earnings forgone. In both cases, there is an element of 'incentive' about the extra earning. Without a bit more money, people might have no incentive to do nasty jobs, or jobs which involve a lot of training. But they are equalizing incentives, not justifications of inequality. Indeed, it should be clear that the kinds of unequal remuneration that would be justified on these grounds are going to look very different from those produced by the market. At the moment, broadly speaking, the more pleasant or satisfying or interesting one's job, the more one earns. Since people typically enjoy exercising their talents, they hardly need to be paid more, as a compensating differential, for doing so. This kind of argument would give greater rewards to those whose lack of talent condemns them to work with special burdens – such as boredom or unpleasant working conditions.

Upon close inspection, then, the maximin (or difference principle) justification of inequality looks less straightforward than it might seem at first sight. If we have to choose between equality and maximin, as we do in the real world, we may prefer the latter; 25:40 may be better than 20:20. But why do we have to choose? Why do we need inequality to get the worst off up from 20 to 25? Why can't we divide the resources in our preferred society equally, opting for 32.5:32.5 rather than 25:40? The answer is, mainly, that other people do not believe in maximin. They believe in maximizing the return on their natural assets. This looks inconsistent with the reasoning behind maximin thinking, which holds that such assets are morally arbitrary and as such cannot justify inequalities in rewards.

Here we reach two closely related and quite general issues: (1) the relation between people's beliefs about the rules that should govern the structure of their society and their beliefs about how they can justifiably act within that structure, and (2) the extent to which it is legitimate for people to pursue their partial interests – not necessarily their own selfish interests; they might include the interests of their friends, families, etc. – rather than acting impartially. The position I've been outlining holds that it is incoherent to say: 'I agree with Rawls. The talented are just lucky, and, for that reason, we should set up rules so that inequalities only exist if they help the worst off. However, as an individual operating within a system governed by those rules, I am justified in exploiting my own good luck to earn as much money as the rules permit.' Others disagree. For them, different kinds of thinking are appropriate in different contexts. As a citizen, thinking about what justice requires at the structural level, I must be impartial and not seek rules that work to my benefit just because I happen to be lucky. But, as an economic agent, it is perfectly appropriate for me to pursue my own partial interest and to maximize the return to my own good luck. Different kinds of thinking appropriate in different contexts? Or plain old hypocrisy? Others say that while maximizing my narrowly selfish return to my own good luck is unjustified, there may be good moral reasons – say my loving desire that my children can fulfil their apparent musical potential (for which they need instruments and lessons) – for me to demand some above-average return to my work, if I can get it. Inappropriate bias towards the interests of my children? Or proper parental concern? Such questions are currently attracting a good deal of attention.

One thing is clear, and it reflects a fundamental difference of perspective between the academic political philosopher and the practising politician. Politicians typically see themselves as in the business of devising rules that work as well as they can, taking people – hypocritical, self-interested, partial, and all the rest of it – as given. Furthermore, politicians also have to get elected before they can enact their preferred rules, which gives them further reason to compromise with the values and attitudes of their electorate. Philosophers have a different brief. They offer reasons why people should think and act differently, better. Great politicians have occasionally managed to do some of that too.

Conclusion

On the one hand, equality is an uncontroversial starting-point for any political philosophy – or political party – worth taking seriously. Whatever our other differences, as citizens we are equal to one another. The state must treat us as equals – taking everybody's interests equally into account, not regarding some people as more important than others. This is the 'egalitarian plateau' on which nearly all political debate is now conducted. On the other hand, a concern with equality is bizarre, perhaps even perverse. Why care that people be equal to one another, rather than that they all have enough, or be as well off as possible? One source of confusion, then, is the difference between equality as a distributive idea – to do with how well or badly off people are – and the kind of equality that asserts people's fundamentally equal standing as members of the political community. But this is only one source. Now add in the practical or 'real world' parts of the story, such as the plausible view that inequality may be needed to achieve the distributive goals we have good reason to care about. No wonder people get confused.

'Do you believe in equality?'

'Well, yes, I believe that all people are equal in some fundamental moral sense, so the state should be equally interested in the well-being of all its citizens. But, no, I don't think it makes sense to seek an equal distribution of well-being rather than making sure that the worst off have as much as possible. However, I am fully sensitive to the ways in which particular aspects of a person's well-being – say their health – may be affected by particular kinds of inequality. Moreover, for some goods – where there is a positional aspect – the only way to help the worst off could be to distribute the good equally. Of course, inequality is functionally necessary – especially given the global context in which we operate. But we shouldn't forget that, insofar as inequality is needed to promote the well-being of the worst off, this is only because people are selfish. Were we all saints, it wouldn't be necessary. A certain amount of self-interested or partial behaviour is doubtless perfectly reasonable, but not the amount that we see reflected in salary differentials today.'

'Answer the question, Prime Minister. Do you believe in equality? Yes or no?'

It would be nice to think that politicians' reluctance to use the 'E' word resulted from an appreciation of this kind of complexity. It would be nice, too, if more politicians realized that arguments for redistributive policies need have nothing to do with envy or levelling down – indeed nothing to do with distributive equality at all – and everything to do with improving the lives of those whose lives most demand improvement.

Further reading

The single most useful collection on equality is Matthew Clayton and Andrew Williams (eds.), *The Ideal of Equality* (Macmillan 2002), closely followed by Louis P. Pojman and Robert Westmoreland (eds.), *Equality: Selected Readings* (Oxford University Press 1997). These contain many of the best-known and most important papers that examine, in much greater depth, many of the ideas surveyed here.

Joseph Raz's views on equality are in *The Morality of Freedom* (Oxford University Press 1986). Important contributions, critical of 'luck egalitarianism' and arguing for the importance of equality as a characteristic of social relationships, are Elizabeth Anderson's 'What is the Point of Equality?', *Ethics* (1999), and Samuel Scheffler's 'What is Egalitarianism?', *Philosophy and Public Affairs* (2003). The Anderson piece is also in Clayton and Williams (eds.), *Social Justice* (Blackwell 2004). Paula Casal's 'Why Sufficiency is Not Enough', *Ethics* (2006) is a good critique of sufficientarianism. Ronald Dworkin's *Sovereign Virtue* (Harvard University Press 2000) collects in one volume his influential articles arguing from 'equal concern and respect' to 'equality of resources' (and against 'equality of welfare').

Although only the last chapter is about the question in its title,

G. A. Cohen's *If You're an Egalitarian, How Come You're So Rich?* (Harvard University Press 2000) is as entertaining and provocative as that title suggests. The argument about incentives is most accessibly pursued in his 'Incentives, Inequality and Community', which is in Stephen Darwall (ed.), *Equal Freedom* (Michigan University Press 1995). The utopian market can be found in Joseph Carens's *Equality, Moral Incentives, and the Market: An Essay in Utopian Politico-Economic Theory* (Chicago University Press 1981). Thomas Nagel's *Equality and Partiality* (Oxford University Press 1991) elegantly explores the conflict between those two ideas.

Debra Satz's 'Gender', in David Estlund (ed.), *Oxford Handbook of Political Philosophy* (Oxford University Press 2012), and Will Kymlicka's chapter on 'Feminism' in his *Contemporary Political Philosophy: An Introduction* (2nd edn, Oxford University Press 2002) are good short overviews. Susan Moller Okin's *Justice, Gender and the Family* (Basic Books 1989) and Clare Chambers's *Sex, Culture and Justice: The Limits of Choice* (Penn State Press 2008) are the places to go next.

At the less philosophical end of the scale, John Baker et al.'s *Equality: From Theory to Action* (2nd edn, Palgrave Macmillan 2009), Anne Phillips's *Which Equalities Matter?* (Polity 1999). and Alex Callinicos's *Equality* (Polity 2000) are all stimulating reads. The adverse effects of inequality on health are most easily approached through *The Spirit Level: Why Equality is Better for Everyone* (Penguin 2010) by Richard Wilkinson and Kate Pickett. Stuart White's *Equality* (Polity 2006) is an excellent textbook.

Part 4

Community

The French revolutionaries of 1789 were inspired by the slogan 'liberty, equality, fraternity'. Today, 'fraternity' – literally 'brotherliness' – is quaint and politically incorrect. 'Solidarity' – the gender-neutral equivalent – turns the mind towards trade unions and picket lines. But 'community' is still in fashion. It is warm, caring, and nobody knows what it means. This combination of qualities has helped it to spawn its own 'ism': communitarianism, which is a complete hotchpotch. (It's only fair to say that political philosophers like me are suspicious of all 'isms'. They are messy things, tending to combine ideas that change over time, pull in different directions, and can easily be made to come apart. From our point of view, it is an unfortunate feature of the world that actual politics involves ordinary people, who think in terms of untidy and shifting constellations of beliefs called things like 'conservatism' or 'liberalism'. How much easier and clearer everything would be if they were all philosophers, affirming or denying discrete and precise propositions. Still, 'communitarianism' really is unusually ill-defined, even by the standards of other 'isms'.)

Recent talk about 'community' has been of two distinct kinds. On the one hand, there has been an academic debate, in which the positions developed by liberal philosophers, such as Rawls, have been accused by other philosophers – especially Michael Sandel (American, b. 1953), Charles Taylor (Canadian, b. 1931), Michael Walzer (American, b. 1935) and Alasdair MacIntyre (Scottish, b. 1929) – of neglecting the significance of community. This debate has covered a range of complex philosophical issues: conceptions of the self or person, whether the state can or should seek to be neutral, whether principles of justice apply universally or are culture-specific, and so on. Much of this 'communitarian critique' of liberalism was based on misrepresentation and misunderstanding. But few would deny that it also contributed a good deal to our understanding of some fundamental issues in political theory.

Alongside this 'philosophical' communitarianism, there has been something else: 'political' communitarianism. This is communitarianism as a political movement, the kind – associated primarily with the Israeli-American Amitai Etzioni (b. 1929) – that issues manifestos, proposes policies and tries to influence politicians. Here the talk is about responsibilities balancing rights, the defects of a litigious culture, the importance of the family, the urgent need to rebuild local communities. The target is not a philosophically mistaken conception of the person, or anything so abstract or abstruse. It is a culture of egoism, of individualism, of self-gratification. This, in some versions of the argument, is claimed to be leading to social disintegration and a world in which atomized individuals, bereft of communal ties, live meaningless, alienated lives. Political communitarianism has had some success – if that is measured by the extent to which leading politicians appeal to 'community' in their speeches and writings. For a while it looked as if 'community' was going to be the Big Idea which the centre-left had been looking for (as part of, or alongside, the 'Third Way' or the 'stakeholder society'), but it is also invoked by 'compassionate conservatives' on their right.

The relation between these two 'communitarianisms' – philosophical and political – is complex. It is not an accident that the two developed simultaneously; they overlap in some places, and political communitarians often invoke the ideas of their philosophical counterparts. Nonetheless, the differences are more striking than the similarities. None of the leading philosophical communitarians has subscribed to Etzioni's 'communitarian platform', and some have actively distanced themselves from it. It is often alleged – and sometimes accepted – that philosophical communitarianism has no clear policy implications at all. In fact, the issues that exercise political communitarians tend either to be philosophically rather straightforward and uncontroversial (e.g., that rights should be balanced by duties or responsibilities) or to have little or no distinctively philosophical component at all (e.g., that community-based initiatives are the best way to combat poverty and crime). So, much of the time the two are simply talking about different things.

Confusing. To make matters worse, philosophical and political communitarianism are each made up of diverse and sometimes inconsistent ideas. Sandel, Taylor, Walzer and MacIntyre argue against different targets. Some aim specifically at Rawls, others are concerned with contemporary moral culture in general. Some focus on liberalism's conception of the self, others object to its supposed neglect of cultural traditions and practices. To be fair, it was others who grouped them together as 'communitarians'. They are not keen on the label – though this is partly because they don't want to be identified with communitarianism as a political movement.

Political communitarianism is itself something of a mixed bag. In some versions, the community that matters is the state, a real community is one that treats its members as equals, and equal membership has an economic dimension. 'Community' is then invoked to defend the welfare state and the redistributive taxation it implies. Others, such as advocates of the 'Big Society', are concerned rather with self-help groups, voluntary associations and local communities; the welfare state – impersonal, bureaucratic, fostering a culture of dependency – is the problem, not the solution. Many invoke 'community' simply to express the elementary thought that people should care about others. Some hold the much stronger view that the 'community' is a legitimate source of moral authority in such a way that the government is justified in promoting particular ways of life (e.g., family values, heterosexuality rather than homosexuality).

My strategy for getting a handle on this mess comes in two parts. First, I show that those who couch their positions in terms of something they call 'community' typically do so by contrasting it with some alternative – sometimes called 'liberal individualism' – which is presented as morally impoverished, philosophically naive and/or sociologically ill-informed. An opposition or confrontation is thus set up between liberals, who care about individuals, and communitarians, who care about communities. But this appearance of confrontation is misleading. Those who endorse liberalism and are interested in the well-being of individuals can say most of what those who emphasize 'community' want them to. The second part of the strategy is to discuss some problems for liberals that survive this process of clarification. Communitarian writings have done more than force liberalism to make explicit things that were previously taken for granted. They have raised deep and crucial issues that remain central to the philosophical agenda.

Correcting misunderstandings and misrepresentations

I've grumbled about how all 'isms' are messy combinations of different ideas that change over time and, though members of the same family, can be quite widely divergent and sometimes incompatible. Liberalism is no exception. (For my purpose – explaining how liberals need not make the mistakes of which they are accused – this is an advantage. I can concede that some in the liberal tradition may be guilty as charged, while pointing to others who are not.) Nonetheless, it is helpful to identify a core claim at the heart of liberal theory, so here it is: liberals are primarily concerned with the freedom and autonomy of individuals. Recall, from Part 1, Rawls attributing to people in his original position a 'highest-order interest in the capacity to frame, revise and pursue a conception of the good'. Though they differ in all kinds of detail, what liberals have in common is a concern to protect and/or promote something like that capacity.

If that's what liberals care about, it's easy to see how they might look uninterested in – or even antagonistic to – community. They are interested in individuals, not communities. They think that people should be free to choose for themselves how they live, apparently without regard to whether the choices they make are good ones, the values of their community, or how their free choices affect others. This, surely, is a political philosophy for egoists, one that sees people as out for themselves, with little or no concern for anybody else. Those in the original position, choosing principles to regulate their society, are presented as 'mutually disinterested', concerned only for themselves. Here, it seems, is liberalism's vanguard theorist acknowledging that the liberal state is one to which people agree simply because it suits them best. And the Rawlsian construction makes explicit two more core liberal mistakes: that people choose their values, and that they do so in some way detached from the communities – the cultures and subcultures – in which they are raised and live. How else are we to understand the oddly disembodied and depersonalized contractors in the original position, motivated above all to protect their freedom to choose how they live?

Liberalism's emphasis on individual freedom seems to set it on a collision course with the value of community. Rawls's hugely influential articulation of liberal ideas appears to confirm this. A third factor leading in the same – mistaken – direction is the confusion of liberalism as that is understood by political philosophers with something that became known as 'economic liberalism' or 'neo-liberalism'. This latter – a core component of the 'New Right' – is a doctrine about the importance of keeping markets free from distortion, regulation and state interference. It combines empirical claims about the superior efficiency and productivity of market mechanisms with moral claims about the importance of private property and individuals being free to engage in economic exchanges. (The latter were discussed in Part 2.) The confusion of economic liberalism with liberalism in general is especially common in post-communist states. It is easy, there, to think in terms of a crude contrast between 'communism' (which mistakenly believes in equality) and 'liberalism' (which rightly believes in individual freedom). 'Freedom' is equated with 'market freedom', 'liberalism' with the 'liberalization' of the market – i.e., a shift from state control and regulation to 'free markets'. The result is that liberals, by definition, believe in a laissez-faire economy. It is those states that have most to gain from a proper understanding of what liberalism does and does not involve. (In the US, on the other hand, liberalism is normally identified with support for the welfare state. I told you these labels were problematic!)

Here, in roughly increasing order of complexity, are seven objections to liberalism that sometimes are made in the name of community:

1   Liberals assume that people are selfish or egoistic.
2   Liberals advocate a minimal state.
3   Liberals emphasize rights rather than duties or responsibilities.
4   Liberals believe that values are subjective or relative.
5   Liberals neglect the way in which individuals are socially con-
    stituted.
6   Liberals fail to see the significance of communal relations,
    shared values and a common identity.
7   Liberals wrongly think that the state can and should be neutral.

All of these objections are misplaced (though some are more misplaced than others). Let's consider them in turn. As we do, try to bear in mind that I'm not trying to defend liberalism. I'm just trying to explain what is and is not implied by endorsement of the core liberal claim identified above.

Objection 1: Liberals assume that people are selfish or egoistic

Politicians sometimes invoke 'community' when they want to say that people should care about one another, not just about themselves. In contrast to the crude 'individualism' of the New Right – an ethos allegedly captured by slogans such as 'greed is good' or 'there is no such thing as society' – community means that people shouldn't simply look out for number one. Rather than pursuing unbridled self-interest, they should have a sense of solidarity with other members of their community, identifying with them sufficiently to be willing to make some sacrifices for their sake. Here, talk about 'community' is essentially code for talk about morality. Morality requires that we act not simply as egoists, but recognize that others may have claims on us.

Why speak in code? Because, for politicians, talking explicitly about morality is dangerous. It is seen as preaching, as inappropriately high-minded. It is often equated with the prescription of a particular and well-specified conception of how people should lead their lives. People don't like politicians telling them how they should live, and politicians are usually keen to avoid even the appearance of doing so. Since politicians must justify their policies, and since all justification of policy is ultimately moral justification, they resort to code. Which is where 'community' comes in. (All justification of policy is ultimately moral because whenever a policy is presented merely technically, as simply the most practical or efficient means to achieve a particular end, it is always relevant to ask whether the end in question is itself morally desirable.)

There are two misunderstandings in all this. The first is held by communitarians who think one needs to invoke 'community' to talk about morality. They fail to see that, on any plausible interpretation, liberalism is itself a moral doctrine. It does not endorse the unrestrained egoistic pursuit of individual self-interest, but has plenty of room for the idea that people have moral claims against one another, some of which – those that entail duties on the part of others – the state can enforce. 'Individualism' (what matters is the well-being of individuals) or 'liberal individualism' (the freedom and autonomy of individuals are essential to their well-being) are not egoism. If individuals matter, then all individuals matter – not just me. I can pursue my self-interest only to the extent compatible with the moral requirement that I treat others justly. To endorse liberalism is not to endorse a culture in which individuals put the gratification of their own desires before everything else. It is to endorse a system of rules and laws that constrain egoism precisely to ensure that all are treated with the concern and respect due to them as autonomous individuals.

The second misunderstanding is held by those who see talk of morality as the prescription of particular ways of life (heterosexual, monogamous, drug-free . . .). The moral idea at the heart of liberalism is precisely that people should be free to choose for themselves how they live, as long as this is consistent with the concern and respect for all individuals discussed in the previous paragraph. (Which implies, amongst other things, similar freedom for others.)

So liberalism is a moral doctrine. But it is a thin moral doctrine. It does not necessarily specify any particular way or ways in which people should live (except that they should treat one another justly). Communitarians are wrong to think that talking about morality implies abandoning liberal individualism. Politicians and journalists are wrong to think that talking about morality means prescribing, or even endorsing, particular ways of life.

Invoking 'community' may indeed be an effective way to motivate concern for others, to couch claims that would look like preaching, or seem inappropriately prescriptive, if they were presented as 'morality'. Philosophers are in favour of anything that makes people more likely to act morally. But they are also in favour of theoretical clarity. 'Community' can serve as a rhetorical proxy for 'morality' as long as it is understood that 'community' used this way is quite compatible with 'liberal individualism'.

Objection 2: Liberals advocate a minimal state

Liberals agree in seeing the state's job as that of protecting and promoting individual freedom. But different strands of liberalism disagree about what counts as 'protecting and promoting freedom'. For some, a liberal state is a minimal or 'nightwatchman' state. It confines itself to the tasks of protecting people's negative rights – their rights not to be interfered with by others – and providing public goods, such as street lighting and defence. ('Public goods' are goods that everybody wants and, once they are provided, everybody benefits from. The state is justified in supplying them, and forcing people to contribute to the costs because, without that element of organized coercion, it's rational for individuals to 'free ride' on the contribution of others, which would lead to no supply of the good – even though everybody wants it.) In particular, coercive redistribution is not justified. If people with property want to give it to those without, that's fine. Perhaps they should. But it is no business of the state to enforce such a transfer. This is the 'libertarian' variant of liberalism, most coherently set out by Robert Nozick (and discussed in Part 1).

Some people don't like liberalism because they think it implies this kind of state. To be a liberal is to be an advocate of laissez-faire economics and generally to favour minimal state interference in the lives of citizens. As I mentioned, this misidentification is especially common in eastern Europe.

But not all liberals are libertarians. Rawls is not Nozick. A Rawlsian state is a more than minimal liberal state. Upholding liberal justice, enforcing those duties that people have to one another in virtue of their status as citizens with a capacity for autonomy, involves, for Rawls, more than protecting people's negative property rights, providing public goods and collecting the taxes owed for their provision. It involves the state in the business of securing compliance with his principles of justice – not just the protection of the basic liberties but the distributive aspect too: fair equality of opportunity, and the difference principle. Treating citizens with the respect due to them in virtue of their capacity for autonomy means making sure they have a fair share of the goods necessary for its exercise. Different versions of liberalism will imply different precise roles for the state – including different degrees of, and justifications for, redistribution – and there is nothing in the idea of a state founded on the principles of 'liberal individualism' that limits it only to the minimal role advocated by libertarians. Theoretically, coherent liberals can perfectly well support a welfare state, and more. (Now that we're talking about community, and related ideas, recall – from Part 3 – that Rawls thinks that his difference principle provides an interpretation of the principle of fraternity: not wanting to have greater advantages unless this is to the benefit of others who are less well off.)

Objection 3: Liberals emphasize rights rather than duties or responsibilities

The most common complaint from political communitarians is that we hear too much about rights and not enough about duties and responsibilities. This may be true. Perhaps people are too quick to assert rights against others, and too slow to acknowledge duties and responsibilities to or for themselves and others. Perhaps Etzioni was right to urge a 10-year moratorium on the coining of new rights. Perhaps a litigious culture is a bad thing. But, if there is a problem, liberalism is not to blame. As should already be clear, there is nothing in that philosophical approach that denies the significance of either duties or responsibilities.

In the case of 'duties', this is a simple matter of conceptual clarity – of understanding what it means to say that somebody has a right to something. The conceptual analysis of rights can get quite tricky – the American legal theorist Wesley Hohfeld (1879–1918) identified four different ways in which the term 'a right' is used – but for most purposes it is a safe working assumption that 'A has a right to X' means precisely that others have a duty to let A have, or to give him, X. Remember the connection between justice, rights and duties. If A has a right to X, then it is not simply the case that it would be nice for A to have X, or even that A ought to have X. To have a right is to have a justice claim, the kind of claim that implies duties on the part of others.

A very influential approach to rights – that of Joseph Raz – defines rights as follows: 'X has a right if and only if X can have rights and, other things being equal, an aspect of X's well-being (his interest) is a sufficient reason for holding some other person(s) to be under a duty.' This contains two claims that go beyond the brute idea that rights entail duties. First, a claim about what kind of thing it is about a person that gives him a right: an aspect of his well-being (otherwise known as his 'interest'). Second, a claim about how the interest relates to the right: by counting as sufficient reason to hold others under a duty. Does A have a right to X? In Raz's view, we answer that by considering whether A's interest in having X is sufficient to hold another person (or persons) to be under a duty. Do I have a right to that Steinway piano I've always wanted? No, because, though getting it would indeed contribute to my well-being, the well-being contributed is not sufficient to hold anybody under a duty to provide me with it. Do I have a right not to be murdered? Yes, because not being murdered contributes to my well-being to such an extent that it does indeed give us reason to hold others under a duty not to murder me.

Sticking with the elementary thought that links rights and duties, see how it makes a nonsense of the communitarian suggestion that liberalism goes on about one but neglects the other.

On this analysis, every time we make a rights claim, on behalf of ourselves or others, we are simultaneously making a duties claim. The more rights people have against one another, the more duties they owe to one another. The rights and duties come together or not at all. And the duties are owed to individuals. We don't need to abandon 'individualism' in favour of 'community' to talk about duties.

Those who claim rights surely realize that they are thereby making a claim about duties. Presumably the whole point of the rights claim is to demand that people provide whatever it is that is being claimed to be a matter of right. It's possible that some people urge rights for themselves without recognizing that the implied duties apply to them also. But that is just inconsistent. To claim that I have a right to free speech but no duty to respect the free speech of others is, in the absence of a reason why I am a special case, clearly contradictory. If I have a right to trial by jury – so others have a duty to provide me with such a trial – then, presumably, I too have a duty to do my jury service when my number comes up. By the same reasoning, though the empirical claim linking the right to the duty raises more complicated questions, my claiming a right to vote could imply a duty to do so – if my turning out to vote were necessary to sustain the democratic system to which I claim a right.

Nothing I have said so far denies that some people are too quick to coin new rights, too ready to regard as 'rights' claims that do not really have that status. This is the grain of truth in the communitarian position. Perhaps many of the rights that people claim are not really rights at all. But the way to decide that is not to invoke the concept of 'community'. It is to think seriously about what rights individuals do and do not have. This is where an approach like Raz's pays off. Is people's interest in their religion not being blasphemed against sufficient to hold others under a duty not to blaspheme against it? That depends, for Raz, on how harmful blasphemy is to people's well-being, and whether it is sufficiently harmful for us to judge, taking into account the cost to people of their not being able to say or write things they might otherwise have had reason to say or write, that people are under a duty not to blaspheme. Do people have a right not to carry an ID card, not to be subject to random drug tests when driving, or not to undergo an AIDS test when applying to be a dentist? The answers are not straightforward. Nothing in Raz's approach is meant to suggest that they are. But at least he allows us to see what considerations are relevant. Communitarians may be right to reject some of the particular rights that organizations such as Liberty (in the UK) or the American Civil Liberties Union (in the US) assert. But if they are right, it is because people do not have the particular rights and duties in question, not because there is anything wrong with 'liberal individualism'.

Similar points apply to responsibilities. Consider two issues where politicians, under communitarian influence, have talked about the importance of people taking on or acknowledging responsibilities: the responsibility of the able-bodied to take work where it is available (rather than just 'scrounging' off state hand-outs) and the responsibility of parents to support their children (rather than relying on the state to do it for them). In the UK, the first has resulted in changes to the rules on eligibility for unemployment benefit and more stringent disability tests (essentially to distinguish the idle from the genuinely disabled unemployed). The second produced the Child Support Agency, a government agency that tries (and often fails) to get parents, especially absent or estranged fathers, to contribute financially to their children's costs. In both cases the aim has been to redraw the 'responsibility boundary' between the individual and the state, to establish a domain in which the individual takes responsibility for (is held to account for, takes the consequences of) her actions.

Liberals have no problem believing that people should be responsible for the outcomes that result from their own free choices. Of course a lot depends on what counts as a 'free choice'. How many options must be available for a person to choose from? How much information about the likely consequences must the chooser have? And egalitarian liberals are going to emphasize the extent to which people are not responsible for the background conditions (such as their place in the distribution of natural talents) in the context of which they make their choices. Communitarians may be on to something when they bemoan a culture in which people rely on the state to ameliorate outcomes for which they themselves are responsible. It may be true that some strands in liberal thinking, by stressing the extent to which people are at the mercy of factors beyond their control, have contributed to a culture which is too ready to let people off the moral hook. But it can hardly be said that liberal political philosophy ignores the issue of responsibility. Quite the contrary.

Certainly liberals have no problem making rights depend on the agent meeting certain conditions (so that the rights are 'conditional'). This is just a matter of specifying the right with sufficient precision. To say that people have a right to welfare is vague, and suggests that they have such a right irrespective of what they do (or don't do), which encourages the thought that liberal rights-talk lets people off the hook of taking responsibility for themselves. But it is straightforward to hold, for example, that those who need welfare assistance through no fault of their own have a right to it, whereas those responsible for their own neediness have no such right but must bear the consequences of their own actions. Of course, deciding who is responsible for what is extremely difficult. But that has nothing to do with the mistaken claim that emphasizing rights means neglecting responsibilities.

Objection 4: Liberals believe that values are subjective or relative

The American poet Robert Frost (1874–1963) said that a liberal is someone who can't take his own side in an argument. Advocates of 'community' sometimes claim that liberals take values to be just 'subjective', a matter of individual preference with no objective criteria for deciding which are right or wrong. The emphasis on individual freedom of choice, the respect for people's own beliefs about how they should live their lives, is held to result from a kind of scepticism. Only if no ways of life are better than any others does it make sense for people to choose such things for themselves. Imposing, or even encouraging, any particular values is as unjustified as imposing or encouraging a particular flavour of ice cream. Values are just a matter of taste, and the state has no business promoting the ones it happens to prefer. Liberals, it is said, are moral relativists. (And moral relativism, the view that 'anything goes', is the source of many of our social problems: drugs, family breakdown, etc.)

It should be clear that this charge of subjectivism or relativism cannot stick as a claim about all moral values. In believing that individual freedom and autonomy matter, and that the state can enforce those justice-related duties we have to one another, liberalism cannot hold that values in general are merely a matter of taste. Somebody who denies the moral significance of individual freedom is making a mistake, not just expressing a preference. For the objection to get a hold, we need at least to distinguish between two kinds of value: freedom, autonomy, rights, justice (which liberals value, and believe themselves to be objectively right to value) and particular ways of life that might be chosen (which, it might be thought, liberals believe to be a matter of subjective taste).

This looks like the distinction that I mentioned when first pointing out that liberalism is indeed a moral doctrine. I suggested then that politicians are wary of talking about morality because such talk is often, mistakenly, regarded as involving the prescription of particular ways of life. With this distinction clear in our minds, we might want to say that, though not subjectivist about values like freedom and justice, they are subjectivist about what it is that people might freely choose to do with their just share of resources. Would this be right? Confining ourselves now to 'conceptions of the good' – philosophers' term for views about what makes people's lives valuable or worthwhile – must liberals believe, with the hard-nosed utilitarian Jeremy Bentham, that pushpin is as good as poetry? That a life playing video games is as well spent as one grappling with philosophy?

The answer is 'no'. Suppose I am absolutely convinced that life with Plato is, for everybody, objectively better than life with Playstation. Those who disagree with me are not just expressing a different, and equally valid, preference. They are making a mistake. Does it follow that I should abandon my liberalism, renouncing my commitment to a state that upholds people's rights to choose how they live? Not if I also think it valuable for people to make and live by their own choices. Somebody who correctly chooses Plato may have a much better life than somebody who mistakenly chooses Playstation. But it being their own choice is crucial. A state that fails to respect the capacity of people to choose for themselves could be depriving them of a necessary condition for their lives going well. So I can quite consistently urge the state to leave them to it while having no doubts whatsoever that they are getting it wrong. In my private life, as an individual in civil society, I may devote myself to spreading the word about how wonderful Plato is. But liberalism is a doctrine about the justified use of the state, about the policies that it can properly pursue. My own views about how people should live can be regarded as quite irrelevant to that issue – however objectively valid those views may be.

For some critics, this liberal response involves a kind of moral schizophrenia. I'm absolutely certain of and committed to the value of Plato – for all my fellow citizens, not just me – but I'm supposed to ignore that fact when it comes to politics? Replace Plato by God. Imagine that you are committed to the truth of a particular religious doctrine, a doctrine that suffuses your entire way of life, providing you with a sense of identity and meaning, with membership of a particular community. This liberal move tells you to bracket those religious views for the purposes of politics. The worry about schizophrenia moves us in the direction of important communitarian arguments that are discussed later. The point for now is that liberals don't have to be subjectivist or relativist about values; they just have to prioritize the value of individual freedom.

Ironically, perhaps, there is a significant strand of communitarian thinking against which the worry about relativism seems to be much better directed. This is the strand that emphasizes the importance of respecting a community's values, traditions and shared understandings simply because they are those of the community in question. In philosophical terms, this is most closely associated with Michael Walzer, who urges that social justice requires us to distribute goods in accordance with their 'social meanings'. (Alasdair MacIntyre's emphasis on the significance of socially defined roles for individual well-being is similar.) Suspicious of liberalism's supposed pretensions to universality, and its apparent abstraction from social and cultural context – think of Rawls's original position – communitarians have insisted that the proper way to do political philosophy is to interpret and refine those values and principles that are immanent in the ways of life of particular concrete societies.

This is indeed a kind of relativism. In Walzer's formulation, 'justice is relative to social meanings'. It's not that values are subjective in the sense that they are simply a matter of individual taste. Individuals can, on this view, be wrong about them. But what they are wrong about is 'the correct interpretation of their society's shared traditions and understandings' or 'the values implicit in their culture's social practices'. Here we approach very difficult issues in meta-moral philosophy. ('Substantive moral philosophy' is to do with what is right and what wrong. 'Meta-moral philosophy' – also known as 'meta-ethics' – is to do with the status of moral judgements, what we mean when we say that something is right or wrong, and how we know which it is.) Happily, it's not appropriate for me to go into them here. What is worth noting is that communitarianism, in both its philosophical and its communitarian guises, sometimes asserts that the justification of a moral value or principle consists, and can only consist, in appeal to the shared intuitions of the community to whom the value or principle in question is to be justified. Add to this the thought that different communities share quite different intuitions, and the result is a kind of social or cultural moral relativism. This is why some object to communitarian thinking because they take it to imply a kind of conservatism, a rejection of the possibility of a role for political philosophy that is radically critical. We have to be careful here. Even communitarians like Walzer think that there is a 'universal' thin kind of morality that is shared by all, or nearly all, cultures. And Walzer's own prescriptions for the US, based on his interpretation of their 'shared meanings', certainly qualify as 'radical social criticism'. But, overall, this kind of relativism is more usually associated with communitarians than with liberals.

Objection 5: Liberals neglect the way in which individuals are socially constituted

Much philosophical communitarianism focuses on the conception of person supposed to lie at the heart of liberalism. Encouraged in their suspicions by the shadowy, desocialized parties to the contract in Rawls's original position, critics claim that liberals fail to recognize the extent to which individuals are 'socially constituted', embedded in communal relations and formed as the people they are by the communities in which they live. The liberal conception of the person as a free chooser of how to live her life is naively 'individualistic'. It overlooks the individual's dependence on the society in which she lives for her conception of the good (and, indeed, for her conception of herself as an individual choosing a conception of the good). Sometimes this dependence – the priority of the social matrix – is presented as an empirical claim about the significance of socialization processes for the individual's self-identity. Sometimes it is the more philosophical idea that language or thought is impossible outside a social setting.

Either way, the critique is misguided. Liberals may make mistakes, but they don't make mistakes as obvious as these. How could anybody deny that people derive their self-understandings from the societies in which they live? What matters is whether this does anything to knock the liberal insistence on the importance of people being free to think about how they want to live, to live the life of their choice, and to change their mind (subject, of course, to the constraint that they respect other people's doing the same). If people had no choice, if the feeling that we decide how to live our lives were an illusion, then this would indeed be a problem. Liberals would be attributing huge importance to a capacity that people do not in fact possess. But the fact that we choose from a set of socially defined options, and that, as individuals, we are undoubtedly subject to social influences (family, school, media) that lead us to choose some rather than others, does not establish that reflection and choice are illusory. To be sure, when we critically reflect upon our lives, we do so while taking some things as given. Detaching ourselves from all our values would leave us with no basis for judgement. But it still matters that people are free to live a life they believe in, rather than being required to live a life that others choose for them.

The fact that individuals are socially constituted does indeed pose challenges to the liberal. If people derive their understanding of who they are from their membership of particular groups, and if such self-understandings are integral to their well-being, then those concerned with individual well-being may find themselves caring about groups in ways that generate potential conflicts with individual freedom and with a strictly individualistic approach to justice. Perhaps some cultural groups require subsidy if they are to survive? Perhaps their survival depends on their being granted group rights that clash with conventional individual rights? We will discuss such issues shortly. Here the point is just to clear away the mistaken idea that liberals simply fail to acknowledge the social constitution of the self.

Indeed, it's precisely because they do recognize the extent to which the social matrix constitutes people's identities that liberals are likely to care about the conditions under which beliefs are formed. Here there may well be a conflict between 'liberal individualism' and 'community'. Consider the devoutly religious. Suppose they propose to raise their children in a close-knit community, send them to religious schools and generally make sure that they are kept away from those of different persuasions. Can the state permit this? For the liberal, the issue is whether doing so adequately respects citizens' capacity for autonomy. Liberals differ on what this implies. For some it is sufficient that people have the right to leave the community in which they were raised. For others, this is not enough. The state must ensure that its future citizens have exercised their capacity for autonomy and this requires that they should not just be educated into (indoctrinated with?) a particular religious view, but should be taught to think for themselves, and to have some awareness of the range of options available to them (including being taught their civil rights). Quite how much state intervention this involves is a difficult question on which liberals disagree. There are many books – and US Supreme Court cases – about it. In general terms, the problem is that of getting the correct balance between respecting the autonomy of parents (whose conception of the good may include raising their children a certain way) and protecting or nurturing the autonomy of children. The communitarian twist is that respecting the autonomy of parents may present itself as respecting a 'community' (here a religious grouping). (To see that it doesn't have to present itself in this way, imagine eccentric parents who refuse to allow their children to have a normal education because they want them to be social isolates. Here there is no 'community' that would be offended by the state's decision to require those children to learn things their parents didn't want them to. So the issue of what the state should do to guarantee the autonomy of its (future) citizens is only contingently related to the question of respecting 'community'.) Whatever the right answer in these cases, it should be clear that liberal concerns about socialization and education arise precisely because they do indeed acknowledge the priority of the social matrix.

Objection 6: Liberals fail to see the significance of communal relations, shared values and a common identity

Communitarian worries about the liberal conception of the person sometimes take a different tack. Rather than objecting to liberalism's supposed view about the source of people's conceptions of the good, they complain about the particular kinds of content which liberalism allegedly ignores and encourages. Here the charge is that liberalism builds upon and fosters a particular understanding of the individual's relation to her community, seeing society as nothing more than a cooperative venture for the pursuit of individual advantage. Conceptions of the good that are communal in content, that recognize that social bonds and relations with others are intrinsically valuable, are thereby downgraded. Liberals are also accused of failing to give proper attention to shared values and the importance of a common identity.

Contrary to this objection, there are two compatible ways in which liberals can accommodate the thought that communal relations are intrinsically valuable. The first requires us to remember that liberalism is a doctrine about what the state can do to, and for, its citizens. Since the state, in liberal theory, is essentially a means whereby free and equal citizens make and help each other do things, this amounts to saying that it is a doctrine about how people should treat one another as citizens. It is not a doctrine about how people should treat one another in general, in their private lives, or as members of civil society (except where a way of treating another is inconsistent with or undermines that other's standing as a free and equal citizen). So even if it were true that liberal individualism conceived political activity and the state in purely instrumental terms, this would still leave plenty of room for people to pursue communal values. The state provides a framework within which people live their lives. Those lives may centrally involve distinctively communal activity, participation in shared practices and valued membership of particular communities. A 'liberal individualist' does not think that the state should prevent people living a religious life, a life in an artistic commune, a life devoted to the collective pursuit of scientific truth, or a life in which the extended family plays a crucial role. Nor does she deny that any of these are valuable ways to live a life – more valuable than the self-interested pursuit of money or individual gratification. She is concerned to ensure that citizens are free to live lives they believe in. Those lives may perfectly well be communal in content, involving membership of groups or associations aiming at shared ends.

But this picture of the liberal state as providing a framework within which individuals are free to pursue communal conceptions of the good is only part of the story. For liberals need not conceive political activity or the state in purely individualistic instrumental terms. Rather, the liberal state itself might be thought to represent or embody a particular understanding of political community. Citizens of a liberal state share a common aim, and are jointly engaged in its pursuit. The aim is that of creating and sustaining a set of social and political institutions that treats citizens justly. Communitarians who accuse liberals of neglecting the idea of the common good miss the point that liberal justice can itself be a common good. It is a common good when it is shared by citizens and pursued by them together. Combine this with the previous point, and we have a conception of the liberal state as a community of communities. An overarching community, founded upon respect for the individual, which allows its citizens to engage in communal (religious, artistic, familial) activity in pursuit of the more particular ends that they share with others.

True, there is something paradoxical about this idea. The content of the good is communal in the sense that it is something held in common by citizens. Its being held in common is integral to that content. A society in which some citizens did not share the goal of sustaining a just society, but had that goal forced upon them against their will, would be a society in which the good was not achieved. But the content of the good is 'individualistic', in that it concerns the importance of respecting the rights of individuals to pursue the life of their choice, with a just share of resources to devote to their individual, freely chosen, life-plan. The common good is individualism (where that means 'respect for the freedom and autonomy of all individuals', not 'the selfish pursuit of one's own gratification').

Some variants of communitarianism hanker after a conception of the common good that is thicker or stronger than this, one that is more communal and less individualistic. But we have seen that liberals permit individuals to pursue communal conceptions of the good within the framework of justice provided by the state. So, if there is to be any real disagreement, communitarians must be arguing that the state can itself embody – act in pursuit of – values that go beyond respect for the freedom and autonomy of all individuals. For some liberals, however, it is a crucial feature of contemporary Western societies that citizens disagree about which particular ways of life are valuable, with a range of different views seeming no more or less reasonable than one another.

In Rawls's terminology, developed in his second book, *Political Liberalism* (1993), such societies are characterized by 'the fact of reasonable pluralism'. Given this, and assuming that the coercive power of the state is jointly held by all citizens equally, it seems illegitimate for some to get the state to favour their own conceptions of what is valuable. That is, to make the state sectarian, not a tool for the execution of a genuinely communal project. To be the latter, the state must restrict itself to the pursuit of those values that are indeed shared by all. These are liberal values such as freedom, equality, autonomy and justice. Understood in this way, the liberal who recognizes what citizens do and do not share, and permits the state to act only in ways that can be justified by appeal to common ground, is showing more respect for the political community as it actually is than the kind of communitarian who advocates a thicker conception of political community. Leaving people free to choose for themselves how they are to live is the expression of political community appropriate to contemporary circumstances. (The claim that such values are indeed 'common ground' is, of course, problematic. I will discuss the problems with this approach later.)

In their private lives, people may define themselves in all kinds of ways – heterosexual, Christian, artist, sport-lover – but, as members of the political community, they coincide in regarding themselves as free and equal citizens. It is this common identity that is modelled by Rawls's original position. So when real people regard the claims of justice as trumping their more particularistic interests, they are, in effect, treating their 'citizenship identity' – the identity they have in common with their fellow citizens – as more important than their other, more particularistic and differentiated, identities. People are expected to be sufficiently constituted by – sufficiently to identify with – their identity as 'citizen' that, when the demands of that identity conflict with the demands of their other identities, the role of citizen takes priority. So liberals do recognize the importance of a common, shared identity.

Objection 7: Liberals wrongly think that the state can and should be neutral

The idea that the state should be neutral between its citizens is often associated with liberalism. It fits with the idea of the state as an impartial umpire, providing a level playing-field, a fair framework within which the individual is left free to pursue her own good in her own way. It is not legitimate for the state to make judgements about how people should lead their lives, even if those judgements are made democratically, for that involves the community imposing its will on individuals in a way that violates the requirement that they be treated with equal concern and respect. Whenever the state promotes, or discourages, particular ways of life, it is not acting neutrally. So the British state, which discourages gambling (through taxation), encourages the arts (through subsidy) and gives special standing to the Anglican Church, is not, in this sense, a neutral state. Similarly, the US federal government, despite its official commitment to individual freedom, deliberately encourages specific ways of life: it subsidizes national parks and the

National Endowment for the Arts, and encourages religious activity by making donations to churches tax-deductible. Both countries have tax laws that support marriage (though they differ in the extent to which they are biased in favour of *heterosexual* marriage, an area where things are changing fast).

One obvious problem is that it isn't at all clear what kind of neutrality is being claimed for a so-called 'neutral' state. Since it explicitly promotes certain values – such as individual freedom and autonomy – how can the claim to neutrality be anything other than a sham? To make good their claim, neutralist liberals will typically invoke a distinction between (a) the individual's capacity to choose and pursue her own conception of the good and (b) the conceptions of the good she might choose and pursue. They are not neutral about (a), but they are neutral about (b). Indeed, in some versions, it's precisely because they care so much about (a) that neutrality about (b) matters. Since individual freedom and autonomy are so important, the state should restrict its role to that of guaranteeing fair background conditions. It shouldn't itself encourage or discourage any particular conceptions of how people should live.

Sometimes this is put as a distinction between 'the right' and 'the good'. The state should uphold justice and people's rights as citizens (which derive from their capacity for autonomy) but it should not get more involved than it needs to in questions of 'the good' (how people should lead their lives). Recognizing that even a theory of justice does in effect presuppose some conception of how people should live and what is good for them, Rawls puts the distinction as follows: the state may act on a 'thin' theory of the good, for this is neutral in the sense that it is common ground between citizens and it applies solely to the political sphere. He accepts that his liberalism involves a political conception of the good (or a conception of the political good). But the state may not act on particular comprehensive doctrines – full-blown views about how people should lead their lives in general – that are endorsed by some but rejected by others of its citizens. For Rawls, members of today's advanced societies disagree in their comprehensive doctrines. But they nonetheless coincide in affirming the core liberal values of freedom (spelled out in terms of the capacity to frame, revise and pursue a conception of the good) and equality. There is, for him, an 'overlapping consensus' on these distinctively political values. These can therefore be worked up – via a modelling device like the original position – into a theory of political justice. That theory is 'neutral', then, in the sense that it builds on 'common ground'. It appeals only to reasons that all in some sense share (and not to reasons grounded in particular and controversial doctrines about which people reasonably disagree).

The difficulties raised by this Rawlsian approach will be discussed later. For now, it is important to see that some variants of liberalism are not committed to neutrality between conceptions of the good (or comprehensive doctrines) at all. It is tempting to think that a state that takes no view about how its citizens should live – beyond how they should treat one another as citizens – is more 'liberal' than one that does. On that view, the current US federal and British states are less liberal than they would be if they refrained from subsidizing the arts or encouraging marriage. Though this has some intuitive appeal – and some liberals would indeed endorse this claim – it is dangerous to see it as a matter of definition, as if liberalism and state neutrality necessarily go together.

There are two reasons why it is dangerous. The less important one is that even Rawls thinks that some state action in favour of particular comprehensive doctrines can be justified. What is not justified is for such conceptions to influence state action where it involves constitutional essentials and matters of basic justice. As long as those are in place, and in the appropriate sense neutral or 'political', people may vote for state policies that fit with their own comprehensive doctrines, and the state may act on the outcome. So a Rawlsian state can subsidize art galleries and museums and national parks, if that's what its citizens vote for. What it can't do is ground its constitutional arrangements, or its conception of basic justice, in any particular comprehensive doctrine. (It's worth mentioning that Rawls has changed his mind on this. In 1971, even subsidizing art galleries was ruled out.)

The more important reason why we should not identify liberalism with the idea of a neutral state is that doing so would blind us to kinds of liberalism that do not want neutrality at all. On such views, nothing in the liberal picture tells against the state acting to encourage its citizens to live valuable lives and discourage them from living worthless ones. It matters that people live autonomously, that they are the makers or authors of their own lives, rather than being subject to the will of others. But it also matters that the lives they live are valuable in their own right. The mere fact that somebody has chosen to live her life a certain way doesn't mean that that way of life is good, even for her. Choice, though necessary for individual well-being, is not sufficient. It matters also that she makes good choices. If the state can help her choose well, then it is justified in doing so.

This, in a nutshell, is the kind of 'perfectionist liberalism' most systematically developed by Joseph Raz. In his view, liberalism is not essentially a doctrine which restricts the state's role to that of providing a level playing-field, avoiding judgements about how people should live their lives. It is a doctrine that permits, and in some cases may require, the state to make and act on such judgements. By subsidizing (and in other ways encouraging) valuable ways of life, and taxing (and in other ways discouraging) worthless or empty ones, the state can promote the well-being of its citizens. Being a liberal state, it cannot force people to make good choices, and it shouldn't prevent them from acting on their bad ones. But subsidizing the arts is not forcing people into theatres and art galleries. Encouraging marriage is not requiring people to get married. Taxing gambling is not banning it.

To see the difference between neutralist and perfectionist kinds of liberalism, consider the case of legislation in relation to sexuality. According to neutralist liberals, the state should concern itself solely with justice, leaving people free to act sexually as they wish. People cannot, of course, harm others, and the protection of children is a legitimate concern of the state. So, if they believe that 16 as the age of consent for homosexual sex would be more likely to harm children than would the same age for heterosexual sex, they could argue for different ages on neutral grounds. What neutralist liberals cannot do is argue for different treatment on the grounds that some kinds of sexual activity are intrinsically more worthy (or depraved) than others. As individuals, we may have views about that. Perhaps such views derive from our religious beliefs. But those beliefs should be kept out of our thinking about how, as citizens, we should treat one another. Some people find it odd that Tony Blair, whose children were educated in Catholic schools, should have supported lowering the age of consent for gay sex to 16. But even if Blair's religious views were of the kind that regarded gay sex as worse than straight sex, he might still think that those views were irrelevant to the political issue of how the state should act. (In the US, former Senator Ted Kennedy opposed restrictions on abortion, despite being a Catholic.)

Perfectionist liberals, on the other hand, think that it is appropriate for us to use the state to get one another to live better rather than worse lives. If – and it is a very big if – straight sex is more valuable than gay sex, then the state might be justified in promoting heterosexuality and discouraging homosexuality. It would not be permissible for the state to seek to enforce a ban on homosexual acts. We're still dealing with a fundamentally liberal perspective, and that kind of ban would violate citizens' autonomy. But, because, unlike the neutralist, she does not exclude perfectionist considerations in principle, a perfectionist leaves more on the agenda for political decision.

Take another example: 'family values'. One might promote such values on the ground that it is intrinsically better for people to live their lives in stable heterosexual marriages than in alternative arrangements. This would be a perfectionist reason, and neutralists would regard it as inappropriate when it comes to deciding state policy. But there might also be other 'neutral' reasons for thinking it legitimate for the state to encourage family values. Perhaps other family forms are more likely to harm the children raised in them, or to produce children likely to harm others (e.g., by becoming delinquent). (Of course, there is going to be disagreement about what counts as 'harm', and about what counts as evidence that harm is caused. The point is not that it's easy to decide whether state support for family values can be justified on neutral grounds. It's simply to bring out the difference between two kinds of argument for such support.) Something similar applies in the case of pornography. If – perhaps not such a big if this time – pornography harms women, then the neutralist liberal will consider state measures against it. What she won't countenance is state policy directed against pornography on the ground that it is inherently degrading or bad for the person consuming it. As an individual, I may think that those for whom the consumption of pornography plays a central role are living lives that are less worthwhile, less valuable for them, than would be a life without it. But – in the absence of harm to others – that is not a reason for the state to take action against it.

What has any of this to do with community? After all, the idea that the state may be permitted, or required, to act on perfectionist judgements about the value of ways of life favoured by some of its citizens has no inherently communal content. (One might, of course, add the claim that 'communal' ways of life are more valuable than 'solitary' or 'individualistic' ones. But nothing in the argument supposes this. It could be accepted by somebody who thought that the life of a hermit or reclusive artist was valuable and worthy of promotion by the state for that reason.) This discussion of neutrality is relevant because it concerns the proper relation between the political community and the individual. The perfectionist thinks it justified for the political community collectively to make and act on judgements about what will make the lives of its individual members go better or worse. The neutralist thinks that such judgements should be left rather to individuals, with the state merely acting to provide an appropriately impartial set of rules and institutions. In this particular sense, then, perfectionist liberals might be thought to be more 'communitarian' – and less 'individualistic' – than their neutralist counterparts.

Summary

This section correcting misrepresentations and misunderstandings sometimes committed in the name of 'community' began with some elementary clarifications. Liberalism is not a doctrine of egoism, nor does it imply (by which philosophers mean 'necessarily imply') a minimal state. Things got a bit more interesting when I pointed out that, despite what some communitarians have suggested, liberals are interested in duties and responsibilities, need not believe that values are merely subjective (not even values concerning the best way to live one's life) and can perfectly well accommodate the ways in which individuals are 'constituted' – made the particular individuals they are – by the social context, or community, in which they live. The further suggestion that some versions of liberalism have no problem according significance to communal relations, shared values and a common identity brought out the sense in which liberalism could itself be understood as a theory of the 'common good'. Finally, we moved closer to the frontier of current philosophical debate as I introduced the idea that liberals need not limit the role of the state to that of providing a level playing-field, a neutral framework that leaves to individuals all judgements about what makes people's lives better or worse. Here the discussion connected with the concerns of some communitarians who are concerned to halt what they diagnose as a process of moral decline.

I have introduced two importantly different strands in liberal thinking: Rawls's 'political liberalism' and Raz's 'perfectionist liberalism'. Rawls is the one saying that, at least in regard to constitutional essentials and matters of basic justice, the state must restrict its role to the pursuit of those values in some sense shared by all: the thin or political theory of the good which is to do with justice, equality, freedom, autonomy. This kind of liberalism is 'communitarian' in seeking to build only on 'neutral', common ground. Raz's conception of liberalism does not realize community in this sense. As long as it is indeed helping its citizens live better lives – lives that are better for them not just for the rest of us – the state need not confine itself to this common ground; it may make and act on more controversial judgements. This is communitarian in a different way. Here the political community may legitimately promote the well-being of its members even where this takes it beyond neutrality.

I admitted, early on, that my attempt to defend liberalism from attacks by communitarian critics would take advantage of the diversity that liberalism shares with all other 'isms'. The reader may feel that I've gone so far as to cheat. It is true that I have allowed 'liberalism' to refer to two different positions. But both these doctrines hold that the freedom and autonomy of individuals is essential to their well-being (the rough definition I offered at the beginning). So it is legitimate to invoke both in order to counter the charge that liberals neglect the significance of 'community'. In any case, despite their differences, both can be seen to regard liberalism as a theory of community, a community concerned with the promotion of a common good, the good of a just society. A society whose members care not solely about themselves or their families, but about the autonomy of all their fellow citizens, and who are prepared to limit the pursuit of self-interest to the extent that the duties owed to their fellow citizens require it (e.g., by accepting redistributive taxation from the better off to the worse off), is a society characterized by solidarity, fraternity and community.

Outstanding issues

That is not, unfortunately, the end of the story. Stopping now would give a misleadingly one-sided account of things, suggesting that communitarian thinking has contributed nothing but error and confusion. In fact, as well as forcing clarification of what liberalism amounts to – or, rather, the variety of different things it might amount to – the communitarian critique has thrown up a number of crucial issues that remain unresolved. Communitarians have sometimes been guilty of uncharitable interpretations of liberal writings. But a charitable reading of what communitarians have to say would see them as raising deep and important questions that are still very much up for grabs. (A charitable reading of a text is one that interprets it so as to make as much of it as true as possible. Especially where somebody disagrees with you, it is usually a good idea to see whether there is any way in which what, or some of what, they are saying could be true. It's likely to be more intellectually productive than the opposing strategy, which is exactly what politicians are trained to do: they deliberately avoid whatever is good in their opponents' arguments and home in on – and rubbish – the bad bits.)

1 Liberalism, neutrality and multiculturalism

Recall our discussion of liberal neutrality. Not all variants of liberalism want the state to be a neutral umpire, but some do. As we saw, those who do have to deal with the obvious objection that a liberal state can't be neutral about everything. They typically respond by admitting that this is indeed obvious and that the kind of neutrality they are interested in is a specific kind of neutrality. Neutrality not on justice, rights, autonomy and equality – what Rawls calls a thin theory of the good – but neutrality on the ways that people might choose to live within a just state. They sometimes add that of course their preferred state is not neutral in terms of the effects it has on the different kinds of life that people might live. Expensive lifestyles, for example, which might thrive if there were an unjust distribution of resources, will tend to be less popular once everybody has only her fair share. So too will ways of life that depend for their survival on people not being properly free to reject them – those that can attract adherents only when people are denied a proper sense of the options available to them. But, neutralist liberals will say, it makes no sense for a state to pursue neutrality of effect. How could it possibly take into account the likely effects of its policies on all the different ways of life endorsed by its citizens? Rather, the kind of neutrality it is arguing for is neutrality of aim or justification. What matters is that the state's reasons for action should not be a judgement about some ways of life being better than others, but should be reasons that are neutral between them (reasons such as those appealing to the value of individual freedom and autonomy).

Will this do? It seems simply to invite the same challenge in another form. 'OK,' the objection now goes, 'I see that you don't want the state to be neutral on matters of "the right" – or what some of you call a "thin" theory of the good. I see that you don't claim that it can be neutral in its effects on how people choose to live. But in that case I don't see why you think this is neutral in any sense that matters. Why not just admit that it embodies a substantial and substantive set of values? Your talk about "neutrality" is a bit of rhetoric supposed to persuade us that your state is an impartial arbiter, above the fray of competing visions of how society should be organized. But that is a dishonest way of presenting things.'

Neutralist liberals are thus presented with a dilemma. They can straightforwardly argue for the importance of the values – individual autonomy, etc. – they endorse. Or they can try to defend some version of their claim to neutrality. If they pursue the former strategy, they are in effect accepting that the state cannot present itself as a neutral umpire. It must justify what it does by direct appeal to the claim that the values it promotes are true, or valid, and those who do not endorse them are making a mistake – a mistake of the kind that, if necessary, warrants coercive state action to correct it. Many liberals think that this is indeed the right strategy to pursue – liberals should stand up for liberal values without hiding behind any claim to significant neutrality. But some, most notably Rawls, have tried to take the other tack. In Rawls's view, the first strategy is unacceptable because it presents liberalism as 'just another sectarian doctrine'. What should matter to liberals is that the coercive power of the state – being power held jointly by citizens who are free and equal – is used, at least where constitutional essentials and matters of basic justice are concerned, only in ways that can be justified to those forced to do what it says. It's not enough that liberal values be objectively 'true' or 'valid'. If they are to inform state action, they must qualify as 'common ground'. They must be part of the political 'overlapping consensus' on which citizens can agree despite their other differences.

Do people coincide in affirming these political values? Many do. There are indeed many religious believers, and advocates of other comprehensive conceptions of the good, who hold those doctrines in a liberal spirit. They believe their doctrines to be true, but those doctrines themselves accord individual freedom and autonomy sufficient importance for them not to want the state to deny its citizens liberal rights. If all those living subject to the authority of the liberal state held doctrines of this kind, then Rawls's claim to be building only on common ground might be valid. But, though many do, not all do. Some of those subject to its authority subscribe to doctrines in which individual freedom is of little or no value, certainly not valuable enough for them to regard it as taking priority in cases of conflict. Consider the case of Salman Rushdie, whose novel *The Satanic Verses* was thought to ridicule elements of the Islamic faith. Protecting Rushdie's freedom of expression was held by some (by no means all) British Muslims to be less important than protecting Islam from blasphemy. Returning to an earlier example, consider the claims of those who want to raise their children in accordance with a particular religion, blissfully ignorant of the other options those children might misguidedly choose to pursue if they knew about them. Most liberals take their commitment to autonomy to require them to advocate at least some state intervention, in the name of children's autonomy. How does Rawls deal with the fact that some members of today's multicultural societies do not affirm the overlapping consensus on liberal values?

His response is to say that they are 'unreasonable'. It is reasonable to disagree about comprehensive doctrines – Catholicism, Islam, utilitarianism, a life dedicated to art. That is partly why it matters that people be free to choose which of them to pursue. But it is not reasonable to disagree about the political values of autonomy, freedom and equality. Someone who denies those is indeed outside the overlapping consensus. But that is her problem. She is outside it because she is unreasonable. The consensus that counts is the consensus of reasonable comprehensive doctrines.

But this means that Rawls's strategy of building only on common ground turns out to be not that different from the first – 'stand up and fight for liberal values' – strategy. When it comes to the crunch, when he comes up against those who do not, in fact, endorse liberal values in politics, he has to put them beyond the pale by describing them as 'unreasonable'. That may be the right thing to say. But it is pushing things a bit to say that and simultaneously claim that the state one favours builds on ground that is 'common' to the doctrines endorsed by the citizens it is to govern. To those who do not buy in to the overlapping consensus – whose comprehensive doctrines themselves involve a denial of the supreme importance of liberal values in politics – even Rawlsian liberalism will look like 'just another sectarian doctrine'. This is why the multicultural nature of today's liberal democracies, the fact that the societies we live in are characterized by such deep and far-reaching doctrinal differences, poses a major justificatory problem for liberals – as, of course, it does for everybody else.

What has any of this to do with community? Well, one strand in the defence of liberalism as itself a theory of 'community' depended on the idea that it recognized the significance of communal relations, shared values and a common identity. Recall the suggestion that citizens of a liberal state share a common aim and are jointly engaged in its pursuit. Once we acknowledge the presence of

citizens who do not share the aim, and experience the requirements of the liberal state as the enforced imposition of majority
opinion, that happy description looks rather less apt. For liberals
wanting to regard the state itself as a community, multiculturalism
can be a problem. It brings with it the kind of incompatibility of
world-view that cannot easily be reconciled with the idea of political community as the collective realization of shared values.

Furthermore, the liberal state may itself be regarded as inimical
to a more particularistic or localized form of community. This will
happen whenever that state's commitment to individual freedom
and autonomy requires it to interfere with a community's own
preferred way of doing things. Should members of a religion be
permitted to raise their children as they wish, protecting them
from the spiritually impoverished and grotesquely sexualized mass
culture? Or is the state justified in protecting the autonomy of its
(future) citizens by requiring that they be educated in such a way
that they are genuinely (not just formally) free to leave that community if they wish? Can a cultural group – say the Francophone
community in Quebec – deny individuals living within 'its' city
the freedom to advertise their businesses in English? Can Native
American communities collectively decide to prevent their individual members from selling land to outsiders? Putting it in general
terms, should we tolerate groups that regard the survival and
flourishing of a particular culture as more important than individual autonomy? Or should we uphold the rights of all citizens to
revise and question traditional cultural practices? For those whose
primary focus is on the value of religious, ethnic, linguistic or cultural communities, the liberal state may look more like the enemy
than the embodiment of 'community'.

Communitarian arguments in political philosophy have focused
on the moral and political significance of groups or collectives.
They pose deep challenges to views conventionally associated with
liberalism. But it would be wrong to think that liberals deny that
significance altogether. One fruit of the communitarian critique
has been an increased sensitivity to the way in which individual
well-being depends on group-level factors, such as culture. The
Canadian philosopher Will Kymlicka, for example, has argued
that the very autonomy that liberals care so much about depends

upon cultural membership, on individuals being brought up within a reasonably rich and secure cultural structure. Someone raised within a community that is withering away before her eyes lacks meaningful options and will be unable to make informed and reflective judgements about how she is to live her life. On this view, liberals have reason to help minority groups, such as the Inuit or French Canadians, protect their community's way of life where they face an unfair struggle against the dominant culture.

On the one hand, then, liberals are concerned to protect individuals from too much community – from practices that stifle the individual's freedom to choose for herself how she lives her life. On the other hand, liberals may acknowledge the importance of cultural self-preservation and accord minority groups collective rights against the majority where that is required by their commitment to individual autonomy. The multicultural nature of the advanced democracies poses deep challenges to the liberal framework, challenges that I have no more than sketched out here. Freeing liberalism from communitarian misunderstanding and misrepresentation allows us to see more clearly the force and significance of those challenges, and to confront what is genuinely valuable in communitarian thinking.

2 Liberalism, the nation-state and global justice

The fact that today's liberal democracies are multicultural, with citizens holding deeply divergent values and doctrines, presents one problem for liberal theory that has been put into focus by communitarian writings. Another problem concerns the scope of liberal principles. Even if states were culturally homogeneous, we would still need to know why liberal principles of justice apply only within states and not across humanity as a whole.

Leaving aside the issue of multiculturalism, a defence of liberalism might run as follows: far from being hostile or inimical to community, liberalism can itself be understood as a theory of community. It allows particular (religious, ethnic, artistic) communities to flourish within the framework of a state built upon respect for individual autonomy. More importantly, the state itself is a community: a collective enterprise in which citizens jointly achieve the common good of a just society. In a properly functioning liberal society, we regard our 'citizenship identity' as sufficiently important that we are prepared to act solidaristically, pursuing our self-interest and our conception of the good only to the extent that this is compatible with doing justice to – respecting and promoting the autonomy of – our fellow citizens. People's shared identity of 'free and equal citizen' must take priority over their more particularistic religious, ethnic or cultural identities. And it must trump their economic self-interest: those who would be better off without it must be willing to endorse however much redistributive taxation is demanded by justice.

This 'liberal community' response certainly refutes some of the more confused objections to 'liberal individualism'. But the sophisticated communitarian is unlikely to be satisfied. In her view, this response cheats: it trades on a hidden premise of just the kind that she regards as important – a premise about the moral significance of particular communities, about the importance of people identifying with their particular community. 'True,' she might say, 'a liberal state can be presented as a political community in the way you outline, a collective enterprise in which citizens jointly provide the common good of justice to one another. But nothing in your account so far explains why those who happen to live in the same state – under the same political rules – owe justice to one another rather than to everybody else. Nor do I think it at all likely that the idea of liberal citizenship, on its own, can motivate people to act justly. In both these ways, from both a philosophical and a practical point of view, your story is not self-sufficient. You must be relying on some more particularistic claim about the moral and motivational significance of the particular community in which people live.'

The problem, then, is that the liberal argument seems to depend on the importance of the individual's capacity for autonomy. It is this feature of my fellow citizens that I am required to respect and promote. But it isn't only my fellow citizens who possess this capacity. So too, presumably, do all other human beings. In that case, why do I owe autonomy-promoting redistributive taxation to disadvantaged fellow Brits but not to the starving of the Third

World? There is a theoretical gap between the abstract and universal terms of the liberal argument and its presentation as a theory of citizenship, applicable to relations between members of particular political communities.

Here we approach from another angle some of the issues broached at the end of Part 1 (pp. 48–54), when I talked about the difference between 'social' and 'global' justice. (Readers wanting to think seriously about those issues would do well to go back and connect up the two discussions.) We need to be careful. For a start, those liberals who think that we owe more extensive duties to our fellow citizens than we do to other human beings will probably accept that we also owe some duties to those others. An advocate of liberal community at the level of the state is unlikely to deny that human beings as such have any claims against one another. She will probably insist only that I owe more to my fellow citizens than I do to others. (Perhaps, in the case of foreigners, I am obliged only to respect their negative rights and to help to avert extreme suffering, whereas I owe members of my own political community compliance with more demanding distributive principles.) It is also important to be clear that some liberals do indeed extend the 'liberal community' argument to the world as a whole. These are 'cosmopolitans', philosophers who think that principles of justice, and conceptions of community, must apply globally. They may keep the concept of 'citizenship', but will radically alter its implications by talking about 'world citizenship', demanding that distributive justice apply not just within existing states but across the world as a whole.

It's also worth making explicit that even cosmopolitans can accept that we owe some duties to the members of our political community, to our fellow citizens, that we don't owe to everybody else. After all, as citizens we are collectively engaged in the process of governing ourselves, of making laws, self-imposed constraints on what we, as individuals, might otherwise choose to do. If I am obliged to obey those laws, then presumably the obligation is owed not to mankind as a whole, but to those who, with me, made the laws, and are similarly obliged to comply with them. There are lots of reasons why somebody might obey a law of their state. Because they don't want to get caught breaking it. Because they think it is the right thing to do anyway. (Most people don't murder others because murder is wrong, not because there is a law against it.) But some people sometimes obey the law for the specific reason that they believe they owe it to their fellow citizens to do so. There is a lot to be said about why they might owe it to them. A chapter on what philosophers call 'political obligation' would say some of it. Here the point is simply that this kind of obligation – the obligation to obey the laws of one's state – if it exists, is indeed plausibly owed to one's fellow citizens and not to anybody else. Cosmopolitans can accept this. What they don't accept is that the rights and duties of distributive justice are claimed against, and owed to, the members of one's political community.

As I said, we need to be careful. Now let's get back to those liberals who do think that, though we owe some duties to all humans, we owe more demanding justice-based duties to our fellow citizens. Respect for the capacity for autonomy on its own can't be enough to explain the difference. There must be something morally special about common citizenship, membership of the same state, that explains why they owe each other more. On this view, it is membership of the same political community – not the 'community of humanity' – that determines people's more substantial rights against, and duties to, one another. We don't have much trouble with the idea that members of a family are in the kind of particularistic relationship that generates special moralities. We feel obligations to help our parents, children and siblings in ways that go beyond the help we owe to others. Blood is thicker than water. Something analogous applies in the case of membership of the same state. The bonds of citizenship are weaker, doubtless, than those we have to our family, but stronger than those we have to mankind as a whole.

But how is the state, the political community, like a family? And can the abstract and universal liberal ideals of autonomy, equality and freedom generate the kind of identification with others, the sense of solidarity or community, that will indeed motivate people to discharge the duties that liberals believe they owe to one another? Here we turn towards the second strand in the communitarian objection – the suspicion that, if 'liberal community' is to work, if people are to be willing to restrain the pursuit of their self-interest for the sake of treating their fellow citizens justly, they must share a sense of common identity that is richer and more inspiring than that of mere 'citizen of the same state'. If it's true that I care about my fellow citizens more than I care about other human beings, that's not because we subscribe to the same abstract principles, and are jointly involved in the project of sustaining a liberal state. It's because my fellow citizens are also my fellow countrymen (and -women). It is because they are British like me, with a shared language, shared traditions, a common history, that they are special to me – special in the required sense that I identify with them enough to accept the rights and duties that the liberal story tries to account for merely in terms of common citizenship. It is our shared national identity, our identity as British citizens, not the idea of citizenship in the abstract, that is needed to do the motivational work. (Of course, the idea that the British do have a common identity – and, to the extent that they do, where it comes from and how it is sustained – is itself controversial. In practice, communal identities are multiple, overlapping, and constantly being reshaped, partly by political developments – such as the European Union. The politics of collective identity is hugely complicated. My aim here is simply to lay out the general shape of the issue as it arises in political philosophy.)

Although it presents itself in universalistic and abstract terms, the idea of a 'liberal community' is, the objection goes, premised on something more particularistic, something more like the family. As with the family, our sense of ourselves as members of a nation is based on a belief in a common history. It gives us a sense of who we are. And it generates particularistic moral ties. We identify with our state, our political community, because, or to the extent that, it coincides with our nation. If our nation and our state do not coincide, we might well try to change things so that they did. (The conflicts in Europe since the collapse of the Soviet Union have been mainly about people who identify with one another as members of the same nation looking to make state and nation coincide.) On the communitarian account, then, the idea of a 'liberal community' is not self-sufficient. One cannot account for the special moral relationship, or expect people to be motivated as egalitarian liberals want them to be, without invoking a conception of community that goes beyond the bare idea of doing justice to one's fellow citizens. People's identities must be 'constituted' by something more particularistic than the abstract idea of 'citizenship'. Which is the kind of thing communitarians were saying all along.

As with everything else in this book, this is the beginning, not the end, of the story. Some liberal theorists accept that social justice should be pursued within particular states, and that fellow citizens owe special justice-based duties to one another. They may also recognize that achieving justice will necessitate state action to promote a sense of patriotism, countering the divisive influence of class, culture and all the other things that tend to encourage sectional thinking. Some pursue the cosmopolitan route. They accept that people may feel closer to their compatriots than to foreigners, but think that this is a feeling that ought to be transcended. Just as people, though often tempted, should not show too much favouritism to their children – avoiding nepotism and observing principles of equality and impartiality when filling jobs, for example – so they should not allow the mere fact of common nationality too much weight in their moral deliberation, perhaps none at all. In any case, isn't nationality usually a myth – an 'imagined community' – constructed, sometimes deliberately, to foster a sense of common identity where none would otherwise exist? Moreover, we all know how dangerous the idea of nationhood can be. (It's significant that recent attempts to revive the moral significance of the nation talk about 'nationality' not 'nationalism'. Contemporary advocates of nationality are very keen to distance themselves from the fanatic excesses of 'blood and soil' nationalism.) Notice, also, that even cosmopolitans can argue that it makes sense for the world to be organized into discrete states, that such states work best when they coincide with national groupings, and that members of such states may be best placed to help one another. This will be the case if they accept the impracticability of a single 'world state', think that the way to get closest to global justice is for each state to look after its own members, and believe that those who share a common national culture are more likely to do so. Here, nationality, and the world being divided into individual states constituted by groups of citizens with shared identities, are valued instrumentally – as a means to a different goal – not because people do really owe their fellow citizens, or ,their fellow countrymen (and -women), more than they owe anybody else.

What generates a sense of common identity? What leads people to feel the kind of solidarity towards one another that is required for them to be motivated to treat each other in accordance with the demanding principles of redistributive liberalism? Wars are good. It is no accident that support for the British welfare state peaked just after the Second World War. There's nothing like a war to build a sense of common purpose, of being in the same boat, and to generate the kind of interaction between people that breaks down divisive social boundaries. As that feeling has weakened – and as society has become more pluralistic and diverse, less culturally homogeneous – so the case for some kind of national or civic service has grown stronger. It is easy now for people not to feel themselves to be members of their state, to identify essentially with more local and particularistic groupings – ethnicity, religion, lifestyle. Requiring them to devote a year of their lives to something conceived and presented as 'national service' – even if this were discharged at the local level – might foster in them a sense of 'citizenship identity'. This would, of course, restrict their freedom. Some liberals might object to it on those grounds. But liberals don't just care about freedom, they care also about justice. If people will be motivated to act justly only towards those with whom they share a sense of common identity, and if compulsory national service would be conducive to that sense, then the liberal should be willing to accept the freedom-restricting implication. (For the cosmopolitan, on the other hand, the promotion of national or citizenship identity is likely to seem illegitimately parochial – part of the problem, not the solution.)

Conclusion

Political communitarians may feel that this discussion has missed the point. It has focused on the dispute (or apparent dispute) between liberalism and its philosophically communitarian critics. It has explained how liberalism sees the state as a community. And it has suggested a way in which this conception may be parasitic on a sense of common identity – arguably threatened by deep cultural diversity – that the liberal tends to leave out of the story. For some, this will all seem too abstract and general. The kind of community they are interested in is smaller-scale, more particularistic and more local – the family, the church, the neighbourhood. I have said that liberalism has a problem explaining why we should care especially about our fellow citizens rather than humanity as a whole. But it might be objected that only an out-of-touch philosopher could think that that was the problem. The real issue is that the state or nation is already too diffuse and distant for people to feel a sense of belonging and fellow feeling of the kind that will prevent them sliding into individualism of the wrong – alienated, egoistic – kind.

On this view, the redistributive state justified by appeal to the idea of common citizenship is not motivationally sustainable. For a time, after the war, there was indeed, in the UK, a sense of national solidarity and common purpose, realized in – and to some extent fostered by – the welfare state. But that couldn't last. Moreover, because it took over the functions of local and voluntary associations, the welfare state undermined the more particularistic forms of community that are better able, in the long run, to provide people with a sense of themselves as more than isolated individuals. The individual's conception of herself as 'citizen' does indeed imply membership of a particular community, but the community it implies membership of – the state – is too bureaucratic, impersonal and distant to counter the disintegration of society into individuals, or at best nuclear families, seeking their own private self-interest, unhappy because they feel that their lives lack the sense of meaning and purpose that comes from involvement in political activity and participation in what political theorists call 'civil society'. National politics is too remote to be of interest. Politics must be returned to its proper, human, level if we are to combat growing alienation and apathy. This kind of communitarian wants the reinvigoration of what the Irish conservative Edmund Burke (1729–97) called the 'little platoons', forms of civil association between the family and the state. That and the strengthening of local communities, the restoration of a 'sense of community' in individual neighbourhoods:

community policing, community schools, community politics, community development, community activism.

Few would deny the value of the individual's sense of belonging, of identification with and attachment to others beyond her immediate family. But we are here moving in the direction of empirical questions, better answered by the political sociologist than the political philosopher. What kinds of belonging, identification and attachment are sustainable, under what conditions, and how do they relate to one another? Are they mutually reinforcing? Do people who leave the private sphere sufficiently to get involved in local community initiatives tend also to take the wider view more generally? In that case, their membership of and participation in this kind of community-based activity form no obstacle to their manifesting solidarity and fraternity at the level of the state also. Are local associations schools for citizenship? Or do local and national community pull in opposing directions? Community is about membership and inclusion. But that means it is also about non-membership and exclusion. Local neighbourhoods are relatively homogeneous, both culturally and economically. Those of similar race, religion and wealth tend to live close to one another. If it does indeed matter, as it must to national politicians, that there be a feeling of common identity across the citizenry as a whole – so that it makes sense to a rich Catholic in one area that some of the money she earns in the market be redistributed to an unemployed Muslim in another – we must not lose sight of the potentially divisive and unequalizing consequences of too much emphasis on the local community, or on other identities that might tend to pull people away from their common citizenship.

Meanwhile, as 'globalization' gathers pace and technological developments make it easier to identify with people across the world, the idea that even the state or nation represents a 'community' of any great moral significance can itself start to seem outdated. If individuals are to transcend their particular selfish interests, taking the wider view and adopting a more other-regarding perspective, then it is the 'community of humanity' that should be the proper subject of their concern. Indeed, for many of my students, motivated above all by environmental issues, that 'community' extends not only beyond their fellow citizens or fellow nationals, but also beyond the living. It compasses also future generations.

Further reading

Shlomo Avineri and Avner de-Shalit's (eds.), *Communitarianism and Individualism* (Oxford University Press 1992) helpfully gathers together bite-sized chunks from the leading protagonists in the so-called liberal–communitarian debate. It is the most efficient way to read most of the key primary texts on the philosophical side. John Rawls's political liberalism, and Joseph Raz's perfectionist liberalism are set out in *Political Liberalism* (Columbia University Press 1993) and *The Morality of Freedom* (Oxford University Press 1986) respectively. Stephen Mulhall and Adam Swift's *Liberals and Communitarians* (2nd edn, Blackwell 1996) provides chapter-length accounts of their positions, as well as fuller discussion of the other issues touched on here. Their 'Rawls and Communitarianism', in Samuel Freeman (ed.), *The Cambridge Companion to Rawls* (Cambridge University Press 2002), is a useful overview. Daniel Bell's *Communitarianism and its Critics* (Oxford University Press 1993) is written as a dialogue set in a Paris brasserie, and is correspondingly fun to read.

On the political communitarian side, the key text is Amitai Etzioni's *The Spirit of Community* (Crown Publishers 1993), which includes 'The Responsive Community Platform'. Elizabeth Frazer's *The Problems of Communitarian Politics* (Oxford University Press 1999) is difficult, but a great attempt to integrate and disentangle the bewildering variety of things that get called 'communitarianism'. http://communitariannetwork.org takes you to 'The Communitarian Network'. Will Kymlicka's *Multicultural Odysseys: Navigating the New International Politics of Diversity* (Oxford University Press 2007) is an excellent collection of essays by a leading philosopher of multiculturalism. *Culture and Equality* (Polity 2000), by Brian Barry, is an entertainingly scathing critique of much that gets said in the name of multiculturalism, and is itself subject to entertainingly scathing criticism by contributors to *Multiculturalism Reconsidered* (Polity 2002), edited by Paul Kelly. Among Barry's critics is Bhikhu Parekh whose *Rethinking*

Multiculturalism: Cultural Diversity and Political Theory is well worth a read (2nd edn, Palgrave Macmillan 2005). David Miller's *Citizenship and National Identity* (Polity 2000) provides sophisticated but clear discussions of what it says it's about.

Part 5

Democracy

Democracy really is the 'motherhood and apple pie' of politics. Who objects to it? The fact that all sorts of doubtful regimes call themselves democratic testifies to the moral and rhetorical force of the idea that political power should be in the hands of the people (Greek *kratos* = 'power', *demos* = 'people'; so, literally, 'people power'). Indeed, the conventional wisdom has it that it's universally valuable, good for everybody. So good, indeed, that some states have come to regard exporting it as a legitimate goal of foreign policy.

Meanwhile 'democracy' has become rather blunt as an ideal, because it is often invoked as a catch-all term referring to any aspect of a political system, or of a society, that the speaker thinks good. Sometimes, of course, this attempt to profit by its rhetorical appeal is so blatant as to become ridiculous. There can't have been many who agreed with the insistence of the pro-hunt lobby that the law to ban hunting with hounds deprived the British people of a democratic right. Perhaps there is a right to hunt, and perhaps the government did wrong not to recognize it. But was that law, announced in a manifesto and carried by a majority of the House of Commons, undemocratic? Or think about the alleged right to carry guns in the US. One may accept or reject that right, and one's grounds for doing so may or may not invoke the Constitution. But it's hard to see how a society that allows its members to carry guns is more democratic than one that (democratically) decides not to.

This universal reverence for democracy, and this tendency to call all good things democratic, is rather ironic. Today it seems obvious, a matter of simple common sense, that democracy is a good thing. For most of human history the opposite has been the case. It was obvious to any clear-thinking person that democracy, should it ever come about, would be a disaster. How on earth could anyone think it desirable to give power to the people – to the unruly, ignorant, self-interested mob? The people were poor, and there were lots of them. Any state foolish enough to put power in their hands would quickly self-destruct as the wealth and civilization built up over centuries by an aristocratic elite were destroyed in a short-term feeding frenzy by the uneducated masses.

That history should give us pause. Don't worry. I'm not going to try to persuade readers that they don't really believe in democracy after all. But, given this widespread and rather unthinking endorsement, it does seem appropriate to spark some anti-democratic intuitions, if only to clarify why exactly we want it – and how much of it we want. For some, the reason why the pessimists were wrong – the reason why democracy did not lead to destruction – is that we don't have all that much of it. For others, though, the problem is quite the reverse. What needs exposing is excessive complacency about the extent to which Western 'liberal democracies' realize the values of democracy. For them, the discussion that follows may reveal how far we are from enjoying membership of a genuinely democratic state.

One important issue – the scope of democratic principles – will not be addressed. I explained in the introduction that this book would focus on politics in the conventional sense that links it to the relation between citizens and states. That focus will be too narrow for some, and there are indeed important issues about whether democratic thinking should apply more widely. Within states, perhaps it should apply to workplaces, firms, families. A fully democratic society, perhaps, would see democratic values permeating our understandings and practices of the institutions of civil society. Beyond states, there has recently been a good deal of interest in the idea of global or cosmopolitan democracy (analogous to global or cosmopolitan justice discussed at the end of Part 1.) Policies adopted in one country can have huge impacts on members of others (think about environmental issues, for example) and it's plausible to think that decisions should be made by all those whose interests will be affected by them. So there are obviously big and important questions about who exactly constitutes the '*demos*' in 'democracy' (including, incidentally, members of future generations who aren't around to speak for themselves.) Although I can't get into them, I hope at least that this chapter will help readers when they come to think about these other questions.

What is democracy?

'Rule of the people, by the people, for the people.' The definition of US President Abraham Lincoln (1809–65) is a good place to start – as long as we're clear that it's the 'by the people' bit that is important. All systems of government are going to be government of the people; it is the people who are being governed. And, in principle, a benevolent dictator or an enlightened aristocracy could rule for the people. True, we might think those scenarios a bit improbable. A democratic regime is perhaps more likely to rule for the people than a dictatorship or an aristocracy, and that might be a good reason for preferring democracy. But what one is then preferring is precisely rule *by* the people – a political system in which the people govern themselves.

If this is what democracy means, then one is immediately confronted by a problem. Even those polities that have the best claim to call themselves democratic can hardly be seen as pure examples of collective self-rule. What really happens is that every now and again there are elections during which a subset of the population votes to decide which microscopically small subset of the population is going to be making the decisions for the next few years. The winners of the election have typically attracted only a minority of those who actually vote, and an even smaller proportion of the electorate as a whole. These elections happen in a context where much of the media is owned by a wealthy elite with clear political interests of its own and where political parties are free to spend on advertising whatever people are willing to give them. Is this way of governing really 'people power'?

The obvious response to this scepticism is to preach practicality. Genuine 'rule by the people' might have been viable in small city-states, where citizens really could assemble to deliberate collectively, and as equals, on their collective affairs, but the size and complexity of today's polities make this kind of direct democracy quite unrealistic. Few see any prospect of getting away from indirect or representative democracy and returning power to the people in any thoroughgoing way. The time that political decision-making would take, and the expertise that it would require to do it at all well, make that a non-starter. The issue on the political agenda is how to get people to bother to vote once every four or five years. In that context, any suggestion of a move towards more direct and egalitarian forms of democracy (at least on the national scale) can look utopian. The citizens of ancient Athens may have been able to assemble and deliberate, but they were effectively gentlemen of leisure – it was women and slaves who did the work – and the issues they were deciding were far simpler and less technical than those confronting contemporary polities.

It's important to keep principled considerations separate from feasibility constraints. It's especially so in the case of democracy, because it's so hard to do. Of course, in the end we have to go for the best realization of democracy that we can get, the best that's within our feasibility set. There will be a lot of disagreement about what is and is not feasible. Much political argument is about what can be made to work (rather than about what would be good if it could be made to work). There's nothing wrong with that. But, when we do political philosophy, it's important not to worry about feasibility constraints too early in the process, as it were, important not to let them interfere with our understanding of where the values lie. First we should think about democratic values and how, in principle, they might best be realized. Then we should look at the world and work out what kind of democracy is most likely to get closest to the ideal.

The key point about 'rule by the people' is that it is a procedure for making political decisions. It directs our attention away from their content to the way laws are made – in particular, to who makes them. Conceiving democracy as a decision-making procedure is a good way of keeping clear about the various arguments for and against it. Is it indeed good that the people themselves should make the laws they are to live under? We can divide answers to that question into two kinds. A procedure can be valued instrumentally, because of the outcomes it is likely to produce. Or it can be valued intrinsically, for its own sake, on grounds independent of the outcomes it tends to produce. Perhaps democracy is good for both kinds of reason. Perhaps it tends to produce good decisions, or stable government, or enlightened citizens, and it respects people's right to participate in collective decision-making or is the fairest way of distributing political power. Perhaps not. Much of this chapter will be exploring these different kinds of justification.

Regarding democracy as a procedure throws up a possible tension between democracy and political philosophy. The philosopher tries to deliver right answers, whereas the democrat wants us all to contribute equally to delivering an answer. That tension finds its clearest expression in Plato's *Republic*, where the father of philosophy explicitly rejects democracy in favour of rule by a philosopher-king. (That's obviously a terrible idea. Plato (Greek, c.427–347 BC) thought that only philosophers possessed the expertise safely to guide the ship of state into harbour. The ones I know have problems remembering where they left their bicycles.) What we want, according to Plato, are wise political decisions, correct answers to the thorny questions that confront even relatively small and homogeneous Greek city-states. But, for many, democracy isn't about making wise political decisions. It's about the people making their own decisions. The legitimacy of law, for many democrats, depends not on its being right, but on its being a proper expression of what the people want, of the popular will – whether or not that would stand up to philosophical scrutiny.

Here we are talking about the difference between correctness and legitimacy. And one important thing that philosophers try to offer is a correct theory of legitimacy. What is it that makes democratic decisions indeed legitimate? What kinds of responsiveness to the popular will are in fact necessary or sufficient for a law to be justified? These are unavoidably philosophical questions. The legitimacy of a decision can indeed be independent of its rightness – but there can still be a right answer about what makes a decision legitimate. And, of course, one can perfectly well have views about what makes a decision legitimate and about what would be the right decision for a political community to take on any particular issue. Most of us have both of these. So philosophers, and everybody else, can quite coherently argue and vote for a particular outcome as the right answer while also insisting that only some ways of making such decisions are legitimate – and insisting that decisions made that way remain legitimate even if they are incorrect. The core issue in democratic theory is why it is valuable that people, or 'the people', should be involved in making the rules to which they are subject.

Degrees of democracy

As a way in, let's think about the various ways in which the democraticness of a political system is a matter of degree. It's tempting to think that either a state is democratic or it isn't. In fact, however, exploring the different ways in which decisions, or states, might be less or more democratic helpfully forces us to get clear on what we mean when we talk about democracy in the first place. One lesson that some learn from the exercise is that, even though democracy is indubitably a good thing, they do not want too much of it.

Here, then, are four dimensions along which it seems that societies, or political systems, or the decisions produced by those systems, can be considered less or more 'democratic'.

1 Directness or indirectness of the decision

Decision-making is directly democratic when the people as a whole vote directly on the issues under consideration. It is indirectly democratic when they vote for representatives who make the decisions on their behalf. The US and the UK operate systems of representative democracy. Occasionally the UK holds a referendum on a particular issue, where the matter is felt to be sufficiently important or controversial to require a direct mandate from the people as a whole for the decision to be legitimate. Decisions made by referendum, where the people's will is expressed directly, are in an obvious sense more 'democratic' than those made by representatives. That is not, of course, to say that they are better in any way. They may not be better decisions. Referenda may not even be a better way of making decisions. But they are a more democratic way.

The indirectness of a decision lessens the extent to which the present will of the majority of the voters controls political outcomes, and the extent to which a decision is direct or indirect is itself scalar ('scalar'= 'not all-or-nothing but admitting of degree'). Imagine a polity where the electorate as a whole votes for an assembly which votes for an assembly which votes for an assembly . . . The more levels of mediation between the people themselves and the decisions that emerge, the less directly democratic, and the less democratic, the system.

It's worth thinking about the relationship between 'direct democracy' and 'participatory democracy'. Important strands in democratic theory are suspicious of representative government and insist on the importance of a genuinely participatory political system, where the people as a whole engage in political debate and are directly involved in political decision-making – rather than merely choosing representatives, who decide things on their behalf, every few years. Discussion of this approach typically focuses on its feasibility rather than its desirability. 'Well, it would be nice if we could all assemble and deliberate and decide issues for ourselves, but of course that's completely impractical in the modern world. The issues are far too complex to be decided by ordinary voters and in any case people nowadays just don't have the time to devote to political affairs.'

But the reality is that, given where we have got to with information technology, direct democracy is perfectly feasible. It would not be hard to equip all households with computer terminals through which all people of voting age could directly register their votes. We could have an elected Parliament to debate issues and frame legislation, but all proposed laws would be put to the people as a whole for endorsement. In effect, there would be a referendum on all decisions that are currently made into law by representatives. Call this 'teledemocracy'. Such a system would be a more direct form of democracy than we have at the moment. And it would, on the account offered here, be more democratic.

But would it qualify as a participatory democracy? That is not so clear. It's quite possible that voters in a teledemocracy would get to decide directly what the laws are without any participation in politics beyond the clicking of a computer mouse. They don't need to be informed about the issues; they don't need to have heard or engaged in any debate. They don't need to have done any of the things typically regarded as important by theorists of participatory democracy. Of course, one might hope that making democracy more direct would also lead to its becoming more participatory in these other senses. Given a greater say in politics, it is often argued, citizens will become more involved, engaged and active; current low levels of interest in politics are the result of the way decisions are made and can be expected to change over time as ordinary people are trusted more. Maybe. But the conceptual point stands: the directness of a decision-making process is a rather formal property, telling us nothing about the input to decisions other than that it is a direct expression of the people's will. Advocates of participatory democracy typically want something more or other than direct democracy – they want an engaged citizenry getting involved in politics in ways that go beyond registering a vote.

Distinguishing in this way between direct democracy and participatory democracy may make the former less attractive. If it would indeed act as a catalyst for political involvement of other kinds, then perhaps moves towards teledemocracy would be a good thing. But taken on its own, and given current low levels of political awareness, many would be doubtful about the merits of such a way of making decisions. I don't trust 'the people' to use their interactive vote wisely when choosing between would-be popstars in TV shows; it's got to be risky letting them make laws by similar means. Suppose the choice were between (a) genuine but short-lived participation in choosing representatives who then make laws and (b) direct votes on laws via computer terminal by citizens with little or no knowledge or interest. The latter may be more 'democratic', but the former would be better.

2 Accountability of representatives

Assuming we have some kind of representative system — and remember that even my teledemocracy has representatives to frame the legislation on which we all vote — there is an issue about the extent to which those representatives are accountable to their electorates. At one extreme, we could imagine a system where all representatives were subject to immediate recall. As soon as they did anything their constituents didn't like, those constituents could haul them back and replace them with others more responsive to the popular will. This would give constituents full democratic control over their representatives. The representatives would effectively be turned into delegates, mandated to vote particular ways. At the other extreme, we could imagine a system where representatives were indeed elected, but they were elected for life. Once in post, they would have complete independence, and would be free to decide issues as they saw fit, without any further democratic check on their authority. That procedure would be more democratic than one in which there is no vote on who gets to make the decisions, but less democratic than one in which representatives are accountable to those who elected them. In between these two extremes lies something like our current system, which we may think of as retrospective recall: voters get the chance to cast judgement on their representatives at elections, and throw the rascals out if they don't like them — electing a different set of rascals in their place.

Here too we might not want too much democracy. A system in which representatives act as delegates, mandated to vote along lines fixed in advance by their constituents, or in which they are subject to immediate recall (i.e., sacked as soon as they do anything their constituents don't like), is very democratic, but not obviously very sensible. For many, the reason to have representatives in the first place is that they are likely to be in a better position to make good decisions than their constituents are. This was certainly the view of the Irish philosopher (and politician) Edmund Burke (1729–97). Addressing the voters of Bristol in 1774, Burke famously told them: 'Your representative owes you, not his industry only, but his judgment; and he betrays instead of serving you if he sacrifices it to your opinion.' But why might one think a representative's judgement likely to be any better than that of the people who voted for him?

A conventional answer to that question holds that the whole point of parliamentary debate (from *parler*, French for 'to talk', so a parliament is not badly translated as a talking shop) is that it tends to yield wiser judgements than would be achieved by the mere aggregation of pre-reflective preferences. Representatives mandated to vote a certain way, or liable to be recalled as soon as they depart from their constituents' wishes, are hardly going to be engaging in a careful, disinterested attempt to filter out bad arguments and act on good ones. OK, given the way parties and political patronage works, one can be sceptical about the extent to which existing parliaments follow this kind of deliberative ideal. But one would have to be extremely cynical about contemporary politics not to acknowledge any epistemic value in the kind of debate that goes on among representatives in parliamentary systems. ('Epistemic' = 'involving knowledge'.)

Does this kind of argument for representative government, and against too much accountability, presume that representatives are inherently wiser than, or in other ways superior to, their constituents? Not necessarily. It could simply be that they are given the time to think about the issues and process relevant information. Representative government could be justified simply by appeal to the division of labour. Many political issues are complicated and technical. Rather than have everybody devote scarce time to thinking about them, it makes sense to identify a few hundred and pay them to do the thinking, full time, for us. Taken on its own, of course, this argument suggests that it would be all right for our decision-makers to be selected randomly. If the case for representative government were entirely that it's efficient to give some people the specific job of doing our political decision-making for us, then a random cross-section of the electorate could be expected to do the job perfectly well. (Some have suggested that the British second legislative chamber, the House of Lords, be replaced by a body of this kind.) If you have doubts about that kind of selection procedure, that's probably because you do in fact believe that elected representatives are likely to be different from − better at decision-making than − the average citizen.

3 Equality (of opportunity) for influence

A political system is more democratic the more its citizens have equal opportunity for political influence. Equality will reappear soon, as a core democratic value, but we can begin to get a sense of its centrality by noting that the degree to which democracy itself is achieved seems to depend, in part, on the extent to which citizens participate equally in the making of political decisions. Imagine two societies, both with the same institutions of representative government, the same electoral laws, and each respecting the democratic idea of 'one person, one vote'. In one of those societies all citizens have been educated to a level where they are able to read the newspapers, to understand and assess the arguments put to them by those competing for votes, and to contribute to political discussion if they want to. All also have jobs that give them roughly equal amounts of money and leisure. In the other society, half the population has acquired the education they need to make and weigh up political arguments, but the other half is innumerate and illiterate. This division is matched by jobs that yield very unequal amounts of money and leisure: half the population earns a comfortable living from jobs that yield ample time off for political reflection, while the other half works all hours just to keep the wolf from the door. Both countries hold general elections at the same time. Which result is more democratic?

If some are so poor that they spend all their time worrying about where the next meal is coming from, while others are trained from birth to think about and study political issues, and to develop the skills needed to present their views in a coherent and plausible manner, then they are hardly able to act as equal citizens in the process of self-rule. The political decisions that are made will not reflect the views of the people as a whole − they will reflect the views of that subset of the people who have the time and energy and skill to devote to them. Those decisions are less than fully democratic.

This is, of course, the beginning rather than the end of the story. Interesting detailed issues remain. We know, for example, that there is a significant correlation between people's socioeconomic position and the likelihood of their voting, and, in the US, between that position and their even being registered to vote. Does this show that socioeconomic inequality impacts on the extent to which people have equality of opportunity to vote? Not necessarily. It shows that economic inequality translates into equality of political input, but, taking the 'opportunity' bit seriously, we have to admit the possibility that some of those who choose not to vote (or to register) are doing just that: choosing. When assessing the democraticness of political decision-making along the equality dimension, is it equality of political input that we should be interested in, or equality of opportunity for input? And how can we tell when two people have really had the same opportunity?

There is also a more general question about whether we should conceive democratic citizenship in egalitarian or sufficientarian terms. (If you don't know what this means, look at pp. 131–2.) Does it really matter whether citizens have equality, whether of political input or of opportunity for such input? Or is the real point that all should reach some threshold level? Some theorists resist the suggestion that equality understood in a strict and distributive sense has implications for the extent to which a political regime, or particular decision, can be said to be democratic. Rather, for them, what matters is that all have whatever they need to act properly as citizens – the requisite freedoms, the education to enable them to assess options, and so on. As long as all have that threshold of 'citizenship-goods', then the society can be said to be fully democratic. Others disagree. Equality really does come into the story, because it really is important that citizens are able equally to take part in political decision-making. And political influence is to some extent a positional good. (See pp. 124–7.) How influential my views will be depends not just on my input, but on my input relative to that of others. If one party has very wealthy supporters who can fund big advertising campaigns, while another has to rely on donations from ordinary citizens, then the latter will be less influential than it would be in a more equal situation. Reforms aimed at limiting campaign contributions in the US should not be thought of as simply levelling down. Those with fewer political resources at their disposal are made better off – the extent to which they can influence public debate is increased – when others are deprived of the opportunity to drown them out. (Rawls thinks something like this. Although he puts political rights like freedom of expression in his first principle of justice, which suggests that they cannot be traded off for distributive goals, he also insists that the political liberties must be given their 'fair value', and recognizes the impact on that value of the resources that citizens can use to back them up. Rawls is in favour of campaign finance reform, and, more generally, has grounds for restricting inequality where that undermines the fair value of people's political liberties. The US Supreme Court continues to hold that attempts to limit political contributions violate the constitutional right to freedom of expression, while US politicians show no interest in limiting inequality on democratic grounds.)

4 Scope of authority of democratic will

However democratically we make our decisions – whether directly or indirectly, whatever the accountability of our representatives, and however equally or unequally citizens are able to influence the decisions that are made – there is an issue about which decisions should be made by democratic procedures. Judging what should be the scope of democratic decision-making is a separate matter from thinking about how decisions within that scope should be made. One could be keen on thoroughly democratic procedures, but think that they should apply only to a narrow range of issues. Or one could believe that a very wide range of matters should be decided by democratic means, but insist that those means should be less democratic than others would like.

The real issue here is the proper scope of politics. Which matters are 'public', where that means something like 'legitimately up for political decision and state action', and which 'private', a matter for individuals to decide for themselves? This, of course, is a huge question. The point for now is simply that the issue of which matters should be decided democratically typically arises only after one has decided which should be decided politically. So we might well think that a person's sex life is a matter for them alone. A polity does not have a collective sex life of the kind that would make it appropriate to decide such matters politically. In that case, we would not want decisions about who went to bed with whom to be decided democratically. But that would be because we did not want that issue on the political agenda at all. It wouldn't be an argument against democracy in particular. And democracy might still be the best way of deciding those matters that are indeed public or political – where coordination is required or where we as citizens have a legitimate interest in regulating one another's actions.

Restrictions on the scope of democratic decision can usefully be divided into two kinds. Some are justified by appeal to the ideal of democracy itself. Suppose that the citizenry of a state collectively decided to deprive some subgroup of the right to vote, or the right to stand for office, or the right to freedom of expression. That decision would itself deny members of that group those things that constitute the ideal of democracy. Though the decision might be made democratically, it would nonetheless violate democratic principles. Allowing its members to vote, or stand for office, or say what they think about the powers that be, is part of what it means for a state to be democratic in the first place. To deny members those rights would, in effect, be to deny them membership of a democratic state, and a state that denied some of those subject to its laws the right to participate in making those laws would then cease to be a democracy. Most theorists hold that democratic authority does not extend to self-abolition – so the people cannot legitimately decide, even by democratic means, to deprive themselves of those rights that are constitutive of democracy in the first place.

But not all restrictions on the scope of the democratic will derive from the ideal of democracy itself. I suggested in Part 1 that there might be nothing undemocratic about a polity's deciding to deprive its members of freedom of sexuality (or of religion). A democratic decision to deprive homosexuals of the right to campaign politically for changes in the law would itself contravene themselves. Let's explore this distinction between instrumental and intrinsic justifications of democracy.

It's helpful to think of democracy as essentially a procedure for making political decisions. The question is whether democracy is a good way of making decisions – or at least the best we've got. (Winston Churchill (1874–1965), British Prime Minister during the Second World War, famously said that democracy is the worst form of government except for all the others that have been tried.) What criteria should we use to assess decision-making procedures? We know that we want the best way of making decisions. But does this mean we want the way that will make the best decisions?

For some, the answer is a straightforward 'yes'. On their view, what makes a decision-making procedure good or bad is precisely the quality of the decisions that it tends to produce. If it produces good decisions, then it is a good procedure for making decisions. If not, not. This makes a lot of sense. After all, we are talking about procedures for making decisions. How else are we going to judge them, if not by considering how likely they are to get those decisions right? As the American philosopher Richard Arneson (b. 1945) has put it: 'Democracy, when it is just, is so entirely in virtue of the tendency of democratic institutions and practices to produce outcomes that are just according to standards that are conceptually independent of the standards that define the democratic ideal.' What's wrong with teledemocracy, on this kind of view, is the fact that making laws by getting millions of uninformed people to click on a computer screen or via their interactive TV is likely to result in some dreadful laws. A procedure that involves careful weighing of the evidence, judicious deliberation among informed and engaged politicians, is, on this view, a better procedure precisely because it is more likely to result in good decisions.

But others think that we should evaluate procedures in a rather different way. Rather than seeing them in instrumental terms, as means to ends, or in terms of their likely output or consequences, we should evaluate them in terms of their intrinsic value – in terms of the values embodied in the procedures themselves. If democracy is good, from this perspective, that's not because democracies tend to make good laws but because the democratic way of making laws itself realizes certain values – such as fairness, equality or autonomy.

This distinction between intrinsic and instrumental value can be confusing. To clarify what's going on here, let's suppose equality to be a value intrinsic to democratic procedures. This means that democratic procedures are intrinsically valuable insofar as they treat people as equals, their views as equally worthy of respect, or something along those lines. It's crucial to see that we are still giving a reason why democracy is intrinsically valuable – in this case it's because that is the procedure that respects people's equality as citizens. The fact that democracy is valuable because it realizes or embodies the value of equality does not mean that democracy is valuable only instrumentally, only as a means to the end of equality. For democracy to be instrumentally valuable, it would have to be valued in terms of its consequences. But the equality we have in mind here is not a consequence of democracy. It is not something that democracy tends to produce. We don't have to wait to see what results from democracy in order to judge that it realizes the value of equality. Democratic procedures embody or realize that value in themselves, intrinsically. The same goes for the value of autonomy or self-rule. We can judge that democratic decision-making embodies the value of self-rule, in a way that being ruled by a dictator would not, without knowing anything about the likely outcomes of democracy in action.

Although it's important to keep the two kinds of argument distinct, the case for democracy need not be based exclusively on either intrinsic or instrumental justifications. The same goes for particular specifications of the idea that the people should rule themselves. There's no incoherence in evaluating procedures for making decisions in terms of both kinds of value, favouring that which seems to give the best overall balance. Thus, for example, we may think that some degree of equality of opportunity for political input is essential to a law-making procedure's being justified, and favour democracy over rule by a wise elite for that reason. But we may also think it worth sacrificing some amount of equality if doing so is likely to produce better decisions. Something like that may be the trade-off made by those who prefer parliamentary democracy to teledemocracy.

Notice that democratic decision-making has consequences other than the decisions that get made. It may be a bit misleading to think of these other consequences as 'outputs', but they may well be relevant to the evaluation of the procedure that produces them. Some, for example, have argued for democracy on the grounds that being involved in the making of political decisions tends to develop citizens' intellectual and moral capacities. (John Stuart Mill famously claimed something along these lines.) Or perhaps it is more important that the laws that get made are respected and complied with than that they are good in terms of their content. A not-so-great law that everybody is willing to obey might be better, all things considered, than an otherwise great law that fails to command widespread support. (Tocqueville runs this argument in his analysis in *Democracy in America* (1835).) This is certainly an important consideration, but bear in mind that the same thing could be said for absolute monarchy, where the people as a whole regarded that as the proper way to make decisions and couldn't be doing with this dangerous and new-fangled idea of democracy. Stability and compliance may be good things, other things equal, but other things aren't always equal. Sometimes insurrection or revolution are precisely what is required.

Is democracy paradoxical?

According to a well-known article by the British philosopher Richard Wollheim (1923–2003), there is a paradox at the core of democracy. It is, I think, easily resolved – perhaps it's not even a paradox at all – but outlining and resolving it is a useful way of explaining the difference between a decision's being correct and its being legitimate.

Suppose I am a democrat. There is a vote on some matter – let's say it's the question of who should be the Member of Parliament for my constituency. I vote for Ms Wise. I do so because I think she is the right person (at least of those standing) to be our MP. I lose the vote, and Mr Foolish is elected. Since I am a democrat, I now think that Mr Foolish is the right person to represent my constituency in the House of Commons. Have I changed my mind? Or do I somehow – and apparently incoherently – think both that

Ms Wise is the right person for the job and that Mr Foolish is? This teaser – sometimes called the puzzle of the minority democrat – shouldn't be too puzzling. There is no deep paradox, since the two candidates are 'right' in different senses.

Before getting clear on what they are, let's dispose of the idea that what happens is that I change my mind about which of the two would be better at the job. Sure, the fact that I lost the vote might lead me to change my mind. I might not have much confidence in my own judgement, and might regard the fact that many other people had a different opinion from me as evidence that my own initial view was mistaken. Certainly I've taken part in votes where that's happened – where I've been unsure as to which way to vote, and seen my being outvoted as a sign that I made the wrong call. But those have been rather special cases. They've been cases where I had reason to think that my fellow voters were at least as likely as I was to make a good judgement about the matter being voted on (e.g., on decisions about whom to appoint to jobs at my university). Where that's the case, the fact that one is in the minority does indeed give one grounds for thinking one made a mistake. (More on this later, when I explain Condorcet's Jury Theorem – which shows that as long as the average person is more likely to be right than wrong, the majority is even more likely to be right.) But I've never changed my mind in an election for my Member of Parliament. I haven't regarded my losing the vote as a sign that I made the wrong call in those elections. Rather, I continued to argue for my preferred candidate, explaining to anybody who would listen that we (i.e., they) had made a big mistake. No, the element of paradox arises precisely where the minority democrat does not change her mind. Only then do we get the apparent conflict between two incompatible judgements.

Apparent, but not real. There are two distinct judgements involved here, judgements on two different issues: correctness and legitimacy. Ms Wise remains the right person to be our representative in the sense of being the person who would do that job best. That is the issue we are voting on, and my vote registers my belief that she is that person. When I endorse the democratic decision, my claim is not that Mr Foolish was a good choice. It is that he is our legitimate representative. I am accepting that the proper procedure for deciding who represents us is a democratic vote. The fact that the procedure selected him means that he is the right person to be our MP – even though (I continue to think) he will be terrible at the job. An outcome of a procedure can be legitimate – one can have moral reason to endorse and abide by that outcome – simply in virtue of its having been the outcome of a legitimate (or, we might say, legitimizing) procedure. And it can be legitimate in that sense without being correct by any procedure-independent standards of correctness.

The idea that a decision might get its legitimacy from the procedure by which it was made, even if it is, in fact, a bad decision, is familiar from sport. We know perfectly well that referees and umpires make mistakes, sometimes glaring ones; but we also understand that there is good reason to have decisions made that way (rather than, say, by a vote amongst the players), and regard those decisions as legitimate for that reason. The same goes for the decisions made by juries in court. Juries get things wrong. Innocent defendants are victims of miscarriages of justice. But as long as the proper procedure was followed (no witnesses were nobbled, the jury wasn't rigged, the prosecution didn't conceal crucial evidence), those decisions remain legitimate.

There's nothing particularly troubling, then, about the idea that decisions that are wrong in one sense can be right in another. It can be right to convict someone just because a jury judged them guilty, even if the jury got that decision wrong. But what is it that makes a procedure the right kind to legitimize a decision? In the sports and courtroom case, it looks as if we choose our procedures with at least one eye on the likelihood of their getting them right. We do in fact change our decision procedures from time to time, when we judge that other procedures would be more likely to issue in the right decision. Cricket has introduced a third umpire, to adjudicate run-outs and stumpings via a television monitor. Juries in the UK will no longer adjudicate on some complex fraud cases, where they are deemed unlikely to have the expertise needed to understand the issues at stake. It's true that considerations other than 'tendency to produce the right answer' play into our assessment of decision-making procedures. (In the sporting case, we don't want to slow the game down too much.) Still, their tendency to produce better rather than worse decisions is an important part of the way we judge the legitimacy of decision-making procedures in these areas.

Does the same apply to democracy? When I endorse Mr Foolish as my representative, is that because I think that, on the whole, democracy is a good way of making good choices? 'OK,' I might think, 'they've messed up big time on this occasion. Still, generally speaking, democratic procedures tend to result in good decisions. That's why I should regard this idiot as my legitimate political representative.' If I do think like this, then I am invoking an instrumental justification of democracy. I am making its legitimizing role hang on a belief about its (likely) consequences. Or is my reason for regarding him as legitimate intrinsic to the democratic procedure by which he was elected? Perhaps the majority view is legitimate simply because all my fellow constituents are equally entitled to a say in who their representative is, and going with the majority is the best way to reflect their equality of standing in relation to that decision. That would have nothing to do with any tendency of democracy to produce good decisions. Again, we are back to the distinction between intrinsic and instrumental justifications of democracy.

Subjectivism, democracy and disagreement

All this talk about 'right answers' and 'mistakes' may be troubling some readers. 'Yes,' you might be thinking, 'I can see that there may be right answers to the questions decided by umpires or juries. I can see also that there might be right answers to technical political questions – about what policies will best achieve particular aims (low inflation, efficient social services or whatever). But, as you told us in your introduction, political decisions aren't just technical. They are also, at least implicitly, decisions about what aims we should be pursuing in the first place. That makes them, ultimately, moral questions. Are there really "right" answers to those? If not, how can it make sense to talk about a political decision being right or wrong?'

One aim of this book has been to highlight and challenge the prevalence of subjectivism or scepticism in much contemporary thinking about moral (and hence political) issues. Many of my students endorse (or think they endorse) some variant of this position, holding that opinions on moral or political matters are essentially matters of opinion or preference only. Many, it seems, believe that the main reason why we should have democracy is precisely that there are no right answers to many political questions. All views about what the law should be are equally valid, so the proper thing to do is simply to add up what people think. Indeed, so the thought sometimes goes, if there were moral knowledge about political matters, then democracy would be a very strange way of reaching it. Endorsing democracy as a means of making laws means treating each person's view – educated and uneducated, wise and thoughtless – as equally good. And that only makes sense if there's nothing for them to be right or wrong about.

This is a bit like the thought allegedly connecting liberalism and moral subjectivism, which I unmasked in Part 4: the idea that it only makes sense to allow people to choose their conception of the good if no conceptions are better than any others. As in that case, one can't be a subjectivist about all values and simultaneously believe that democracy is the legitimate way to make political decisions. If no moral judgements are true or false, what makes democracy more legitimate than dictatorship? That view must invoke some moral claims: perhaps that there's some value to the people ruling themselves. This is a collective variant of the liberal view that what matters is not so much that people choose rightly as that they choose autonomously. And, like that view, it is quite consistent with the idea that some choices are better than others. We can perfectly well be democrats even if we do think that there are better or worse answers to political questions, and even if we don't think that democracy is particularly well suited to reaching them.

Democrats need not, then, believe that all opinions as to what the law should be are equally good answers to that question. They might believe something similar but crucially different, such as that everybody's opinion about the answer should be fed into the legislative procedure on equal terms. Opinions could be equally valid as inputs to the legislative decision without being equally good answers to the question of what law would be best. This might be because all citizens have a right to take part in the law-making process on equal terms. It might be because there is no other appropriately public or legitimate basis for deciding which answers are better than others. Whatever the specifics, the basic point is that there are more goods than epistemic goods. So even if we believed that there was a right answer in any particular case, and even if we believed that it could be identified, we might still prefer a decision-making procedure that we thought less likely (than, say, the decision of moral experts) to produce it.

The fact that people usually disagree about which laws should be made is certainly of huge significance for the issue of which decision-making procedures are legitimate. But that significance is often misunderstood. It is not, as many believe, that disagreement – even deep and apparently interminable disagreement – proves that there is nothing to be right or wrong about. That is a non sequitur. The fact that people disagree about something does not necessarily mean that there's no right answer to the question of which of them (if any) is right. Disagreement is significant not because it implies that any decision would be as good as any other, but because there's a moral problem – a problem of legitimacy – in making people comply with policies they disagree with. The state is a coercive agent. It uses its coercive apparatus to force citizens to go along with its decisions. What happens, in effect, is that one subset of the population imposes on everybody else its view about how things should be. The claim that the view in question is the right one does not justify that imposition.

Why not? The answer has something to do with people's equal standing as citizens, as members of the polity. Perhaps the idea of respect for my fellow citizens is part of the story. But if we think about it that way, we need to tread carefully. I have very little respect for the opinions of some of my fellow citizens. Perhaps I'm arrogant, but I'm not inclined to regard the fact that they hold views different from mine as strong evidence that I'm wrong. Nor does our disagreement lead me, in the sceptical direction, to doubt that there's anything for us to be right or wrong about. But, though far from respectful of their views, I respect their standing as my fellow citizens. I accept that their views, however misguided, should feed into our collective decision-making processes on equal terms with mine. That is the fair way to make political decisions given disagreement between people with equal standing. The distinction here is between respecting their views (which I don't) and respecting them as equal members of our political community (which I do).

A few pages back I cited Arneson's instrumental approach to the justification of democracy. For him, to repeat: 'Democracy, when it is just, is so entirely in virtue of the tendency of democratic institutions and practices to produce outcomes that are just according to standards that are conceptually independent of the standards that define the democratic ideal.' Jeremy Waldron (b. 1953, in New Zealand) thinks that this misses the point: 'Any theory that makes authority depend on the goodness of political outcomes is self-defeating, for it is precisely because people disagree about the goodness of outcomes that they need to set up and recognize an authority.' Knowing what would be the right law is quite consistent with recognizing that others disagree in a way that would make it illegitimate for you to impose your view on them. The very fact that people disagree about what's right, and yet all are to be ruled by the laws that are made, means that we need a mechanism for dealing with that disagreement. That mechanism must itself be morally justified. Most philosophers hold that, in one form or another, democracy is such a mechanism.

The values of democracy

So far I have talked in rather general terms about the distinction between those values intrinsic to democratic procedures and those values that democratic procedures might help to realize instrumentally. Now it's time to be a bit more systematic about the different considerations that might be adduced in each category. Remember that these are all values that are claimed to tell in favour of democracy understood as a procedure. What kind of democracy one favours is likely to depend on which of them one thinks does the justificatory work. If your main reason for being a democrat is that democratic procedures respect citizens equally, then you may want a different kind of democracy from those who favour it because they think it tends to produce better citizens. If you value democracy because it yields political stability, then you will probably worry about different aspects of the procedure from those who care about its producing good decisions. If you think that several – or even all – of these arguments have something going for them, then you're going to end up with the difficult job of deciding which kind of democracy yields the best overall package of these different, and sometimes conflicting, values.

Intrinsic 1: freedom as autonomy

Back in Part 2, I set out various conceptions of positive freedom, one of which I called 'freedom as political participation'. If you haven't read that, or don't remember it, then it would be worth having a look now (pp. 69–73). The basic idea is Rousseau's, that 'freedom is obedience to a law we give ourselves'. People living under laws that they have made for themselves enjoy a kind of freedom (the kind of freedom called autonomy – 'self-rule') not enjoyed by people whose laws were made by others. This is so even if the two sets of laws are exactly the same. This kind of freedom is intrinsic to democratic procedures. We don't need to know anything about their consequences to say that they give citizens the opportunity to rule themselves. (Another way of thinking about this value is in terms of the idea of freedom-as-non-dependence. Freedom, on this view, means not being dependent on the will of others. Though different theorists develop these ideas in different ways, and freedom-as-non-dependence has attracted quite a bit of attention recently, for our purposes these are similar enough to be discussed together.)

The conception of freedom that is intrinsic to democratic procedures is very specific and rather controversial. We are not talking about the kind of freedom that might, or might not, be allowed to people by the content of the laws that are made. A liberal dictator might make laws that grant her subjects a good deal of individual negative freedom. Perhaps she has very relaxed views about what kinds of religious or sexual activity are tolerable. Perhaps her views are more tolerant than are those of the great majority of her subjects. In that case, democratic law-making would result in less negative freedom for the individual than would be enjoyed under dictatorship. Of course, it's plausible that democratic decision-making procedures are more likely to secure negative freedom than are dictatorial ones. That may indeed be a good reason to favour democracy. But if that is the argument, then it's consequentialist – and it invokes a different conception of freedom from the one we're thinking about now. Democracy is valued as a means to the end of freedom-as-non-interference. That is quite different from the claim that democracy intrinsically realizes freedom-as-autonomy (or freedom-as-non-dependence).

What should we make of that claim? Well, it's a problem that the outvoted minority do not rule themselves – at least not in any straightforward sense. 'The people' as a whole may enjoy the power to determine their collective affairs, by contrast, say, with dictatorial rule, or rule by a foreign power. (Nationalist movements, seeking to throw off the yoke of colonial rule, are often motivated by a sense that their 'people' have the right to self-determination.) But an individual member of a self-determining nation who has been outvoted on an issue does not live under a law she gave herself. She lives under a law that was given to her by her fellow nationals. That may be different, morally speaking, from being given a law by a ruling elite or a colonial power. But does the difference really have anything to do with autonomy? As far as the outvoted individual is concerned, she is not free to follow her own will. She is subject to the will of others.

There is, of course, a general tension between the law or the state and individual autonomy. That's the tension emphasized by philosophical anarchists, who argue that the very idea of authority is incompatible with autonomy. Since the individual owes it to herself to do what she thinks is right at all times, she can never be justified in deferring to the judgement of others, and the state can never be right to demand her obedience. No kind of state, democratic or otherwise, can have legitimate authority over the individual. Now the issue of whether a state can be justified at all is, of course, a big question, and not one I'm going to venture into here. Our question is more specific: assuming that state authority can be justified, what kind of decision-making procedure best respects the autonomy of individuals? This is something like the question Rousseau sets himself: how can we live under law and yet be free?

We know that the state will require some people to do things they would not have chosen to do. It's because people disagree about what should be done that we need a state in the first place. So, unless we go the anarchistic route, we must accept that there will be members of a state who are not getting exactly what they would have wanted. So the argument for democracy that we're considering now cannot claim that democracy gives all people autonomy in the sense of their never being subject to the will of others. It must hold, rather, that, given the inevitable conflicts that states exist to manage, democracy is the decision-making procedure that best respects people's autonomy overall. Democracy gives more people more autonomy than would any other system.

That's one way of approaching the issue. Here's another. An outvoted minority, forced to comply with the will of the majority, still enjoys something not available to those living under a dictator: the opportunity to take part, on equal terms, in making the laws they live under. That opportunity does seem valuable, and helpfully conceived as a variant of freedom-as-autonomy (or non-dependence), even where one is outvoted. One's opinion has been fed into the decision-making procedure on the same basis as everyone else's. One has had the opportunity to persuade others to vote differently. One has played a full role in the making of the collective decision. This is so even for those who are members of a persistent minority. It's sometimes claimed that majoritarian democracy is maximally consistent with autonomy because, although everybody will be outvoted from time to time, the law of averages means that the individual's view will prevail more often than not. Other things equal, that is indeed true. But, as we all know, other things are often not equal. It can easily arise that some subset of the population is outvoted time after time, hardly ever seeing its views make it into legislation. The suggestion here is that, in a democracy, even the members of that subset enjoy a kind of self-rule that they would not have if the laws were made by a dictator or a foreign power.

This argument for democracy is under the 'intrinsic' heading because it gives us reason to value democratic decision-making procedures on grounds independent of the content of what gets decided. Respect for people's right to rule themselves does indeed look like a value that might properly constrain the pursuit of right answers about what the law is. As noted earlier, there is a clear similarity to a core idea of liberalism here. It matters not so much that people choose rightly as that they choose for themselves. Democracy looks like the same idea applied to politics. People should individually determine their own individual affairs (liberalism), and they should collectively determine their collective affairs (democracy). We might, then, think of liberalism and democracy as friends, rather than enemies. As Waldron has emphasized, the fact that liberalism and democracy emerged at roughly the same time suggests that they share a common deep grounding, despite the superficial tensions between them. It is only as people come to be conceived as possessed of the capacity for rational self-determination, which is recognized by liberal rights, that they are conceived also as sufficiently rational to be capable of taking collective responsibility for themselves, which makes democracy – rather than monarchy or aristocracy – the appropriate mechanism for making political decisions.

This all looks plausible. But we must not move too fast. The analogy between liberalism and democracy is far from perfect. Why should we think that we have a right to an equal say in determining the coercive rules that significantly affect how other people live their lives? It may indeed be that we have a right to control our own lives – to the extent that exercising that right is consistent with respecting it in other people. If we want to screw up our own lives, that is our prerogative. But why think that we have a fundamental moral right to exercise significant power over the lives of others? If there are indeed good reasons to favour democratic procedures, it might be thought, then those must invoke the claim that democracy is a good way of making good laws. One can think that people have the right to make mistakes about how they live their own lives without thinking that they also have the right to make mistakes about how others live theirs.

Intrinsic 2: self-realization

The idea that there's a kind of freedom achieved through member-ship of a self-governing political community is sometimes associ-ated with the idea that participation in collective decision-making is an essential part of a fully flourishing human life. This thought also came up in Part 2, when I noted that some theorists have equated freedom with self-realization and have claimed that self-realization consists, at least in part, in involvement in the life of one's polity. One of the distinctive features of human beings is their capacity to get together and decide how they want their collective affairs to be organized. Ants have extremely complicated and well-ordered patterns of interaction. Bees are very good at building hives and giving each other the low-down on where to find nectar. But non-human animals cannot reflect on and discuss with each other and collectively determine what rules are to govern their interac-tions. That capacity is something specially human, and you're not fully human unless you do it. Man is a political animal. (In Greek, the word for 'private' is *idios*. In ancient Greece, anyone who con-cerned himself only with his own affairs, declining to take part in public life, was deemed an idiot!)

Only in a democracy do all citizens get to participate fully in political life – realizing their nature as creatures capable of politi-cal creation. This value, too, might explain some of our antipathy to the model of teledemocracy outlined earlier. People unthink-ingly clicking on a computer screen during a commercial break are hardly enjoying the kind of self-realization that human beings achieve by sharing in the shaping of their collective affairs. It matters, on this justification of democracy, that citizens deliberate about how things should be. Only then are they making full and proper use of their distinctively human capacities.

I'll say a bit more about the significance of deliberation soon. Here it's worth being clear that we're talking now about the kind of self-realization that is achieved in the very act of participation.

It's not a consequence of that participation. There is a different way of thinking about self-realization that makes it something people achieve progressively, through and as a result of political involvement. Taking part in politics is good for people, on this view, because it acts as an educational or developmental process, enlarging their intellectual and moral powers. This idea is sometimes invoked to suggest that really giving political power to the people wouldn't be as dangerous as it seems, since the very experience of making decisions tends to make people better at it. I'll leave it to the reader to evaluate that suggestion. What matters, in our current context, is the kind of argument it is. It appeals to democracy's consequences – its beneficial effects on citizens. True or false, that is different from the claim that participating in politics is itself an essential part of a flourishing life for human beings.

Intrinsic 3: equality

The idea that democracy is the law-making procedure that most respects the equal standing of citizens is, for many, the very heart of the democratic ideal. Even if there are better and worse decisions, we disagree about which are which, and we disagree about which of us is more likely to make those decisions well. The only fair way to deal with that disagreement is to give everybody an equal say. With the exception of children, the mentally impaired and criminals (who are widely thought to have forfeited their claim to participate in collective decision-making), all should be equal not only in their treatment by the law, but also in their input to it.

We've already seen that the idea of an 'equal say' can be interpreted in various ways, with less or more radical distributive implications. That discussion was all about equality as a property of the democratic procedure, not of the outcomes it generates. Whether democracy produces egalitarian policies depends on what policies people vote for. Certainly a significant strand of anti-democratic thought has worried that democracy would tend to result in more equality than the anti-democrats judged desirable. And for some it's something of a mystery why democracy hasn't led to more equality than it has. (Do most of the people believe that inequality is actually a good thing? Are they ideologically conned into accepting its inevitability? Do we not in fact have the kind of procedural equality that would lead to more egalitarian outcomes?) A procedure with equal inputs might be expected, other things equal, to lead to more equal outputs than a procedure in which inputs are not equal – assuming that those doing the inputting care about the way outputs affect them. But this is just an empirical tendency. Conceptually, equal influence in making the law is quite consistent with that law leaving lots of distributive inequality.

So far so good. A genuinely equal or fair procedure may generate distributively unequal outcomes. That's true. But suppose we think that a fair procedure requires more than that all have the formal right to vote. Suppose we believe it requires also that citizens really do have an equal opportunity to influence political decisions. And suppose we think that this condition is satisfied only when all are properly educated, or when none suffers the kind of poverty that effectively excludes them from the political process. (We might think that taking equality of political opportunity seriously has even more radical implications, but this will do to make the point.) In that case, the maintenance of fair procedures itself sets limits on distributive outcomes. A polity that fails properly to educate all its members, or allows some of them to live in severe poverty, is effectively denying itself the possibility of making decisions by fair procedures. Of course, in the real world, political decisions aren't made by that kind of procedure in the first place. For some, this may be enough to render all such decisions illegitimate. But the point is that even in the ideal case – where all did genuinely participate in collective decision-making on equal terms – the importance of sustaining proper procedures would significantly constrain the range of possible outcomes. The general lesson is that the more content we build into our specification of democratic procedures, the less we leave open to democratic decision. If democracy may not legitimately abolish itself, or undermine its own democraticness, then some issues – those that constitute a political system as democratic – cannot themselves be up for democratic grabs. At the limit, we could come up with such a thick understanding of what makes a democratic procedure legitimate that we'd end up taking nearly everything off the agenda for democratic decision.

Leaving aside that paradoxical possibility, notice that talk about equality of input leaves open the issue of what form that input takes. One way of treating citizens equally is simply to give all their preferences equal weight in the process of aggregation to form a collective decision. Another is to give them an equal chance to influence collective deliberation, by presenting their reasons for preferring the decisions they prefer, and giving them equal opportunity to persuade everybody else. Here we touch on a key fault-line that runs through democratic theory. For some, the basic idea of democracy is that the people get what they want. The problem is that people want different things, and what we need is a legitimate way of combining their different preferences into an overall decision. This approach, sometimes called a 'social choice' approach, worries about how best to aggregate individual prefer-ences. (Some working in this tradition worry a lot about whether there can indeed be legitimate – fair or non-arbitrary – ways of aggregating them.) Other theorists come at the issue from a rather different angle. For them, democracy is not about adding up what people want, it's about collective deliberation. Democracy is not merely a means of turning preferences into policies; it's a means of transforming preferences themselves. Through a process of democratic debate, argument, reflection, hearing other people's point of view and responding to objections, democracy can, and should, be a way of changing – and improving – people's views, not just registering and combining them. This approach, which has become especially popular among theorists in recent years, favours 'deliberative democracy'.

On one view, democracy is like a market in which politicians and policies respond to what people want. On another, it is – or should be – a forum where citizens deliberate together about matters of common concern. If we hesitate to embrace telede-mocracy, that may be because we hanker after at least some of the latter. That the people make the decision, and do so on equal terms, does not seem quite enough. Why not? One answer was offered under the previous heading. If it's true that human beings achieve self-realization through collective debate and deliberation about their common affairs, then only the forum model properly makes politics an arena for that achievement. Another answer takes us into the category of outcome-oriented justifications of decision-making procedures. Perhaps our objection to teledemocracy is fundamentally a worry about the quality of the decisions it is likely to produce. Giving all citizens' votes the same weight is indeed a way of treating citizens equally. But the idea of equal respect is vague enough to leave open what best counts as respecting them equally, and it may be that the way we choose to do that reflects other concerns. We might think that giving all citizens an equal chance to state their views, to respond to objections, to take part in the deliberative process, is a way of respecting them equally that also tends to produce good decisions.

We shouldn't underestimate the extent to which political inequality has a damaging impact on the quality of decisions. Most of those who object to it do so on fairness grounds. It does seem unjust that citizens are so unequal in their capacity to influence the affairs of their state. But inequality of input also has a negative impact on the quality of political deliberation. The louder some voices are able to shout, the more other voices are drowned out. Political influence is in large part a zero-sum game. The more we hear one argument, the less we hear the others. That's not a recipe for making good decisions.

The democracy–equality relationship raises other issues that can get only a mention here. One concerns the legitimacy of majority rule. There's a straightforward connection between equality and majoritarian decision-making. Going with the majority view seems implied by the requirement to count each vote equally. The alternatives involve giving the minority's votes greater-than-equal weight. Perhaps, however, we shouldn't just add up preferences on a one-person-one-vote basis. Perhaps we should take into account how much people care about the issue under consideration. We should factor in the intensity of preferences, and not just how many people have them. That might do something to protect minorities from the tyranny of the majority, but it's not going to help if a majority really wants to oppress a minority. Factoring in intensity could help with lukewarm majorities, but it doesn't avoid the deep problem. Better, perhaps, may be the move, sketched above, that seeks to derive respect for individual rights, as trumps against majoritarian decision-making, from the same concern for equality that justifies that procedure in general.

Another issue concerns the arguments over direct and indirect (or representative) forms of democracy. It seems obvious that direct democracy embodies equality more fully than does indirect democracy. In the former, all citizens get to vote on laws directly. In the latter, they get to vote only for representatives who make those decisions on their behalf. This two-tiered aspect introduces a kind of inequality, and I suggested early on that this can be thought of as compromising the democraticness of the system. All this is true in principle. In practice, however, it's not absurd to think that our system of voting for representatives actually does better, in terms of equality, than would a direct procedure for making decisions. If all issues were decided by referenda, would people actually bother to vote? Some would. An unrepresentative minority of political activists would doubtless devote their time and energy to the business of making laws. But that hardly seems a good way of taking account of all citizens' views equally. For all its faults, a system in which the polity as a whole deliberates intensively every few years about who should make decisions – and those elected know that they will have to stand for re-election in a few years' time – may actually better embody equality of political influence than would a system that allowed the possibility of mass participation but actually consisted of minority activist rule. (OK, given current turn-outs, it's pushing it a bit to suggest that national elections in the UK or the US count as 'intensive deliberation by the polity as a whole'. But you get the idea.) As so often in politics, what looks justified in principle may turn out rather differently in practice.

Instrumental 1: good or correct decisions

Let me turn now from values that might be realized intrinsically by democratic procedures to those that might justify those procedures on instrumental grounds. First up is the suggestion that democracy is a good procedure for making good decisions. A lot of relevant ground has already been covered. I've challenged the idea that democratic procedures make sense only when there is no right answer. And I hope I've explained how one can regard democratic decisions as legitimate even if one thinks that there are right answers to political questions and that democracy is not particularly good at finding them. For many, the quality of decisions is simply beside the point.

Still, there are important strands in democratic theory that do appeal to democracy's tendency to produce right answers. One is associated with the French philosopher and mathematician, the Marquis de Condorcet (1743–94). Condorcet showed mathematically that if the average person is more likely to be right than wrong about something, then the majority opinion is very likely to be right about it. Quite how likely depends on how many people are consulted and how much better than random is the judgement of the average individual, but the probabilities get startlingly high surprisingly quickly. (For example, if the average individual has a 55 per cent chance of being right, then 399 people taken together have a 98 per cent chance of being so.) From this perspective, then, democracy is a good way of finding the common good (or whatever it is one is trying to identify) just because the laws of large numbers mean that many heads are better than one. There is a wisdom in crowds that makes consulting them a good way of ascertaining right answers. (We came across this idea earlier, when I suggested that being outvoted on something might give one reason to change one's mind – not just to accept the legitimacy of the majority view.)

Not convinced? If so, that may be because you're not willing to grant the crucial premiss. Condorcet's Jury Theorem works if one assumes that the average voter is more likely to be right than wrong. To be fair, Condorcet's approach doesn't require us to assume that all voters have this level of competence. We don't need all our fellow citizens to have a better than 50 per cent chance of making the right judgement. We need only average competence over 50 per cent (and normal distribution around that average). Still, it's obviously open to question whether voters are on average better than random. If they aren't, then Condorcet's theorem will immediately give grounds for rejecting democracy. If the average person is more likely to be wrong than right, then the last thing you want to do is give the decision to lots of people, as they are very likely to get it wrong. And there are other problems in applying Condorcet's indisputable mathematics to the real world. One is that the result requires the inputs to be independent of each other. It's because you are aggregating independent inputs that many heads are so much more likely to be better than one. But in practice it may be that many people vote as members of factions or parties, in which case they are not feeding their own independent opinion into the procedure. (Rousseau opposed factions on the grounds that they hindered the emergence of a general will. Some interpretations see him as gesturing towards this Condorcetian thought.) Another difficulty is that Condorcet's result applies only to dichotomous choices – where voters are choosing between just two options. Most voting in real democracies is more complicated than that.

It's not a good objection to the Condorcetian approach to reject the whole idea of right answers altogether. His maths shows only that if there are such answers, and the average voter is more likely to be right than wrong about what they are, then majorities are very likely to be more right than wrong. Still, applying that result to real democratic decisions, and invoking it to defend the claim that those decisions are likely to be right (and legitimate because they are likely to be right), is far from straightforward. Condorcet's approach works if all votes can be treated as judgements on the same issue. But it's unlikely that voters in contemporary elections do in fact see their votes in the same way at all. When I vote, I take myself to be giving my opinion about which of the options on offer would be best, all things considered, for my fellow citizens collectively (or something pious like that). But it's hardly crazy to wonder whether my fellow voters are not registering a judgement about that at all. Call me cynical, but I sometimes suspect that some of them are voting for whichever option they take to be in their own best interests. In that case, what is being aggregated by the voting procedure is not a set of judgements about the same issue at all. If so, we certainly cannot assume that the winning outcome is also likely to be the right one.

If we're willing to grant Condorcet's assumptions, then his approach does indeed suggest that democracy is a good way of making good decisions. His theorem is about how, given those assumptions, we can aggregate individual views into a view more likely to be right than any individual is. But there's a second way of seeing democracy as having epistemic value. On this perspective, the point is not simply to aggregate or count views and appeal to the laws of large numbers. Democracy is a deliberative procedure. Through discussion, reflection and debate, citizens' initially uninformed and possibly selfish views are changed for the better – into judgements closer to the 'right answer'. We've already come across this idea, when discussing the different ways in which one might treat citizens' input equally.

How does collective deliberation improve the quality of decisions? Well, discussion and debate are good ways of gathering good information relevant to the decision in question. Political decisions typically involve judgements about complicated empirical issues, and different people will have different views about the likely consequences of any particular policy. The process of critical cross-examination, of empirical claim and counter-claim, is a valuable means of sifting through the relevant evidence and coming to an informed view about what is indeed likely to happen if a particular policy is put into action. More interesting, perhaps, is the suggestion that discussion in the public forum improves the quality of the moral thinking that implicitly underpins political decisions. There can be sensible and rational debate about the relative importance of different values that might be promoted or hindered by the various policy options on the table. Indeed, some have suggested that collective deliberation encourages people to be public-spirited, motivated to pursue the common – rather than their own, particular – good. The very enterprise of defending one's political views in the public forum requires one to conceive and present them in terms acceptable to others. It just won't do for someone to defend a policy on the selfish grounds that it will make her (or people like her) better off. And even if many claims to be furthering the common good start off as hypocritical or disingenuous, the very requirement to frame one's views in ways that present them as good overall, not just good for oneself, gradually alters one's perspective on politics. The idea that democratic procedures may tend to improve the quality of political decisions has, then, both an informational and a moral aspect. Deliberation helps us to discover which are the best means to which ends, but it also helps us work out which ends are better than others.

The Condorcetian and the deliberative approaches posit quite different mechanisms by which democracy might tend to produce good decisions, but they are not mutually exclusive. Condorcet says nothing about how individuals come to their political judgements. It is quite consistent with his mathematics that citizens should formulate their views about how to vote through a process of debate and critical reflection with one another (as long as each ends up voting for what she really thinks, not simply toeing a party line). And although the deliberative account might posit unanimity as the ideal – if we talk about it long enough, we'll all end up agreeing – in any real-world situation there is bound to be some residual disagreement and need for a vote. So there's nothing incoherent about a conception of democratic decision-making that reaps the benefits of both stories. First we each try to work out, through careful reflection and debate with one another, what is the right thing to vote for. If the deliberative account is right, that process of deliberation will tend to improve our judgements, making it more likely that the average person is more likely to be right than wrong. Then we have a vote. If deliberation has improved our individual judgements sufficiently, then the majority is very likely indeed to be right. So this hybrid model is justified on the grounds that it tends to produce right answers.

Two final points about this kind of justification. First, the claim is not that democracy is legitimate because it always gets the answer right. It's justified because it is more likely to do so than is any other procedure. It is in virtue of the procedure, not the outcome, that the decision is legitimate; but what makes the procedure legitimate is its epistemic value – its tending to produce better rather than worse decisions. On this account, then, it is perfectly coherent to accept the legitimacy of a democratic decision while believing it to be wrong. But its legitimacy depends not simply on its emerging from a fair procedure, or one that respects citizens' capacity to rule themselves. (Those would be intrinsic justifications.) What makes it legitimate is the fact that the procedure by which it was made is more likely to get it right than is any alternative procedure.

Rousseau thought that as long as everybody was genuinely voting for the common good then the minority must simply have made a mistake. (Actually Rousseau says various inconsistent things, but this is certainly one of them.) That's not quite right. The minority might be right. The reason why the minority should abide by the democratic decision, on this epistemic account, is not that they must have made a mistake. But nor is it that the decision emerged from a procedure justified on intrinsic grounds. It's that the decision emerged from the procedure most likely to have got it right.

Finally, the justifications of democracy considered under this heading see it as an instrument for producing right answers. Right answers here mean 'answers that are correct by standards independent of those that define the democratic ideal'. This approach does assume that there are right answers in this sense. But it does not assume that we can identify them by means other than democratic procedures. It's perfectly coherent to regard democracy as a good procedure for making decisions without having any idea about what would be a good decision in advance of the procedure. When people talk about democracy having epistemic value, they mean precisely that it can increase our knowledge, that it can be a way of discovering things. It's not simply a way of legitimizing decisions that we already knew, or even could have known, to be right.

Instrumental 2: intellectual and moral development of citizens

For some theorists, what's good about people making political decisions for themselves is not so much that they will make good decisions as that their making the decisions will make them better people. A system in which laws are made for some by others not only deprives those subject to those laws of the good of autonomy or self-rule, it stunts their development. Just as children cannot evolve into capable adults unless they are gradually given the opportunity to make their own decisions, so non-democratic systems are infantilizing, depriving adults of the chance to develop their intellectual and moral powers. There is an important overlap between this justification and the previous one. Citizens who have been given the opportunity to develop their powers and capacities are going to be better at making political decisions. They'll be less selfish (that's the moral development bit) and better at gathering and assessing information (that's the intellectual development bit). But, analytically at least, we can distinguish the quality of the decisions from the quality of the people who make them. This argument suggests that giving people self-rule is the best way to help them grow up.

This justification of democratic procedures is also rather similar to the intrinsic one that appeals to self-realization, to the claim that human beings achieve a kind of flourishing through the very act of participating in the political life of their community. What we're talking about under this heading is the consequentialist version of that idea. The thought now is not that citizens achieve self-realization immediately, in the very act of participating. It's that participation is conducive to development; it acts, over time, to change people for the better. This is not only a different kind of claim, analytically speaking; it's a less substantial or controversial one also. The suggestion that democratic participation tends to have beneficial impact on citizens – and even that it makes them more fully realized human beings – involves less metaphysical baggage than the idea that such participation just is, in itself, an essential element of self-realization for human beings.

One feature of this justification gives it an element of paradox. The benefits to citizens that come through participation cannot be achieved if those benefits are their reason, or at least their only reason, for participating. Suppose you meet someone on her way to a political rally or demonstration. You ask her why she is there, and she says it's because she thinks it will be good for her moral and intellectual development. Something has gone wrong. She has reduced politics to the realm of self-help and personal growth. There's no problem, I suppose, in her believing that the activity will have that beneficial effect, but it seems very odd for that to be the reason that motivates her to go. Her motivating reason ought to be something to do with the content of the principle or cause for which she is demonstrating. Citizens are supposed to care about outcomes, yes; but those are the policy outcomes they are arguing about or demonstrating and voting for, not the outcome in terms of their own personal development. Indeed, since she wouldn't actually care what the policy outcome was, someone who took part in politics only for the sake of personal development would not be getting much of it. She wouldn't be seriously engaging with the arguments of others or responsibly exercising her agency as a member of her political community. The beneficial effects that come under this heading have to be by-products or side-effects of political engagement undertaken for other reasons, so it's hard to see how these in-process benefits could play a major justificatory role.

Instrumental 3: perceived legitimacy

When my father was being trained as an officer in the British Army, he was told that it was more important that he should make clear and confident decisions than that he should get them right. ('Nobody gives a damn what you decide, Swift. Just stop blithering and bloody well decide.') It mattered that his subordinates should regard him as knowing what he was doing, and so be willing to follow his commands. What would be the right order if everybody complies with it could lead to disaster if nobody does. Something similar applies in politics. It matters not only what decisions are made, but what people think of those decisions. Decisions need to be regarded as legitimate. Of course, there are ways of getting people to obey laws they reject as illegitimate. States can use the police or army to enforce compliance, and sometimes even democratic states have to do this. But that is expensive, and can't be sustained for long without serious moral cost also. It's a valuable feature of democracy that its decisions tend to be perceived as legitimate.

Of course, the reasons why democracy might tend to be perceived as legitimate have a lot to do with the reasons why it might indeed be legitimate. Presumably, people are willing to comply with democratic decisions because they respect the procedure that made them, and presumably they respect that procedure because they see that it realizes equality, or autonomy, or self-realization, or tends to produce good decisions. That's true, but it shouldn't lead us to blur the distinction between legitimacy and perceived legitimacy. A regime could be regarded as legitimate by those subject to it even if it was not in fact of a kind where they had good reason to do so. For many centuries, England was ruled by monarchs who claimed to be God's representative on earth and to rule by divine right. Many of those subject to their commands accepted that claim and obeyed for that reason. Those kings, and their commands, had perceived legitimacy. But that legitimacy rested on the inculcation of false beliefs in such a way that we would now want to say that their rule was not, in fact, legitimate.

Since most of us believe that democracy, at least in some form, could be legitimate, this point may seem academic. (That's 'academic' in the pejorative sense that condemns my profession to the elucidation of irrelevant niceties.) True, there is a definite analytical difference between the legitimacy of democracy (which on some views derives entirely from features of the procedure itself) and its decisions being perceived as legitimate and complied with for that reason (which is a consequence of that procedure). But if democracy is indeed legitimate, and is rightly perceived as being so, what's the big deal? One answer is that we shouldn't be too quick to assume that the regimes we live under are in fact legitimate or democratic. To show that democracy can be a legitimate system for making laws is not to show that the system we in the West call 'democracy' is indeed legitimate. Perhaps our way of making laws, though democratic in some respects, is not democratic enough to be legitimate. Perhaps, for example, it lacks the kind of equality of political influence on which true legitimacy in fact depends. Perhaps law-abiding people in contemporary democracies are like the medieval subjects who accepted their king's claim that he had the right to rule them. Perhaps they too are wrong about the conditions that must be satisfied before a law can rightly claim legitimacy.

Conclusion

Democracy is a complex ideal. It stands at the confluence of several different values – and different kinds of value – and it can be very hard to work out which is relevant to what, or how to combine them. Some clarity is gained, I hope, by holding firmly to the idea

of democracy as a procedure. We can then focus on the different ways in which procedures might be justified, intrinsically and
instrumentally, and the different considerations that come under
each heading. But readers shouldn't worry if, having disentangled
things analytically, they don't immediately have a clear picture of
how to fit them together. Most people's views about democracy –
why it's good, which kind is best, how much of it we have, how
much of it we want – turn out to be an intricate and messy mixture
of different thoughts. We are inevitably balancing different kinds
of value: fair procedures against wise decisions, deliberation against
the aggregation of preferences. And in assessing how much 'people
power' we really want, here and now, we quite properly have to
factor in real-world considerations, such as inequalities in political
input, or many people's lacking the skills needed to make political
judgements about hugely difficult issues.

Everybody loves democracy, and most people think we've got
it. That can make democracy seem rather innocuous or innocent,
lacking the critical edge of some of the other concepts discussed in
this book. In fact, however, taking democracy seriously – thinking
hard about why it's valuable and what would be needed genuinely
to realize the values that make it so – is an extremely demanding
agenda. If it really matters that citizens rule themselves, and that the
distribution of political influence among them be fair, then democracy
itself demands radical changes to the way we do things. If genuinely
democratic procedures produce good decisions only when citizens
are skilled in the art of decision-making, then that increases those
demands still further. Of course, democratic values, though important, are only some values among many. We may well want to limit
the scope of democratic decision-making, and be content to sacrifice
democratic values in other ways also, for the sake of other good things.
But those politicians who are so keen to tell us how great democracy
is are not wrong. It would be interesting to see them take seriously its
implications for their own societies.

Further reading

Robert Dahl's *On Democracy* (Yale University Press 2000) is a short
and accessible introduction to normative and sociological perspec-

tives. For a fuller version of Dahl's approach, try his *Democracy and Its Critics* (Yale University Press 1991), engagingly written as a dialogue. Ross Harrison's *Democracy* (Routledge 1995) is useful on the philosophical side, while David Held's *Models of Democracy* (3rd edn, Polity 2006) is a clear, nicely organized guide to the different institutional forms generated by different justifications of democracy.

At a more advanced and philosophical level, there are some excellent collections of academic papers on the issues covered here. Best overall for coverage and quality are David Estlund (ed.), *Democracy* (Blackwell 2002), and Thomas Christiano (ed.), *Philosophy and Democracy: An Anthology* (Oxford University Press 2003). Both have very good introductions, and helpfully group the articles they contain under headings indicating the kind of position being argued for. Both also have some papers on deliberative democracy, but the most extensive collection on that approach is James Bohman and William Rehg (eds.), *Deliberative Democracy: Essays on Reason and Politics* (MIT Press 1997).

For readers with the energy for more, the following books are particularly important and/or interesting: David Estlund's *Democratic Authority: A Philosophical Framework* (Oxford University Press 2009), Thomas Christiano's *The Constitution of Equality: Democratic Authority and its Limits* (Oxford University Press 2008), Jeremy Waldron's *Law and Disagreement* (Oxford University Press 1999), Amy Gutmann and Dennis Thompson's *Why Deliberative Democracy?* (Princeton University Press 2004), and Daniele Archibugi's *The Global Commonwealth of Citizens: Toward Cosmopolitan Democracy* (Princeton University Press 2008). James Surowiecki's *The Wisdom of Crowds* (Little, Brown 2004) fascinatingly explores Condorcetian themes without mention of Condorcet.

Conclusion

Since this book hasn't made an argument, it can't really have a conclusion. I have not tried to persuade the reader of a particular position. Rather, my aim has been to set out, and clarify, the issues that arise when philosophers discuss some key political concepts. Of course, what I call 'clarification' has an argumentative aspect to it. I am arguing against those who have confused or vague views. And sometimes a view clearly stated is immediately less plausible than it was when hazy. But, primarily, I've been arguing against the confusion or vagueness, not against – or for – any of the substantive positions that come in confused or vague form. Those positions can more clearly be understood and assessed when that confusion is sorted out, or when what was fuzzy has been made more precise. This is just clearing the decks, so that useful relevant argument can begin. For example, some of Part 4 tried to show that many communitarian objections to liberal individualism misunderstand or misrepresent what it is they are attacking. That was an 'argument' of a kind. But the aim was just to get a better sense of where the real differences lie, and what is at stake between those who subscribe to the different views.

If the book does have an overall message, it must be that this process of clarification is useful. That it does indeed help us to understand better what we and other people think about central moral issues in politics, and what we are disagreeing about when we disagree. Nothing I can say in this 'conclusion' will help to persuade the reader of this. It's too late for that now. My discussions of social justice, liberty, equality, community and democracy will have made the case, or failed to make it, already.

I've been quite critical of politicians. They use concepts in vague, imprecise ways. They sometimes like it when it's unclear what words mean, because then they can fudge disagreements and appear to be on everybody's side. They are reluctant to admit that the policies they advocate, though justified overall, will make some people worse off than the policies of their opponents. They misleadingly pretend that all good things go together, so that we don't have to make hard moral choices. They go for the weakest parts of competitors' arguments, and are quite happy to ignore, if they can, the bits that make sense. They will never admit that they have made a mistake, or that they have changed their mind about anything. They can never say 'I don't know'. They are preoccupied with rhetoric and spin, rather than with content or substance; what matters is how things sound, how they play to the electorate, not what they really mean.

Political philosophers, by contrast, hate it when things are unclear and will harass one another until vagueness is dispelled. They have no problem accepting the necessity of difficult choices, or concluding that it is justified to make some people worse off – perhaps much worse off – than they might otherwise be. They understand that intellectual progress is achieved not by easy repetitious exposure of the weak bits of their opponents' arguments, but by painful and productive engagement with cogent criticism. Being committed to the pursuit of truth, they are happy to change their minds, and to admit to changing their minds, when somebody shows them they were wrong. They don't claim to have all the answers. Although apparently and self-indulgently obsessed with words, close inspection reveals the opposite: 'conceptual analysis' is just the only way to get at what people mean when they say things. Once we know the content, the words used drop out as irrelevant.

Both these descriptions are, of course, stereotypes. Some

politicians do actually and explicitly confront the hard choices they talk about. Some political philosophers are famously reluctant to admit that they have changed their minds. ('But that's what I was saying all along. Thanks for helping me to put it more clearly.') Some politicians do accept that they have made mistakes. Some political philosophers ignore or evade the good objections and make a meal of the bad ones. Nonetheless, the descriptions do, I think, capture genuine differences between the two professions. Suppose this is so. The way I've put it could be summarized as 'political philosophers good, politicians bad'. But is that fair? After all, the criteria I am using to assess them are those that philosophers judge to be important. If we think about the comparison from the politicians' point of view, things look rather different. Politicians operate in an environment that imposes constraints far more demanding than those faced by political philosophers. The competitive and confrontational nature of electoral politics means that any admission of ignorance, change of mind, or acknowledgement that one's opponents might have got something right, will be seized on as incompetence, a 'U-turn' or evidence of weakness. The need to win votes, and to present one's party as the representative of the country as a whole, makes it dangerous to concede that one is prepared to make anybody worse off than they might otherwise be. The slightest slip will be spun and exaggerated in the media. Moreover, politicians are expected to come up with concrete policies, not just abstract ideas. Policies that will work if they are implemented, and that have the popular appeal to stand a chance of being implemented. For, unlike philosophers, politicians have to get elected. This restricts their options. In terms of form, things must be kept simple. (Hence their preoccupation with sound-bites, slogans and the continual search for the 'Big Idea' to lend a simplifying rhetorical unity to their position.) In terms of content, they must not be too far removed from current public opinion. (Hence their preoccupation with focus groups.)

We should beware caricature. Political philosophers do consider the practical implications of their work. Many explore what policies would follow from their philosophical arguments in an ideal world, and many go further, taking on board the fact that political decisions have to be made in a context that falls short of the ideal. Nonetheless, consideration of how best to realize the values they argue for, given the real world as it actually is, may well raise questions that go beyond philosophers' expertise. The answers will depend on empirical information – detailed knowledge about how the world works – that the political philosopher may not be in a good position to acquire or judge. Nor do political philosophers want to get too concerned with the sellability, the popular appeal, of their conclusions. For them, that looks like unacceptable compromise. 'Perhaps the truth just is too complicated to be packaged in sound-bites. Why expect the right answers to difficult philosophical questions to be readily intelligible to everybody? Why expect people to agree with our answers if they did understand them? So what if, for example, ordinary people disagree with our belief that conventional desert claims are mistaken – a belief we've thought about long and hard? If they are wrong, they are wrong. We are philosophers, engaged in the pursuit of truth. You can't expect us to take popular opinion into account when coming to our conclusions.'

From the politician's perspective, this is, putting it politely, unhelpful. 'Some of you philosophers say that top athletes don't deserve to earn more than social workers. Suppose you're right. Unless you can tell me the implications for what my government should do – here and now, not in an ideal utopia – you are no help at all. And unless you can show me how to persuade voters that they are wrong to believe what they currently believe, we'd get blown out of the water come the next election in any case. That means not just presenting valid arguments, but presenting them in such a way that they will be seen to be valid, which means that they must be simple and accessible. Oh, and while you're at it, remember that every word will be carefully examined for the possibility of its being twisted into something that our opponents would like us to have said.'

It is hard not to be sympathetic to this response. Political philosophers inclined to grumble about the philosophical failings of politicians must take into account the quite different natures of the two enterprises. Philosophers can take a long-term view, aiming to change public opinion, not merely to accommodate it. Politicians have a more immediate agenda. While not leaving themselves at

the mercy of uninformed popular prejudice, they must, if they
are to be successful, take the electorate with them. They must
also have a realistic sense of what will and will not work, in terms
of policy, given people as they actually are. To take a concrete
example from Part 3, a politician concerned to maximize the position of the worst off must devise tax rates that are informed by
knowledge about people's motivational structures. It would be
no good at all to set rates on the mistaken assumption that people
will work just as hard when they are taxed at 80 per cent as at 40
per cent. But how hard people are prepared to work at what rates
of tax is not fixed. It may be given at any particular time – and
as such be part of the information that feeds in to the politician's
calculations – but it is not given for all time. It depends on people's
attitudes to one another, to their government, to their work, and
so on. These are the very attitudes that more abstract political philosophers can seek to change.

Politics is not a wholly rational activity. It would be naive to
expect the careful exposition of clear arguments simply to triumph
over emotion and prejudice. There may well be good strategic
reasons for politicians to do some pandering to the sentiments,
confusions and false beliefs of those they want to vote for them.
If, by doing so, they get elected and make the world a better
place than it would otherwise have been, those strategic reasons
may also be moral reasons. So I'm not always against politicians
saying things that are vague and mistaken. Sometimes that might
be the right thing to do. But that is an argument for saying vague
and mistaken things. It is not an argument for holding vague and
mistaken beliefs. When it comes to thinking, clarity, precision and
truth have to be better than the alternatives. There may be strategic reasons for politicians not to be too philosophically pure in
the positions they present to voters. But that's no reason for them
to be unclear about what they really believe, about what values
they expect such a strategy to realize, and why they endorse those
values.

It makes sense to go for a division of labour. Those best suited
to abstraction and precision should pursue them. Those adept
at translating abstract ideas into concrete policies should work
on that. Those skilled at selling both ideas and policies to the

electorate should do so. Political philosophers are lucky enough to have the time to work through ideas carefully, and can make mistakes without losing their jobs. For the division of labour approach to be effective, we must make the fruits of our collective efforts accessible to those – voters as well as politicians – who do not enjoy such luxuries. That's what I have tried to do in this book.

Further reading

If you've got to the end of this beginners' guide you're probably ready for the more advanced textbooks mentioned at the end of my Introduction (pp. 9–10). Those with the energy for state-of-the-art survey articles across the full range of political philosophy should try D. Estlund (ed.), *The Oxford Handbook of Political Philosophy* (Oxford University Press 2012) and the *Stanford Encyclopedia of Philosophy* (http://plato.stanford.edu), which is a wonderful, free, online resource.

Index